Columbia British

Papers Connected with the Indian Land Question

1850-1875

Columbia British

Papers Connected with the Indian Land Question
1850-1875

ISBN/EAN: 9783744713542

Printed in Europe, USA, Canada, Australia, Japan

Cover: Foto ©ninafisch / pixelio.de

More available books at **www.hansebooks.com**

BRITISH COLUMBIA.

PAPERS

CONNECTED WITH THE

INDIAN LAND QUESTION.

1850-1875.

VICTORIA:
PRINTED BY RICHARD WOLFENDEN, GOVERNMENT PRINTER,
AT THE GOVERNMENT PRINTING OFFICE, JAMES' BAY.
1875.

CONTENTS.

Conveyance of Land to Hudson's Bay Company by Indian Tribes.

Correspondence between the Secretary of State for the Colonies and Governor Douglas.

Correspondence between the Colonial Secretary and the Chief Commissioner of Lands and Works.

Correspondence between the Rev. J. B. Good and the Colonial Government.

Correspondence between the Lieutenant-Governor and the Secretary of State for the Provinces.

Correspondence between the Indian Commissioner and the Provincial Government.

BRITISH COLUMBIA.

PAPERS

CONNECTED WITH THE

INDIAN LAND QUESTION.

1850-1875.

CONVEYANCE OF LAND TO HUDSON'S BAY COMPANY BY INDIAN TRIBES.

TEECHAMITSA TRIBE—COUNTRY LYING BETWEEN ESQUIMALT AND POINT ALBERT.

Know all men, we, the chiefs and people of the Teechamitsa Tribe, who have signed our names and made our marks to this deed on the twenty-ninth day of April, one thousand eight hundred and fifty, do consent to surrender, entirely and for ever, to James Douglas, the agent of the Hudson's Bay Company in Vancouver Island, that is to say, for the Governor, Deputy Governor, and Committee of the same, the whole of the lands situate and lying between Esquimalt Harbour and Point Albert, including the latter, on the Straits of Juan de Fuca, and extending backwards from thence to the range of mountains on the Saanich Arm, about ten miles distant.

The condition of or understanding of this sale is this, that our village sites and enclosed fields are to be kept for our own use, for the use of our children, and for those who may follow after us; and the land shall be properly surveyed hereafter. It is understood, however, that the land itself, with these small exceptions, becomes the entire property of the white people for ever; it is also understood that we are at liberty to hunt over the unoccupied lands, and to carry on our fisheries as formerly.

We have received, as payment, Twenty-seven pounds ten shillings sterling.

In token whereof, we have signed our names and made our marks, at Fort Victoria, 29th April, 1850.

(Signed)   SEE-SACHASIS his x mark, and 10 others.

Done in the presence of
(Signed)   RODERICK FINLANSON,
   JOSEPH WILLIAM MCKAY.

KOSAMPSOM TRIBE—ESQUIMALT PENINSULA AND COLQUITZ VALLEY.

Know all men, we, the chiefs and people of the Kosampsom Tribe, who have signed our names and made our marks to this deed on the thirtieth day of April, one thousand eight hundred and fifty, do consent to surrender, entirely and for ever, to James Douglas, the agent of the Hudson's Bay Company in Vancouver Island, that is to say, for the Governor, Deputy Governor, and Committee of the same, the whole of the lands situate and lying between the Island of the Dead, in the Arm or Inlet of Camoson, and the head of the said Inlet, embracing the lands on the west side and north of that line to Esquimalt, beyond the Inlet three miles of the Colquitz Valley, and the land on the east side of the arm, enclosing Christmas Hill and Lake and the lands west of those objects.

The condition of or understanding of this sale is this, that our village sites and enclosed fields are to be kept for our own use, for the use of our children, and for those who may follow after us; and the land shall be properly surveyed hereafter. It is understood, however, that the land itself, with these small exceptions, becomes the entire property of the white people for ever; it is also understood that we are at liberty to hunt over the unoccupied lands, and to carry on our fisheries as formerly.

We have received, as payment, Fifty-two pounds ten shillings sterling.

In token whereof, we have signed our names and made our marks, at Fort Victoria, on the thirtieth day of April, one thousand eight hundred and fifty.

        (Signed)   HOOKOOWITZ his x mark,
                  and 20 others.

Done in the presence of
 (Signed)   ALFRED ROBSON BENSON, M.R.C.S.L.
       JOSEPH WILLIAM MCKAY.

SWENGWHUNG TRIBE—VICTORIA PENINSULA, SOUTH OF COLQUITZ.

Know all men, we, the chiefs and people of the family of Swengwhung, who have signed our names and made our marks to this deed on the thirtieth day of April, one thousand eight hundred and fifty, do consent to surrender, entirely and for ever, to James Douglas, the agent of the Hudson's Bay Company in Vancouver Island, that is to say, for the Governor, Deputy Governor, and Committee of the same, the whole of the lands situate and lying between the Island of the Dead, in the Arm or Inlet of Camoson, where the Kosampsom lands terminate, extending east to the Fountain Ridge, and following it to its termination on the Straits of De Fuca, in the Bay immediately east of Clover Point, including all the country between that line and the Inlet of Camoson.

The condition of or understanding of this sale is this, that our village sites and enclosed fields are to be kept for our own use, for the use of our children, and for those who may follow after us; and the land shall be properly surveyed hereafter. It is understood, however, that the land itself, with these small exceptions, becomes the entire property of the white people for ever; it is also understood that we are at liberty to hunt over the unoccupied lands, and to carry on our fisheries as formerly.

We have received, as payment, Seventy-five pounds sterling.

In token whereof, we have signed our names and made our marks, at Fort Victoria, on the thirtieth day of April, one thousand eight hundred and fifty.

        (Signed)   SNAW-NUCK his x mark,
                  and 29 others.

Done before us,
 (Signed)   ALFRED ROBSON BENSON, M.R.C.S.L.
       JOSEPH WILLIAM MCKAY.

CHILCOWITCH TRIBE—POINT GONZALES.

Know all men, we, the chiefs and people of the family of Chilcowitch, who have signed our names and made our marks to this deed on the thirtieth day of April, one thousand eight hundred and fifty, do consent to surrender, entirely and for ever, to James Douglas, the agent of the Hudson's Bay Company in Vancouver Island, that is to say, for the Governor, Deputy Governor, and Committee of the same, the whole of the lands situate and lying between the Sandy Bay east of Clover Point, at the termination of the Swengwhung line, to Point Gonzales, and thence north to a line of equal extent passing through the north side of Minies' Plain.

The condition of or understanding of this sale is this, that our village sites an enclosed fields are to be kept for our own use, for the use of our children, and for those who may follow after us; and the land shall be properly surveyed hereafter. It is understood, however, that the land itself, with these small exceptions, becomes the entire property of the white people for ever; it is also understood that we are at liberty to hunt over the unoccupied lands, and to carry on our fisheries as formerly.

We have received, as payment, Thirty pounds sterling.

In token whereof, we have signed our names and made our marks, at Fort Victoria, on the thirtieth day of April, One thousand eight hundred and fifty.

                    (Signed)   QUA-SUN his x mark,
                                          and 11 others.

Done in the presence of
    (Signed)   ALFRED ROBSON BENSON, M.R.C.S.L.
                     JOSEPH WILLIAM McKAY.

WHYOMILTH TRIBE—NORTH-WEST OF ESQUIMALT HARBOUR.

Know all men, we, the chiefs and people of the family of Whyomilth, who have signed our names and made our marks to this deed on the thirtieth day of April, one thousand eight hundred and fifty, do consent to surrender, entirely and for ever, to James Douglas, the agent of the Hudson's Bay Company in Vancouver Island, that is to say, for the Governor, Deputy Governor, and Committee of the same, the whole of the lands situate and lying between the north-west corner of Esquimalt, say from the Island inclusive, at the mouth of the Saw-mill Stream, and the mountains lying due west and north of that point: this District being on the one side bounded by the lands of the Teechamitsa, and on the other by the lands of the Kosampsom family.

The condition of or understanding of this sale is this, that our village sites and enclosed fields are to be kept for our own use, for the use of our children, and for those who may follow after us; and the land shall be properly surveyed hereafter. It is understood, however, that the land itself, with these small exceptions, becomes the entire property of the white people for ever; it is also understood that we are at liberty to hunt over the unoccupied lands, and to carry on our fisheries as formerly.

We have received, as payment, Forty-five pounds sterling.

In token whereof, we have signed our names and made our marks, at Fort Victoria, on the thirtieth day of April, One thousand eight hundred and fifty.

                    (Signed)   HAL-WHAL-UTSTIN his x mark,
                                          and 17 others.

Done before us,
    (Signed)   ALFRED ROBSON BENSON, M.R.C.S.L.
                     JOSEPH WILLIAM McKAY.

CHE-KO-NEIN TRIBE—POINT GONZALES TO CEDAR HILL.

Know all men, we, the chiefs and people of the tribe or family of Che-ko-nein, who have signed our names and made our marks to this deed on the thirtieth day of April, one thousand eight hundred and fifty, do consent to surrender, entirely and for ever, to James Douglas, the agent of the Hudson's Bay Company in Vancouver Island, that is to say, for the Governor, Deputy Governor, and Committee of the same, the whole of the lands situate and lying between Point Gonzales and Mount Douglas, following the boundary line of the Chilcowitch and Kosampsom families, the Canal de Haro, and the Straits of Juan de Fuca, east of Point Gonzales.

The condition of or understanding of this sale is this, that our village sites and enclosed fields are to be kept for our own use, for the use of our children, and for those who may follow after us ; and the land shall be properly surveyed hereafter. It is understood, however, that the land itself, with these small exceptions, becomes the entire property of the white people for ever ; it is also understood that we are at liberty to hunt over the unoccupied lands, and to carry on our fisheries as formerly.

We have received, as payment, Seventy-nine pounds ten shillings sterling.

In token whereof, we have signed our names and made our marks, at Fort Victoria, on the thirtieth day of April, One thousand eight hundred and fifty.

                (Signed)   CHAYTH-LUM his x mark,
                                        and 29 others.

Done before us,
   (Signed) ALFRED ROBSON BENSON, M.R.C.S.L.
                JOSEPH WILLIAM MCKAY.

KA-KY-AAKAN TRIBE—METCHOSIN.

Know all men, we, the chiefs of the family of Ka-ky-aakan, acting for and with the consent of our people, who being here present have individually and collectively confirmed and ratified this our act. Now know that we, who have signed our names and made our marks to this deed on the first day of May, one thousand eight hundred and fifty, do consent to surrender, entirely and for ever, to James Douglas, the agent of the Hudson's Bay Company in Vancouver Island, that is to say, for the Governor, Deputy Governor, and Committee of the same, the whole of the lands situate and lying between Point Albert and the Inlet of Whoyung, on the Straits of Juan de Fuca and the snow covered mountains in the interior of the Island, so as to embrace the whole tract or District of Metchosin, from the coast to these said mountains.

The condition of or understanding of this sale is this, that our village sites and enclosed fields are to be kept for our own use, for the use of our children, and for those who may follow after us ; and the land shall be properly surveyed hereafter. It is understood, however, that the land itself, with these small exceptions, becomes the entire property of the white people for ever ; it is also understood that we are at liberty to hunt over the unoccupied lands, and to carry on our fisheries as formerly.

We have received, as payment, Forty-three pounds six shillings and eight pence.

In token whereof, we have signed our names and made our marks, at Fort Victoria, on the first day of May, One thousand eight hundred and fifty.

                (Signed)   QUOITE-TO-KAY-NUM his x mark.
                                    TLY-A-HUM his x mark.
                              Descendants of the Chiefs—ancient possessors of this District, and their only surviving heirs—about 26 in number.

Done in the presence of
   (Signed) ALFRED ROBSON BENSON, M.R.C.S.L.
                JOSEPH WILLIAM MCKAY.

CHEWHAYTSUM TRIBE—SOOKE.

Know all men, we, the chiefs of the family of Chewhaytsum, acting for and on behalf of our people, who being here present have individually and collectively ratified and confirmed this our act. Now know that we, who have signed our names and made our marks to this deed on the first day of May, one thousand eight hundred and fifty, do consent to surrender, entirely and for ever, to James Douglas, the agent of the Hudson's Bay Company in Vancouver Island, that is to say, for the Governor, Deputy Governor, and Committee of the same, the whole of the lands situate and lying between the Inlet of Whoyung and the Bay of Syusung, known as Sooke Inlet and the snow covered mountains in the interior of the Island.

The condition of or understanding of this sale is this, that our village sites and enclosed fields are to be kept for our own use, for the use of our children, and for those who may follow after us; and the land shall be properly surveyed hereafter. It is understood, however, that the land itself, with these small exceptions, becomes the entire property of the white people for ever; it is also understood that we are at liberty to hunt over the unoccupied lands, and to carry on our fisheries as formerly.

We have received, as payment, Forty-five pounds ten shillings.

In token whereof, we have signed our names and made our marks, at Fort Victoria, on the first day of May, One thousand eight hundred and fifty.

    (Signed)   AL-CHAY-NOOK his x mark.
                            WE-TA-NOOGH his x mark.
                            CHA-NAS-KAYNUM his x mark.
Chiefs and representatives of the family of Chewhaytsum, who collectively have ratified the sale—about 30 in number.

SOOKE TRIBE—NORTH-WEST OF SOOKE INLET.

Know all men, we, the chiefs of the family of Sooke, acting for and on behalf of our people, who being here present have individually and collectively ratified and confirmed this our act. Now know that we, who have signed our names and made our marks to this deed on the first day of May, one thousand eight hundred and fifty, do consent to surrender, entirely and for ever, to James Douglas, the agent of the Hudson's Bay Company in Vancouver Island, that is to say, for the Governor, Deputy Governor, and Committee of the same, the whole of the lands situate and lying between the Bay of Syusung, or Sooke Inlet, to the Three Rivers beyond Thlowuck, or Point Shirringham, on the Straits of Juan de Fuca, and the snow covered mountains in the interior of Vancouver Island.

The condition of or understanding of this sale is this, that our village sites and enclosed fields are to be kept for our own use, for the use of our children, and for those who may follow after us; and the land shall be properly surveyed hereafter. It is understood, however, that the land itself, with these small exceptions, becomes the entire property of the white people for ever; it is also understood that we are at liberty to hunt over the unoccupied lands, and to carry on our fisheries as formerly.

We have received, as payment, Forty-eight pounds six shillings and eight pence.

In token whereof, we have signed our names and made our marks, at Fort Victoria, on the first day of May, One thousand eight hundred and fifty.

    (Signed)   WANSEEA his x mark.
                            TANASMAN his x mark.
                            CHYSIMKAN his x mark.
                            YOKUM his x mark.
Chiefs commissioned by and representing the Sooke Tribe here assembled.

SAANICH TRIBE—SOUTH SAANICH.

Know all men that we, the chiefs and people of the Saanich Tribe, who have signed our names and made our marks to this deed on the sixth day of February, one thousand eight hundred and fifty-two, do consent to surrender, entirely and for ever, to James Douglas, the agent of the Hudson's Bay Company in Vancouver Island, that is to say, for the Governor, Deputy Governor, and Committee of the same, the whole of the lands situate and lying between Mount Douglas and Cowichan Head, on the Canal de Haro, and extending thence to the line running through the centre of Vancouver Island, North and South.

The condition of or understanding of this sale is this, that our village sites and enclosed fields, are to be kept for our own use, for the use of our children, and for those who may follow after us; and the land shall be properly surveyed hereafter. It is understood, however, that the land itself, with these small exceptions, becomes the entire property of the white people for ever; it is also understood that we are at liberty to hunt over the unoccupied lands, and to carry on our fisheries as formerly.

We have received, as payment, Forty-one pounds thirteen shillings and four pence.

In token whereof, we have signed our names and made our marks, at Fort Victoria, on the 7th day of February, one thousand eight hundred and fifty two.

       (Signed) WHUT-SAY-MULLET his x mark.
               and 9 others.

Witness to signatures,
 (Signed) JOSEPH WILLIAM MCKAY,
      Clerk H. B. Co's. service.
    RICHD. GOLLEDGE, Clerk.

SAANICH TRIBE—NORTH SAANICH.

Know all men, that we the chiefs and people of the Saanich Tribe, who have signed our names and made our marks to this deed on the eleventh day of February, one thousand eight hundred and fifty-two, do consent to surrender, entirely and for ever, to James Douglas, the agent of the Hudson's Bay Company in Vancouver Island, that is to say, for the Governor, Deputy Governor, and Committee of the same, the whole of the lands situate and lying as follows, viz :—commencing at Cowichan Head and following the coast of the Canal de Haro North-west nearly to Saanich Point, or Qua-na-sung; from thence following the course of the Saanich Arm to the point where it terminates; and from thence by a straight line across country to said Cowichan Head, the point of commencement, so as to include all the country and lands, with the exceptions hereafter named, within those boundaries.

The condition of or understanding of this sale is this, that our village sites and enclosed fields are to be kept for our own use, for the use of our children, and for those who may follow after us; and the land shall be properly surveyed hereafter. It is understood, however, that the land itself, with these small exceptions, becomes the entire property of the white people for ever; it is also understood that we are at liberty to hunt over the unoccupied lands, and to carry on our fisheries as formerly.

We have received, as payment [*amount not stated*].

       (Signed) HOTUTSTUN his x mark.
              and 117 others.

Witness to signatures,
 (Signed) JOSEPH WILLIAM MCKAY,
      Clerk H. B. Co's. service.
    R. GOLLEDGE, Clerk.

QUEACKAR TRIBE—FORT RUPERT.

Know all men, we, the chiefs and people of the Tribe called Queackars, who have signed our names and made our marks to this deed on the eighth day of February, one thousand eight hundred and fifty-one, do consent to surrender, entirely and for ever, to James Douglas, the agent of the Hudson's Bay Company on Vancouver Island, that is to say, for the Governor, Deputy Governor, and Committee of the same, the whole of the lands situate and lying between McNeill's Harbour and Hardy Bay, inclusive of these ports, and extending two miles into the interior of the Island.

The condition of or understanding of this sale is this, that our village sites and enclosed fields are to be kept for our own use, for the use of our children, and for those who may follow after us; and the land shall be properly surveyed hereafter. It is understood, however, that the land itself, with these small exceptions, becomes the entire property of the white people for ever; it is also understood that we are at liberty to hunt over the unoccupied lands, and to carry on our fisheries as formerly.

We have received, as payment, Sixty-four pounds sterling.

In token whereof, we have signed our names and made our marks, at Fort Rupert, Beaver Harbour, on the eighth day of February, one thousand eight hundred and fifty-one.

          (Signed)   WALE his x mark.
 Witnesses,   and 11 others.
(Signed)   WILLIAM HENRY MCNEILL, C. T., H. B. Co.
     CHARLES DODD, Master, Steamer Beaver.
     GEORGE BLENKINSOP, Clerk, H. B. Co.

QUAKEOLTH TRIBE—FORT RUPERT.

Know all men, we, the chiefs and people of the Tribe called Quakeolths, who have signed our names and made our marks to this deed on the eighth day of February, one thousand eight hundred and fifty-one, do consent to surrender, entirely and for ever, to James Douglas, the agent of the Hudson's Bay Company on Vancouver Island, that is to say, for the Governor, Deputy Governor, and Committee of the same, the whole of the lands situate and lying between McNeill's Harbour and Hardy Bay, inclusive of these ports, and extending two miles into the interior of the Island.

The condition of or understanding of this sale is this, that our village sites and enclosed fields are to be kept for our own use, for the use of our children, and for those who may follow after us; and the land shall be properly surveyed hereafter. It is understood, however, that the land itself, with these small exceptions, becomes the entire property of the white people for ever; it is also understood that we are at liberty to hunt over the unoccupied lands, and to carry on our fisheries as formerly.

We have received, as payment, Eighty-six pounds sterling.

In token whereof, we have signed our names and made our marks, at Fort Rupert, Beaver Harbour, on the eight day of February, one thousand eight hundred and fifty-one.

          (Signed)   WAWATTIE his x mark
 Witnesses,   and 15 others.
(Signed)   WILLIAM HENRY MCNEILL, C. T., H. B. Co.
     CHARLES DODD, Master, Steamer Beaver.
     GEORGE BLENKINSOP, Clerk, H. B. Co.

SAALEQUUN TRIBE—NANAIMO.

A similar conveyance of country extending from Commercial Inlet, 12 miles up the Nanaimo River, made by the Saalequun Tribe, and signed Squoniston and others.

CORRESPONDENCE BETWEEN THE SECRETARY OF STATE FOR THE COLONIES AND GOVERNOR DOUGLAS.

Extract from a Despatch from the Right Hon. Sir E. B. Lytton, Bart., to Governor Douglas, dated 31st July, 1858.

3. I have to enjoin upon you to consider the best and most humane means of dealing with the Native Indians. The feelings of this country would be strongly opposed to the adoption of any arbitrary or oppressive measures towards them. At this distance, and with the imperfect means of knowledge which I possess, I am reluctant to offer, as yet, any suggestion as to the prevention of affrays between the Indians and the immigrants. This question is of so local a character that it must be solved by your knowledge and experience, and I commit it to you, in the full persuasion that you will pay every regard to the interests of the Natives which an enlightened humanity can suggest. Let me not omit to observe, that it should be an invariable condition, in all bargains or treaties with the natives for the cession of lands possessed by them, that subsistence should be supplied to them in some other shape, and above all, that it is the earnest desire of Her Majesty's Government that your early attention should be given to the best means of diffusing the blessings of the Christian Religion and of civilization among the natives.

Copy of Despatch from the Right Hon. Sir E. B. Lytton, Bart., to Governor Douglas.

(No. 12.)

Downing Street,
September 2nd, 1858.

SIR,—In my Despatch of the 31st July, No 6, I directed your attention to the treatment of the Native Indians in the country which it has so recently been decided to establish as a British Colony. I regard that subject as one which demands your prompt and careful consideration. I now transmit to you the copy of a letter from the Aborigines Protection Society, invoking the protection of Her Majesty's Government on behalf of these people. I readily repeat my earnest injunctions to you to endeavour to secure this object. At the same time I beg you to observe that I must not be understood as adopting the views of the Society as to the means by which this may be best accomplished.

I have, &c.,
(Signed)   E. B. LYTTON.

ENCLOSURE.

To the Right Honourable Sir Edward Bulwer Lytton, M. P., Her Majesty's Principal Secretary of State for the Colonies, &c., &c., &c.

SIR,—As the Aborigines Protection Society have for many years taken a deep interest in the welfare of the Indian Tribes to the west as well as the east of the Rocky Mountains, I am instructed to address you on certain matters affecting not only the rights and interests but the very existence of the numerous Indian population of the new Colony of British Columbia. It appears, from all the sources of information open to us, that unless wise and vigorous measures be adopted by the representatives of the British Government in that Colony, the present danger of a collision between the settlers and the natives will soon ripen into a deadly war of races, which could not fail to terminate, as similar wars have done on the American continent, in the extermination of the red man.

The danger of collision springs from various causes. In the first place, it would appear from Governor Douglas's Despatches, as well as from more recent accounts, that the natives generally entertain ineradicable feelings of hostility towards the Americans, who are now pouring into Fraser and Thompson Rivers by thousands, and who will probably value Indian life there as cheaply as they have, unfortunately, done in California. The reckless inhumanity of the gold diggers of that State towards the unfortunate Indians, is thus described in a recent number of the *New York Times* :—

"The country is perfectly wild, and a dense forest, full of warlike Indians; and,
"with the well known injustice of the miner towards anything of the genus Indian
"or Chinaman, and their foolhardiness, they will get up a series of little amuse-
"ments in the way of pistolling and scalping, quite edifying. It is the custom of
"miners generally to shoot an Indian as he would a dog; and it is considered a
"very good joke to shoot at one at long shot, to see him jump as the fatal bullet
"pierces his heart. And when, in the spirit of retaliation, some poor hunted
"relative watches his opportunity, and attacks a straggling white man, the papers at
"once teem with long accounts of Indian outrages. And yet the men that shoot
"down these poor Indians are not the ruffians we are led to suppose are always the
"authors of atrocities, but the respectable sovereign people, brought up in the fear
"of God by pious parents, in the most famed locations for high moral character.
"The Indian and Chinese murders are more frequently committed by men brought
"up in the quiet country villages of Eastern States, and who return looking as
"innocent as lambs. There never yet existed so bad a set of men on the face of
"this fair earth as a certain class of the highly respectable sovereigns of the states
"who find their way to the frontiers. It is much to be rejoiced at that the Fraser
"River Indians are of a serious turn of mind, and can't take a joke; and in their
"ignorance of the sports and pastimes of the great American nation may deprive
"some of the practical jokers of their 'thatches,' "

The necessity which is imposed upon Her Majesty's Government to adopt measures to protect the Indians against this class of diggers is too obvious to require any further illustration or argument on our part.

But there is another aspect of the question which is of equal importance. The Indians, being a strikingly acute and intelligent race of men, are keenly sensitive in regard to their own rights as the aborigines of the country, and are equally alive to the value of the gold discoveries; no better proof of which could be furnished than the zest and activity with which large numbers of them have engaged in gold digging. Governor Douglas states that in the earlier stages of the gold discoveries they endeavoured to expel the settlers, who were then few in number, and to obtain possession of the fruits of their labour. But he also states that while manifesting a determination to reserve the gold for their own benefit, they yet respected the persons and property of the whites. Other accounts describe the Indians as "quiet and peaceful," but state that "as soon as a miner lays down his pick an Indian stands by to "make use of it for himself, and when he lays down the shovel for the pick the "Indian takes the shovel, and relinquishes the other implement." They are further described as having learnt the full value of their labour; in proof of which it is stated that they now charge five dollars to eight dollars a day, instead of one dollar, for their services as boatmen in navigating Thompson and Fraser rivers.

As, therefore, the Indians possess an intelligent knowledge of their own rights, and appear to be determined to maintain them by all the means in their power, there can be no doubt that it is essential to the preservation of peace in British Columbia that the natives should not only be protected against wanton outrages on the part of the white population, but that the English Government should be prepared to deal with their claims in a broad spirit of justice and liberality. It is certain that the Indians regard their rights as natives as giving them a greater title to enjoy the riches of the country than can possibly be possessed either by the English Government or by foreign adventurers. The recognition of native rights has latterly been a prominent feature in the aboriginal policy of both England and the United States. Whenever this principle has been honestly acted upon, peace and amity have characterized the relations of the two races, but whenever a contrary policy has been carried out, wars of extermination have taken place; and great suffering and loss, both of life and property, have been sustained both by the settler and by the Indian. We would beg, therefore, most respectfully to suggest that the Native title should be recognized in British Columbia, and that some reasonable adjustment of their claims should be made by the British Government.

The present case resembles no common instance of white men encroaching on the lands and rights of aborigines for hunting or settlement. It more than realizes the fabulous feuds of Gryphons and Arimaspians, and no ordinary measures can be expected to overcome the difficulties which duty and interest require to be removed if British Columbia is to become an honourable or advantageous portion of the British Dominions. It would seem that a Treaty should be promptly made between the delegates of British authority and the chiefs and their people, as loyal, just, and pacific as that between William Penn and the Indians of Pennsylvania, but that more stringent laws should be made to ensure its provisions being maintained with better faith than that was carried out on the part of the whites. No nominal protector of aborigines,—no annuity to a petted chief,—no elevation of one chief above another, will answer the purpose. Nothing short of justice in rendering payment for that which it may be necessary for us to acquire, and laws framed and administered in the spirit of justice and equality, can really avail. To accomplish the difficult but necessary task of civilizing the Indians, and of making them our trusty friends and allies, it would seem to be indispensable to employ in the various departments of Government a large proportion of well-selected men, more or less of Indian blood, (many of whom could be found at the Red River) who might not only exert a greater moral influence over their race than we could possibly do, but whose recognized position among the whites would be some guarantee that the promised equality of races should be realized. The adoption of these or similar measures would, we believe, propitiate the goodwill of the Indians; and instead of obstructing the work of colonization they might be made useful agents in peopling the wilderness with prosperous and civilized communities, of which they one day might form a part.

      I have, &c.,
        (Signed)   F. W. CHESSON,
                 Secretary.

Copy of Despatch from Governor Douglas to the Right Hon. Sir E. B. Lytton, Bart.
(No. 17.)   Victoria, Vancouver's Island,
                  November 5, 1858.

SIR,—I have the honour to acknowledge the receipt of your Despatch, No. 12, of the 2nd of September last, transmitting to me a copy of a letter from the Aborigines Protection Society, invoking the protection of Her Majesty's Government on behalf of those people.

2. While you do not wish to be understood as adopting the views of the society as to the means by which that may be best accomplished, you express a wish that the subject should have my prompt and careful consideration, and I shall not fail to give the fullest effect to your instructions on the head, as soon as the present pressure of business has somewhat abated. I may, however, remark that the native Indian tribes are protected in all their interests to the utmost extent of our present means. I have, &c.,
        (Signed)   JAMES DOUGLAS,
                 Governor.

Copy of Despatch from the Right Hon. Sir E. B. Lytton, Bart., to Governor Douglas.

(No. 62.) Downing Street,
December 30, 1858.

Sir,—With reference to my Despatches of this day's date, on the present condition of British Columbia, I wish to add a few observations on the policy to be adopted towards the Indian tribes.

The success that has attended your transactions with these tribes induces me to inquire if you think it might be feasible to settle them permanently in villages; with such settlement civilization at once begins. Law and Religion would become naturally introduced amongst the red men, and contribute to their own security against the aggressions of immigrants, and while by indirect taxation on the additional articles they would purchase they would contribute to the Colonial Revenue, some light and simple form of direct taxation, the proceeds of which would be expended strictly and solely on their own wants and improvements, might obtain their consent.

Sir George Grey has thus at the Cape been recently enabled to locate the Kaffirs in villages, and from that measure, if succeeding Governors carry out, with judgment and good fortune, the designs originated in the thoughtful policy of that vigorous and accomplished Governor, I trust that the posterity of those long barbarous populations may date their entrance into the pale of civilized life.

I have, &c.,
(Signed) E. B. LYTTON.

Governor Douglas to the Secretary of State for the Colonies.

No. 4. Victoria, Vancouver's Island,
9th February, 1859.

Sir,—I have the honor of transmitting herewith for your information, my correspondence with the House of Assembly of Vancouver's Island on the public business of this Colony.

2. The subjects referred to in that correspondence are not of an important nature with the exception of that marked letter, dated 5th February, 1859, which touches on the subject of land reserved near the town of Victoria for the benefit of the native Indian population.

3. Attempts having been made by persons residing at this place to secure those lands for their own advantage by direct purchase from the Indians, and it being desirable and necessary to put a stop to such proceedings, I instructed the Crown Solicitor to insert a public notice in the Victoria *Gazette* to the effect that the land in question was the property of the Crown, and for that reason the Indians themselves were incapable of conveying a legal title to the same, and that any person holding such land would be summarily ejected.

4. In my communication before referred to, you will perceive that I have informed the House of Assembly of the course I propose to adopt with respect to the disposal and management of the Indian Reserve at Victoria; that is to lease the land, and to apply all the proceeds arising therefrom for the exclusive benefit of the Indians.

5. I have but little doubt that the proposed measure will be in accordance with the views of Her Majesty's Government, and I trust it may meet with their approval, as it will confer a great benefit on the Indian population, will protect them from being despoiled of their property, and will render them self-supporting, instead of being thrown as outcasts and burdens upon the Colony.

I have, etc.,
(Signed) JAMES DOUGLAS.

Copy of Despatch from Governor Douglas to the Right Hon. Sir E. B, Lytton, Bart.

(No. 114.) Victoria, Vancouver's Island,
March 14, 1859.

Sir,—I have the honour to acknowledge the receipt of your Despatch, No. 62, of the 30th December last, containing many valuable observations on the policy to be observed towards the Indian tribes of British Columbia, and moreover your instructions directing me to inform you if I think it would be feasible to settle those tribes permanently in villages; suggesting in reference to that measure, that with such settlement civilization would at once begin; that law and religion would become naturally introduced among them, and contribute to their security against the aggressions of immigrants; that through indirect taxation, on the additional articles they would purchase, they would contribute to the Colonial Revenue, and with their own consent, some light and simple form of taxation might be imposed, the proceeds of which would be expended strictly and solely on their own wants and improvements.

2. I have much pleasure in adding, with unhesitating confidence, that I conceive the proposed plan to be at once feasible, and also the only plan which promises to result in the moral elevation of the native Indian races, in rescuing them from degradation, and protecting them from oppression and rapid decay.

It will, at the same time, have the effect of saving the Colony from the numberless evils which naturally follow in the train of every course of national injustice, and from having the native Indian tribes arrayed in vindictive warfare against the white settlements.

3. As friends and allies the native races are capable of rendering the most valuable assistance to the Colony, while their enmity would entail on the settlers a greater amount of wretchedness and physical suffering, and more seriously retard the growth and material development of the Colony, than any other calamity to which, in the ordinary course of events, it would be exposed.

4. In my Despatch No. 4, of the 9th of February last, on the affairs of Vancouver's Island, transmitting my correspondence with the House of Assembly up to that date, there is a message made to the House on the 5th February, 1859, respecting the course I propose to adopt in the disposal and management of the land reserved for the benefit of the Indian population at this place, the plan proposed being briefly thus:—that the Indians should be established on that reserve, and the remaining unoccupied land should be let out on leases at an annual rent to the highest bidder, and that the whole proceeds arising from such leases should be applied to the exclusive benefit of the Indians.

5. The advantages of that arrangement are obvious. An amount of capital would thereby be created, equal perhaps to the sum required for effecting the settlement of the Indians; and any surplus funds remaining over that outlay, it is proposed to devote to the formation and support of schools, and of a clergyman to superintend their moral and religious training.

6. I feel much confidence in the operation of this simple and practical scheme, and provided we succeed in devising means of rendering the Indian as comfortable and independent in regard to physical wants in his improved condition, as he was when a wandering denizen of the forest, there can be little doubt of the ultimate success of the experiment.

7. The support of the Indians will thus, wherever land is valuable, be a matter of easy accomplishment, and in districts where the white population is small, and the land unproductive, the Indians may be left almost wholly to their own resources, and, as a joint means of earning their livelihood, to pursue unmolested their favorite calling of fishermen and hunters.

8. Anticipatory reserves of land for the benefit and support of the Indian races will be made for that purpose in all the districts of British Columbia

inhabited by native tribes. Those reserves should in all cases include their cultivated fields and village sites, for which from habit and association they invariably conceive a strong attachment, and prize more, for that reason, than for the extent or value of the land.

9. In forming settlements of natives, I should propose, both from a principle of justice to the state and out of regard to the well-being of the Indians themselves, to make such settlements entirely self-supporting, trusting for the means of doing so, to the voluntary contributions in labour or money of the natives themselves; and secondly, to the proceeds of the sale or lease of a part of the land reserved, which might be so disposed of, and applied towards the liquidation of the preliminary expenses of the settlement.

10. The plan followed by the Government of the United States, in making Indian settlements, appears in many respects objectionable; they are supported at an enormous expense by Congress, which for the fiscal year ending June 30, 1856, granted the sum of 358,000 dollars for the support and maintenance of the Indians of California alone, and for the four years ending with the 30th June, 1858, the total expenditure for that object came to the large sum of 1,104,000 dollars, and notwithstanding the heavy outlay, the Indians in those settlements are rapidly degenerating; neither would I recommend the system pursued by the founders of the Spanish missions in California.

Their objects, though to a certain extent mercenary, were mainly of a benevolent kind; the Indians were educated and trained in the Roman Catholic faith; they were well fed and clothed, and they were taught to labour; but being kept in a state of pupilage, and not allowed to acquire property of their own, nor taught to think and act for themselves, the feeling and pride of independence were effectually destroyed; and not having been trained to habits of self-government and self-reliance, they were found, when freed from control, altogether incapable of contributing to their own support, and really were more helpless and degraded than the untutored savages.

11. With such beacons to guide our steps, and profiting by the lessons of experience so acquired, we may perhaps succeed in escaping the manifest evils of both systems; the great expense and the debasing influences of the American system, by making the Indians independent and the settlements self-supporting; and to avoid the rock on which were wrecked the hopes of the Spanish missions, I think it would be advisable studiously to cultivate the pride of independence, so ennobling in its effects, and which the savage largely possesses from nature and early training.

12. I would, for example, propose that every family should have a distinct portion of the reserved land assigned for their use, and to be cultivated by their own labour, giving them however, for the present, no power to sell or otherwise alienate the land; that they should be taught to regard that land as their inheritance; that the desire should be encouraged and fostered in their minds of adding to their possessions, and devoting their earnings to the purchase of property apart from the reserve, which would be left entirely at their own disposal and control; that they should in all respects be treated as rational beings, capable of acting and thinking for themselves; and lastly, that they should be placed under proper moral and religious training, and left, under the protection of the laws, to provide for their own maintenance and support.

13. Having touched thus briefly on the prominent features of the system, respecting which you requested my opinion, and trusting that my remarks may convey to you the information you desired, and may not be deemed irrelevant.

I have, &c.,
(Signed) JAMES DOUGLAS,
Governor.

The Secretary of State for the Colonies to Governor Douglas, C. B.

(No. 49.)
Downing Street,
11th April, 1859.

Sir,—I have to acknowledge the receipt of your despatch of the 9th of February, No. 4, transmitting copies of communications which have passed between you and the House of Assembly of Vancouver Island, between the 23rd August and the 5th February last.

I am glad to perceive that you have directed the attention of the House to that interesting and important subject, the relations of Her Majesty's Government and of the Colony to the Indian race. Proofs are unhappily still too frequent of the neglect which Indians experience when the white man obtains possession of their country, and their claims to consideration are forgotten at the moment when equity most demands that the hand of the protector should be extended to help them. In the case of the Indians of Vancouver Island and British Columbia, Her Majesty's Government earnestly wish that when the advancing requirements of colonization press upon lands occupied by members of that race, measures of liberality and justice may be adopted for compensating them for the surrender of the territory which they have been taught to regard as their own. Especially I would enjoin upon you, and all in authority in both colonies, the importance of establishing schools of an industrial as well as an educational character for the Indians, whereby they may acquire the arts of civilized life which will enable them to support themselves, and not degenerate into the mere recipients of eleemosynary relief. If it is to be hoped that by such and other means which your experience will enable you to devise, the Indians may in these, the most recent of the British settlements, be treated in a manner worthy the beneficient rule of Our Gracious Sovereign.

I have, etc.,
(Signed)   CARNARVON,
In the absence of Sir E. B. Lytton.

Copy of Despatch from the Right Hon. Sir E. B. Lytton, Bart., to Governor Douglas, C. B.

(No. 67.)
Downing Street,
May 20, 1859.

Sir,—I have to acknowledge the receipt of your Despatch, No. 114, of the 14th of March, on the subject of the policy to be observed towards the Indian tribes, and containing your opinion as to the feasibility of locating the Indians in native villages, with a view to their protection and civilization.

I am glad to find that your sentiments respecting the treatment of the native races are so much in accordance with my own, and I trust that your endeavours to conciliate and promote the welfare of the Indians will be followed by all persons whom circumstances may bring into contact with them. But whilst making ample provision under the arrangements proposed for the future sustenance and improvement of the native tribes, you will, I am persuaded, bear in mind the importance of exercising due care in laying out and defining the several reserves, so as to avoid checking at a future day the progress of the white colonists.

I have &c.,
(Signed)   CARNARVON.
(In the absence of the Secretary of State.)

Governor Douglas to the Secretary of State for the Colonies.

(No. 24.) Victoria, 25th March, 1861.

My Lord Duke,—I have the honour of transmitting a petition from the House of Assembly of Vancouver Island to your Grace, praying for the aid of Her Majesty's Government in extinguishing the Indian title to the public lands in this Colony; and setting forth, with much force and truth, the evils that may arise from the neglect of that very necessary precaution.

2. As the native Indian population of Vancouver Island have distinct ideas of property in land, and mutually recognize their several exclusive possessory rights in certain districts, they would not fail to regard the occupation of such portions of the Colony by white settlers, unless with the full consent of the proprietary tribes, as national wrongs; and the sense of injury might produce a feeling of irritation against the settlers, and perhaps disaffection to the Government that would endanger the peace of the country.

3. Knowing their feelings on that subject, I made it a practice up to the year 1859, to purchase the native rights in the land, in every case, prior to the settlement of any district; but since that time in consequence of the termination of the Hudson's Bay Company's Charter, and the want of funds, it has not been in my power to continue it. Your Grace must, indeed, be well aware that I have, since then, had the utmost difficulty in raising money enough to defray the most indispensable wants of Government.

4. All the settled districts of the Colony, with the exception of Cowichan, Chemainus, and Barclay Sound, have been already bought from the Indians, at a cost in no case exceeding £2 10s. sterling for each family. As the land has, since then, increased in value, the expense would be relatively somewhat greater now, but I think that their claims might be satisfied with a payment of £3 to each family; so that taking the native population of those districts at 1,000 families, the sum of £3,000 would meet the whole charge.

5. It would be improper to conceal from your Grace the importance of carrying that vital measure into effect without delay.

6. I will not occupy your Grace's time by any attempt to investigate the opinion expressed by the House of Assembly, as to the liability of the Imperial Government for all expenses connected with the purchase of the claims of the aborigines to the public land, which simply amounts to this, that the expense would, in the first instance, be paid by the Imperial Government, and charged to the account of proceeds arising from the sales of public land. The land itself would, therefore, be ultimately made to bear the charge.

7. It is the practical question as to the means of raising the money, that at this moment more seriously engages my attention. The Colony being already severely taxed for the support of its own Government, could not afford to pay that additional sum; but the difficulty may be surmounted by means of an advance from the Imperial Government to the extent of £3,000, to be eventually repaid out of the Colonial Land Fund.

8. I would, in fact, strongly recommend that course to your Grace's attention, as specially calculated to extricate the Colony from existing difficulties, without putting the Mother Country to a serious expense; and I shall carefully attend to the repayment of the sum advanced, in full, as soon as the Land Fund recovers in some measure from the depression caused by the delay Her Majesty's Government has experienced in effecting a final arrangement with the Hudson's Bay Company for the reconveyance of the Colony, as there is little doubt when our new system of finance comes fully into operation that the revenue will be fully adequate to the expenditure of the Colony.

I have, &c.,
(Signed)   James Douglas.

The Secretary of State for the Colonies to Governor Douglas, C. B.

(No. 73.)　　　　　　　　　　　　　　　　Downing Street,
　　　　　　　　　　　　　　　　　　　　19th October, 1861.

Sir,—I have had under my consideration your despatch No. 24, of the 25th of March last, transmitting an Address from the House of Assembly of Vancouver Island, in which they pray for the assistance of Her Majesty's Government in extinguishing the Indian title to the public lands in the Colony, and set forth the evils that may result from a neglect of this precaution.

I am fully sensible of the great importance of purchasing without loss of time the native title to the soil of Vancouver Island; but the acquisition of the title is a purely colonial interest, and the Legislature must not entertain any expectation that the British taxpayer will be burthened to supply the funds or British credit pledged for the purpose. I would earnestly recommend therefore to the House of Assembly, that they should enable you to procure the requisite means, but if they should not think proper to do so, Her Majesty's Government cannot undertake to supply the money requisite for an object which, whilst it is essential to the interests of the people of Vancouver Island, is at the same time purely Colonial in its character, and trifling in the charge that it would entail.

　　　　　　　　　　　　　　　　　　　　　　I have, etc.,
　　　　　　　　　　　　　　　(Signed)　　　Newcastle.

GENERAL CORRESPONDENCE.

Mr. Cox to the Chief Commissioner of Lands and Works.

　　　　　　　　　　　　　　　　　Rock Creek, 12th February, 1861.

Sir,—I have the honour to inform you that I am this day in receipt of a Circular from the Colonial Secretary, by which I perceive His Excellency the Governor has been pleased to appoint me Assistant Commissioner of Lands for this District.

I therefore beg to seek from you some information on the following, viz:—
Laws for controlling Indian Reservations:
Laws for the letting of Agricultural Land to Aliens.

The former I shall thank you much to make me acquainted with as early as convenient; some disputes (for the present amicably arranged) having lately arisen between the natives and white men, concerning ground preoccupied by the former near the northern extremity of Okanagan Lake, on its eastern bank, where some miners and farmers now are.

The land in question has been for many years in possession of the Indians as one of their camping localities or villages. I intend, on receipt of your instructions in this matter, proceeding there and finally measuring out whatever ground you consider the Indians entitled to. Mines have lately been discovered there, hence the altercations.

I shall also feel obliged by you informing me of your wishes as to the survey of this town and disposal of its building lots.

　　　　　　　　　　　　　　　　　　　　I have, &c.,
　　　　　　　　　　　　　　　(Signed)　　　William Geo. Cox.

The Chief Commissioner of Lands and Works to Mr. Cox.

New Westminster, 6th March, 1861.

Sir,—I have the honour to acknowledge the receipt of your communication of the 12th ultimo, requesting information as to the laws for controlling Indian Reservations, also those for the letting of agricultural lands to aliens.

With regard to the former, I have received instructions from His Excellency the Governor to communicate with you on the subject and to request that "you will mark out distinctly all the Indian Reserves in your District, and define their extent as they may be severally pointed out by the Indians themselves." I would, at the same time, beg of you to be particular in scrutinizing the claims of the Indians, as I have every reason to believe that others (white persons) have, in some instances, influenced the natives in asserting claims which they would not otherwise have made, the object of such persons being prospective personal advantages previously covertly arranged with the Indians. To instance this, I heard of men keeping Indian women inducing them or their relations to put forward claims in order that they (the white men) may so gain possession of the land.

As to the law for the letting of "country" lands to aliens, in a recent correspondence with the Colonial Secretary on the subject, I am referred by him to the "Aliens Act, 1859," clause 8, which stipulates that "every alien shall have the same capacity to take, hold, enjoy, recover, convey and transmit title to lands and real estate of every description" as a natural born British subject; and under the "Pre-emption Act, 1860," Aliens, who shall take the oath of allegiance, will be entitled to enjoy the privileges it confers.

I trust that you will, ere this, have received the supply of forms which were forwarded to you from this office on the 7th ultimo, and which, by a careful attention to them, will facilitate much the working of the Land system.

I have to thank you for the promptitude you have shown in complying with the instructions, to which you allude as having received from the Colonial Secretary, and hope that you will communicate frankly to me all that may occur in your District having reference to the Lands and Works Department.

Respecting the laying out of the town you will oblige me much by forwarding to me, at your early convenience, a sketch (no matter how rough) descriptive of the spot on which you suggest the lots (town and suburban) should be picketed out. The breadth of the principal street should be 66 feet and the back streets in proportion. The size of the town lots should be 132x66, and advantage should be taken of level spaces for public squares, etc. Suburban lots nearest the town may vary in extent from one to five acres.

I have, &c.,
(Signed) R. C. Moody.

The Colonial Secretary to the Chief Commissioner of Lands and Works.

New Westminster,
5th March, 1861.

Sir,—I am directed by His Excellency the Governor to request that you will take measures, so soon as may be practicable, for marking out distinctly the sites of the proposed Towns and the Indian Reserves throughout the Colony.

2. The extent of the Indian Reserves to be defined as they may be severally pointed out by the Natives themselves.

I have, &c.,
(Signed) Charles Good,
For Colonial Secretary.

Extract from a Despatch from the Colonial Secretary to the Chief Commissioner of Lands and Works.

Colonial Secretary's Office,
5th April, 1861.

* * * * * *

6. His Excellency further directs me to convey to you his instructions that the position and extent of all spots of land, now set apart as Government or Indian Reserves, are to be forthwith published in three different places in each district where there may be such Reserves, and also in the local newspapers, and should it so happen that circumstances may afterwards render it expedient to relinquish any such reserve, notice of the same is to be likewise published for 2 months at least, before any sale or occupation of the reserved lands be permitted; and His Excellency requests you will furnish him, at your earliest convenience, with a rough general sketch of the country, exhibiting the different districts, and also as near as may be the land already alienated by the Government.

* * * * *

I have, &c.,
(Signed) WILLIAM A. G. YOUNG.

Instructions to Sapper Turnbull.

New Westminster, 1st May, 1861.

SAPPER TURNBULL,—You will take an early opportunity of staking and marking out in the District you are now stationed, all Indian villages, burial places, reserves, etc., as they may be pointed out to you by the Indians themselves, subject, however, to the decision of the District Magistrate as to the extent of the land so claimed by them. Make sketches of the locality and give dimensions of claim, sending them to this office after acquainting the Magistrate of what you have done. Be very careful to satisfy the Indians so long as their claims are reasonable, and do not mark out any disputed lands between whites and Indians before the matter is settled by the Magistrate, who is requested to give you every assistance. Report your progress from time to time.

I have, &c.,
(Signed) R. M. PARSONS, Capt., R. E.

[No reply to this letter can be found.]

The Private Secretary to the Chief Commissioner of Lands and Works.

New Westminster,
15th May, 1861.

SIR,—I am directed by His Excellency the Governor to acquaint you that Mr. Atkins, of Coquitlam Farm, has represented to His Excellency that a misunderstanding has arisen between himself and the Indians of that district, in reference to the boundaries of their respective claims, and to request you will take efficient steps to decide the question at issue, by sending a surveying party to define the boundaries of those claims, and to mark them out without delay.

I have, &c.,
(Signed) CHARLES GOOD,
Acting Private Secretary.

[No reply to this letter can be found.]

The Colonial Secretary to the Chief Commissioner of Lands and Works.

Colonial Secretary's Office,
2nd August, 1861.

Sir,—With reference to the 6th paragraph of the Colonial Secretary's letter No. 36 of the 5th April last, and to which no reply has as yet been received, I am directed by His Excellency the Governor to request you will inform him what measures you have adopted for carrying out the instructions contained in that letter in reference to publishing in every district lists of the Indian and Government Reserves, and also will mention the dates on which such notices were published in each district. His Excellency desires me, further, to draw your attention to the map of such reserves called for in the above mentioned letter, which has not been sent.

I have, &c.,
(Signed)   CHARLES GOOD,
For Colonial Secretary.

[No reply to this letter can be found.]

The Chief Commissioner of Lands and Works to Mr. Brew.

New Westminster,
13th May, 1862.

Sir,—I have the honour to acquaint you that a portion of land, with five chains frontage on the North Arm of the Fraser, has been laid out as an Indian Reserve, at a distance of ten chains west from the Suburban Lots of New Westminster.

I have, &c.,
(Signed)   J. GRANT, Capt., R. E.,
For Chief Commissioner.

The Chief Commissioner of Lands and Works to the Colonial Secretary.

Lands and Works Department,
New Westminster, 27th May, 1862.

Sir,—An Indian named Snat Stroutan, of the Squamish tribe, resident here, desires to purchase, just as a white man would, one of the suburban lots adjoining New Westminster. It is among those that have been put up to auction, and was not bid for, so that it is open to purchase at the upset price. The lot selected by him is at some distance from the town, so that it cannot prove an annoyance, and the man proposes actually to reside thereon.

The above is an interesting turning point in the history of the Indians of British Columbia, and I submit that I be authorized to receive the purchase money, procure him a title deed, and in all respects deal in the matter precisely as I would with a white man. His Excellency's authority is requested early.

I have, &c.,
(Signed)   R. C. MOODY.

The Colonial Secretary to the Chief Commissioner of Lands and Works.

Colonial Secretary's Office,
18th June, 1862.

Sir,—With reference to your letter of the 27th ultimo, on the subject of the purchase of a Suburban Lot of Land by an Indian, on the same terms as it could be purchased by a white man, I am directed by the Governor to inform you that there can be no objection to your selling lands to the Natives on the same terms as they are disposed of to any purchasers in the Colony whether British subjects or aliens.

I have, &c.,
(Signed) WILLIAM A. G. YOUNG.

The Chief Commissioner of Lands and Works to the Colonial Secretary.

Lands and Works Department,
New Westminster, 2nd June, 1862.

Sir,—In compliance with the instructions contained in your letter of the 30th May, 1862, No. 65,* I have to state that among the items for expenditure for services in progress, is that of marking out and surveying the spots occupied by Indians with their villages and isolated "provision grounds." So far as we can ascertain the latter, they are often in hidden spots, and the Indians (possibly distrusting our statements) are loth to show them.

In carrying out this service I am employing from 2 to 3 Indians, sometimes 4, with the 2 Royal Engineers. The Indians on this special service are peculiarly useful in many obvious ways. The cost will not exceed thirty-five Pounds per month, and I request special sanction for the same until further notice from you. I *may* require such aid almost continuously until the end of the season.

I have &c.,
(Signed) R. C. MOODY.

The Colonial Secretary to the Chief Commissioner of Lands and Works.

Colonial Secretary's Office.
9th June 1862.

Sir,—I have received and laid before the Governor your letter of the 2nd instant, making application for sanction for an expenditure not exceeding £35 monthly, until the end of summer, for the purpose of marking out and surveying the spots occupied by Indians with their villages and isolated provision grounds.

2. With reference thereto, I am to state that His Excellency would be glad of some further information on this subject, as he was under the impression that the work of marking out (*not surveying*) the Indian Reserves had been long ago carried out, where requisite, under the instructions conveyed to you by His Excellency on the 5th April, 1861.

3. His Excellency is not aware what necessity may exist for the present *survey* of these Indian Reserves, but unless the reasons are very weighty, His Excellency would not, under the existing heavy pressure on the resources of the Colony, feel justified in authorizing an outlay to the extent you mention, for it appears to His Excellency that for all present purposes, the marking of such Reserves by conspicuous posts driven into the ground would be sufficient, and that the survey thereof could be postponed until the Colony can better afford the expense.

I have, &c.,
(Signed) WILLIAM A. G. YOUNG.

---

* This letter merely contains general instructions to the effect that no money is to be expended on any work without authority having been first obtained.

The Chief Commissioner of Lands and Works to the Colonial Secretary.

Lands and Works Department,
New Westminster, 11th June, 1862.

SIR,—A question has arisen as to Indians pre-empting lands precisely as a white man could. I understood His Excellency to say that there is nothing to prevent their doing so, provided, of course, they fulfil all the terms required by the Pre-emption Proclamation.

I shall feel obliged by receiving official instructions in respect to the above. Such instructions appear to be very necessary in connection with the progress of the survey of the country, the more so as I understand Indians are pre-empting in "extended order" along the River and elsewhere to considerable extent, and that such extent is likely to increase very considerably and very rapidly.

I have, etc.,
(Signed) R. C. MOODY.

The Colonial Secretary to the Chief Commissioner of Lands and Works.

Colonial Secretary's Office,
2nd July, 1862.

SIR,—I am directed by the Governor to acquaint you, in reply to your letter of the 11th ultimo, No. 87, on the subject of the pre-emption of land by the Natives of British Columbia, that it is intended to legislate on this subject hereafter, and provisions will be made for permitting Indians to hold land under pre-emption on the following conditions:—

1st. That they reside continuously on their farms.

2nd. That they build thereon a house of squared logs with shingled roofs, not less than 30 feet by 20 feet, and side walls 10 feet high.

3rd. That they clear, enclose, and cultivate 1st year 2 acres of wood-land, or 5 acres of prairie land. 2nd year and afterwards, till the end of the 5th year, 3 acres of wood-land, or 6 acres of prairie land.

4th. That no power shall be given to convey such land without the consent of the Governor having been first obtained.

I have, &c.,
(Signed) WILLIAM A. G. YOUNG.

The Colonial Secretary to the Chief Commissioner of Lands and Works.

Colonial Secretary's Office,
26th June, 1862.

SIR,—I am directed by the Governor to forward the enclosed tracing, and with reference thereto, to acquaint you that the bearers of this letter by name "Kholasten" and "Scakhalan," Langley Indians, are desirous of abandoning their present abode on the Island opposite Langley, and with their families and some other Indians of settling on another piece of land on the right bank of the river, adjoining the claim of William Cromerty.

2. His Excellency, therefore desires you will be good enough to declare to be an Indian Reserve, a tract of land of 160 acres in area, immediately adjoining William Cromerty's claim, as by the accompanying sketch, and when convenient have the same marked out by corner posts on the ground.

I have, &c.,
(Signed) WILLIAM A. G. YOUNG.

The Chief Commissioner of Lands and Works to Mr. Spalding.

New Westminster,
28th June, 1862.

SIR,—I have the honour to enclose a copy of a letter received by me this day from the Colonial Secretary, respecting the appropriation for an Indian Reserve of 160 acres of land adjoining the reputed claim of one William Cromerty.

I beg to be informed whether any such claim has been recorded in your office, and whether the Indian Reserve laid out as directed, will or will not conflict with the claims of others.

I have, &c.,
(Signed) R. C. MOODY.
[No reply to this letter can be found.]

Mr. Cox to the Chief Commissioner of Lands and Works.

Kamloops, 31st October, 1862.

SIR,—I have the honour to forward you herewith, records of four Indian Reserves. I have, &c.,

(Signed) WILLIAM GEO. COX.

ENCLOSURE.

October 15th, 1862.—Indian Reserve situated on the Bonaparte River between Cache Creek and McLean's Restaurant; is bounded on either side by the mountains, and by Messrs. McLean's land claims on the northern and southern extremities.

The soil is fertile in some places along the river bottoms, which are densely covered with brush and cotton-wood; the boundaries are substantially and prominently marked off by stakes.

October 15th, 1862.—Indian Reserve situated on the Bonaparte River north of McLean's Restaurant, and adjoins Scotty's Farm on the north end and Mc Donald's on the south, and bounded on either side by mountains.

The soil similar to that of the former Reserve.

October 24th, 1862.—Indian Reserve situated at Kamloops, and extends along the North River, east side, for about six miles, and along the Thompson River to the east for about twelve miles more or less, running back to the mountains in both cases.

The soil in some places is of the best description, and the pasture excellent—a quantity timbered with pine and willow.

October 26th, 1862.—Indian Reserve situated on the common road, midway between Kamloops and the Lake Ferry, and a short distance west of River Ceuis; containing about 25 acres more or less.

The soil is very fertile and the pasture of the best nature.

Governor Douglas to the Chief Commissioner of Lands and Works.

New Westminster,
27th April, 1863.

SIR,—An application has been made to me this morning, by the Native inhabitants of Coquitlam River, for an additional grant of land contiguous to the Indian Reserve immediately opposite Mr. Atkinson's premises.

That reserve it appears is so small, not exceeding 50 acres of land, as to be altogether insufficient to raise vegetables enough for their own use.

I beg that you will, therefore, immediately cause the existing reserve to be extended in conformity with the wishes of the Natives, and to include therein an area so large as to remove from their minds all causes of dissatisfaction.

Notwithstanding my particular instructions to you, that in laying out Indian Reserves the wishes of the Natives themselves, with respect to boundaries, should in all cases be complied with, I hear very general complaints of the smallness of the areas set apart for their use.

I beg that you will take instant measures to inquire into such complaints, and to enlarge all the Indian Reserves between New Westminster and the mouth of Harrison River, before the contiguous lands are occupied by other persons.

I have, &c.,
(Signed) JAMES DOUGLAS.

The Chief Commissioner of Lands and Works to His Excellency the Governor.

Lands and Works Department,
New Westminster, 28th April, 1863.

SIR,—I have the honour to acknowledge the receipt of a communication from Your Excellency, dated 27th instant, respecting an application from the Indians on the Coquitlam for an additional grant of land, and you desire the existing reserve be immediately extended.

Before carrying out these instructions, it is proper I should submit the following statements in connection with the immediate point and the remarks in the concluding portion of Your Excellency's letter to me :—

The reserve in question was most carefully laid out, the Indians being present, and after they had *themselves* marked according to their own wishes the bounds, the area was further enlarged. I resisted the appeal of the neighbouring settler, and acceded to the amplest request of the Indians.

The Indians in question have asked of me not for an extension of the *present* boundary, but the privilege of pre-empting *elsewhere*—knowing that to extend the boundary of what they now hold would be merely to grant them swampy ground subject to inundation. As it is a question of pre-emption, they have been referred by me to the Magistrate of the District, within whose sole cognizance are matters of pre-emption of land.

The Roman Catholic priests have moved the Indians to pre-empt as freely as any other persons. This I made known to Your Excellency, in order that such instructions as you desire to be prepared may be given to the Magistrates. It is a growing question that will have to be met.

I have never yet received, nor heard from any source whatever, a complaint from the Indians in reference to the extent of their boundaries. In fact, in every case the wishes of the Indians are carefully consulted, and the bounds are widely extended beyond the limits marked out by themselves.

Any statement, contrary to the above, made to Your Excellency from whatsoever quarter is absolutely without foundation. The interests of the Indian population are scrupulously, I may say jealously, regarded by myself and every officer and man under my command.

I beg leave earnestly to move Your Excellency that some practical measures be adopted in respect to the land as well as to other interests of the Indians, measures that shall effectually guard against any misunderstanding. I do not think this can well be done by my department. It requires also a thorough knowledge of the Indian languages.

Pending better arrangements, if even now for instance I had the able assistance of so judicious a man as the Reverend Mr. Garrett to make himself acquainted with all the villages, number of population in each, and extent of land wished for or requisite, I would attach a man to him with proper stakes, &c., and then, having before me a statement as regards all in the valley of the Fraser, below Yale at all events, these lands would be safe from invasion, could be gazetted at once and surveyed at leisure.

Several full reserves have already been made, but I hear incidentally that there are other Indian villages and potato grounds with the sites of which the Lands and Works Department is not acquainted.

I have, &c.,
(Signed)   R. C. MOODY.

The Chief Commissioner of Lands and Works to Governor Douglas.

(CONFIDENTIAL.)   New Westminster,
28th April, 1863.

SIR,—I endeavoured to carry out through the medium of the Reverend M. Fouquet, R. C., the idea laid down in an accompanying letter as to obtaining the numbers of villages, population, extent of land, etc., and furnished him with stakes all in accordance with that which seemed to be suitable at the time. M. Fouquet conferred with your Excellency in my presence, but 1 very quickly had occasion to desist from such a course from the extreme want of judgment shown by that gentleman, in fact from the operations of the Roman Catholic Missionaries, (philanthropic in spirit no doubt), we are likely to have embarrassments, and I would recommend some special arrangements, distinct from those of the Lands and Works Department, be early devised and carried out.

I shall be only too happy to give every aid in my power.

I have, etc.,
(Signed)   R. C. MOODY.

The Colonial Secretary to the Chief Commissioner of Lands and Works.

Colonial Secretary's Office,
11th May, 1863.

SIR,—I am desired by the Governor to acknowledge his receipt, this day, of your letter of the 28th ultimo, marked "Confidential," relative to the Indian Reserves in British Columbia.

2. In reply thereto I am to acquaint you that His Excellency considers that the instructions contained in his letters to you of 5th March and 5th April, 1861, and 27th April, 1863, cover the whole question, and he requests that those instructions may be carried out to the letter, and in all cases where the land pointed out by the Indians appears to the officer employed on the service to be inadequate for their support, a larger area is at once to be set apart.

3. His Excellency does not see [that it is at all necessary or expedient to employ the Roman Catholic Missionaries to assist in laying out the Indian Reserves, although they no doubt can, and will readily, furnish useful information concerning the numbers composing each tribe.

I have, &c.,
(Signed)   WILLIAM A. G. YOUNG.

The Chief Commissioner of Lands and Works to Mr. Brew.

New Westminster, 11th June, 1863.

SIR,—I shall feel obliged if you will be good enough to inform me when it will be in your power to dispatch a legal functionary to Keatzie, to settle the claim of the Indians as to the bounds of their land. Surveyors shall be sent with him to mark it off by posts so soon as he shall adjust the dispute.

You may remember the interview with the Governor, in which he decided that the Indians, by the present condition of affairs, were defrauded of their just demands; and it appeared that the bounds being moved some moderate distance further east would meet their desires. It was then considered the best way would be to send a sufficiently qualified person up to Keatzie who could understand the Indian.language and rightly interpret the case, and that this Department should carry out on the spot the decision arrived at.

I have, &c.,
(Signed)   R. C. MOODY.

Mr. Brew to Chief Commissioner of Lands and Works.

New Westminster, B. C.,
12th June. 1863.

SIR,—In reply to your letter of the 11th instant, I beg leave to say that I shall dispatch Mr. T. Brew, High Constable, to Keatzie, on Tuesday next, the 16th instant, to try and settle about the Indian Reserve.

I have, &c.,
(Signed)   C. BREW, J. P.

Mr. Nind to the Honorable the Colonial Secretary.

Lytton, 17th July, 1865.

SIR,—I have the honour to address you on the subject of the Indian land claims above Kamloops and in its vicinity.

That branch of the Shuswap tribe, which live on the Upper Thompson and Shuswap Lakes, numbering, I am informed, less than five hundred souls, claim the undisputed possession of all the land on the north side, between the foot of the Great Shuswap Lake and the North River, a distance of nearly fifty miles, where lie thousands of acres of good arable and pasture land, admirably adapted for settlement. I have heard of one cattle-owner who paid their Chief, Nisquaimlth, a monthly rent for the privilege of turning his cattle on these lands.

Another branch of the same tribe, not so numerous as the first, claim all the available land on the North River, extending northward many miles above the mouth, which also possesses attraction to the settler. These Indians do nothing more with their land than cultivate a few small patches of potatoes here and there; they are a vagrant people who live by fishing, hunting and bartering skins; and the cultivation of their ground contributes no more to their livelihood than a few days digging of wild roots; but they are jealous of their possessory rights, and are not likely to permit settlers to challenge them with impunity; nor, such is their spirit and unanimity, would many settlers think it worth while to encounter their undisguised opposition. This, then, has the effect of putting a stop to settlement in these parts. Already complaints have arisen from persons who have wished to take up land in some of this Indian territory, but who have been deterred by Indian claims. At present all the land pre-empted is on the south side of the Thompson Valley for no other cause than this. James Todd, an old settler at Kamloops, is anxious to take up land close to Nisquaimlth's camp; but he is on friendly terms with the chief, and says he can buy him over to his views with a horse or so. I have refused at present to record him the land, particularly as he wants to purchase, in addition to his pre-emption, four hundred and twenty acres, until I put the matter of Indian claims before the Government. It seems to me undesirable that the principle of a settler purchasing or acquiring his right to land from the natives should ever be admitted. I assume that this is the prerogative of the Government of the Colony which should alone be able to confer an undefeasible title to its lands. Certainly what one man might obtain by influence over a chief or intermarriage with a tribe, or other means more questionable, might be refused to another who yet carried out all the requirements of the law. One would live in security; the other would always be subject to molestation and danger. I believe the only method of settling this matter satisfactorily and with equity to both Indians and whites will be for the Government to extinguish the Indian claims, paying them what is proper for so doing, and giving them certain reservations for their sole use. These Indians are now quiet and not ill-disposed to the whites; but they are capable of giving a good deal of trouble if they imagine their rights are invaded.

I have, &c.,
(Signed)   PHILIP HENRY NIND.

The Chief Commissioner of Lands and Works to the Colonial Secretary.

Lands and Works Department,
New Westminster, Sept. 20th, 1865.

SIR,—In reference to Mr. Nind's letter to yourself of the 17th July, which has been referred to me for a report, I have the honor to state that the settlement of the boundaries of Indian reserves is, in my opinion, a question of very material present and prospective importance, and should engage immediately the attention of all interested.

I quite concur in Mr. Nind's remarks on the Kamloops and Shuswap reserves, taking for granted that the premises on which they are founded are correct, but as this department is entirely without official information as to the location or extent of these Indian reserves, I am unable to supply any exact data on this subject.

It appears most advisable that it should be at once constituted the definite province of some person or persons, duly authorized for that purpose, to make a thorough enquiry into this subject throughout the Colony. To ascertain as exactly as practicable what lands are claimed by Indians, what lands have been authoritatively reserved and assured to the various tribes, and to what extent such reserves can be modified with the concurrence of the Indians interested in them—either with or without money or other equivalent.

I am satisfied from my own observation that the claims of Indians over tracts of land, on which they assume to exercise ownership, but of which they make no real use, operate very materially to prevent settlement and cultivation, in many instances besides that to which attention has been directed by Mr. Nind, and I should advise that these claims should be as soon as practicable enquired into and defined.

I have, &c.,
(Signed)   JOSEPH W. TRUTCH.

The Colonial Secretary to the Chief Commissioner of Lands and Works.

Colonial Secretary's Office,
26th September, 1865.

SIR,—I am directed by the Officer Administering the Government to acknowledge the receipt of your letter of the 20th instant, on the subject of Indian Reserves.

His Honor is fully impressed with the importance of defining those reserves throughout the Colony, but he is not prepared, at this late season of the year, to commence a general system such as you recommend. His Honor, however, thinks it very desirable that the Shuswap and Kamloops Reserves should be reduced, without further delay, to reasonable limits, as it would perhaps be a matter of greater difficulty to settle the affair should the route by Kamloops become the main thoroughfare to the Columbia River. I am therefore to request you to inform Mr. Moberly that the Governor is very desirous of reducing the reserves to which Mr. Nind makes allusion in his letter of the 17th July, last, and of which I forward a copy for your information and guidance; and that you will authorize Mr. Moberly to make enquiries on his way down, and to reduce these reserves if he is of opinion that it can be effected without much dissatisfaction to the Indians.

If, however, he should be of opinion that difficulty will arise from such a course, his duty will be to collect on the spot all the information he can on the subject, and furnish you with a full report thereon, in order that the Government may have some data to go by in coming to a decision on the matter.

His Honor further suggests that Mr. Nind be at once requested to furnish Mr. Moberly with a copy of a report from Mr. Cox on this subject; which report His Honor remarks you may remember Mr. Cox stated, in your presence, he had sent to Mr. Nind. I have, &c.,

(Signed)   CHARLES GOOD,
For the Colonial Secretary.

Instructions to Mr. Moberly.

New Westminster,
October 10th, 1865.

SIR,—The Indian Reserves at Kamloops and Shuswap laid out by Mr. Cox, being considered entirely disproportionate to the numbers and requirements of the Indians residing in those Districts, His Honor has instructed me to direct you to make an investigation of the subject on your way back from the Columbia, and to report, on your return to this place, whether in your opinion arrangements can be made to reduce the limits of these reserves, so as to allow part of the lands now uselessly shut up in these Reserves to be thrown open to pre-emption.

I enclose copies of an extract from the Colonial Secretary's letter to me on this subject and of Mr. Nind's letter to the Colonial Secretary, and have requested Mr. Nind to furnish you with a copy of Mr. Cox's report on the location of the reserve, and you will be pleased to take such steps towards the fulfilment of His Honor's instructions in this regard as may appear most advisable to you.

I have. etc.,
(Signed)   JOSEPH W. TRUTCH.

Mr. Nind to Mr. Moberly.

Lytton, 5th October, 1865.

SIR,—I have been desired by the Acting Colonial Secretary to forward to you copy of a letter I received from Mr. Cox respecting Indian reserves; also a sketch forwarded to me at the same time, in illustration by that gentleman.

I have, etc.,
(Signed)   PHILIP HENRY NIND.

ENCLOSURE.

Extract from letter from Mr. Cox to Mr. Nind, respecting Indian Reserves about Kamloops, dated 16th July, 1865.

SHUSWAP RESERVE.—Just before leaving Kamloops, I received instructions from Governor Douglas to mark out all the Indian Reserves in the neighbourhood. The Kamloops Reserve extends about $4\frac{1}{2}$ miles up North River, and about 10 miles up Thompson River. The Shuswap tribes called upon me to do the same for them, as some Frenchmen were encroaching upon their grounds. I could not mark off their boundaries at that time on the ground, but chalked out the position and extent of the Shuswap Reserve at Kamloops, for the chief, and gave him papers to post up. There could be no mistake. I shall send you, herewith, a sketch of same, as well as I can recollect it. The probability is that my papers have been removed, and the grounds allowed by me greatly added to.

(Signed)   W. G. COX.

Copy of paper given by Mr. Cox to Gregoire, and Son, Nisquaimlth.

All persons are hereby cautioned not to cut timber, interfere or meddle in any way with the rights of the Indians, on this Reserve.

Gregoire and Son are the chiefs of the Reserve.

(Signed) W. G. COX, P. M.

Shuswap, 31st October, 1862.

Copy of Notice in possession of Petite Louis, Chief of Kamloops Indians.

KAMLOOPS INDIAN RESERVE.—Bounded by the North and Thompson Rivers, as per stakes and notices defining the boundaries.

All persons are hereby cautioned not to encroach upon or interfere in any way with the rights of the Indians. Any person or persons found or detected cutting timber on the Reserve will be severely punished.

Chelouis or Louis is chief of this Reserve, and will be found an obliging, honest, young man.

(Signed) W. G. COX, J. P.

Kamloops, 31st October, 1862.

The Chief Commissioner of Lands and Works to the Colonial Secretary.

Lands and Works Department,
New Westminster, January 17th, 1866.

SIR,—I have the honour to enclose for the information of the Officer Administering the Government, a copy of a report from Mr. Moberly on the subject of the Kamloops and Shuswap Indian Reserves, an investigation of which was undertaken by him in accordance with my letter of instructions of 10th October. I also enclose a sketch showing the position and extent of these reserves, together with copies of all the papers relating to them that can be found in this Department. On the general subject of these reserves I have already offered an opinion in my letter to yourself of 20th September.

It appears to me that, as stated by Mr. Moberly, these reserves are entirely disproportionate to the numbers or requirements of the Indian Tribes to which they are represented to have been appropriated by Mr. Cox.

Two points remain to be determined, 1st.—Whether or not Mr. Cox's agency in the matter is binding on the Government? And secondly—are the boundaries of the reserves now claimed by the Indians those which Mr. Cox really gave them assurance of?

On the first point I cannot form an opinion, as I am without any information as to the instructions given to Mr. Cox on the subject, but on the second I think there is reason to believe, from what Mr. Cox stated to Mr. Birch in my presence in August last, at Richfield, and from the rough sketch furnished in his own handwriting, a copy of which is enclosed, that the extent of one at least of these reserves, that of the Shuswap Tribe, has been largely added to by the changing of the position of the boundary stakes by the Indian claimants.

It is most important that these questions be enquired into as soon as possible, and if it be decided that Mr. Cox's Reserves are to be observed, and that the tracts claimed by the Indians are only those which were actually made over to them by him, there will remain only to be determined whether it is advisable to purchase back from them such portions of these lands as are valuable for settlement.

Much of the land in question is of good quality, and it is very desirable, from a public point of view, that it should be placed in possession of white settlers as soon as practicable, so that a supply of fresh provisions may be furnished for consumption in the Columbia River Mines, and for the accomodation of those travelling to and from the District.

I have, &c.,
(Signed)   J. W. TRUTCH.

ENCLOSURE.

Mr. Moberly to the Chief Commissioner of Lands and Works.

New Westminster,
December 22nd, 1865.

SIR,—In reply to your letter dated October 10th, 1865, I have to inform you that on my return from the Columbia River on the 2nd November, I took immediate steps to find out the position and extent of the Indian Reserves on the North and Shuswap Rivers, and other particulars connected with the granting of these lands by Mr. Cox, and also if an arrangement could be effected with the Indians for the reduction of these reserves to reasonable limits.

I found that Nisquaimlth, and his father Gregoire, the two Shuswap Chiefs, claim the land on the north bank of the Shuswap River, from a point about sixteen miles above Kamloops, to a point about four and a half miles in a direct line above the foot of the Great Shuswap Lake, and also to the northerly end of Adams Lake; that Che-louis, or Petite Louis, the Kamloops Chief, claims the land from a point about one mile below the westerly boundary of Nisquaimlth's claim to Kamloops, and thence up the North River a distance of about eight miles; and that the intermediate strip of land between the above claims was vacant. The two above reserves embrace an area of about six hundred square miles.

I learnt from the Indians that they claim these lands by virtue of certain papers given them by Mr. W. G. Cox, who they say told them at the time he made the above reservations, that he was acting under instructions received by him from Governor Sir James Douglas, and that such portions of these reserves not cultivated by them would be useful for grazing their cattle upon.

I also ascertained from the Indians that Mr. Cox had seen the position of the different stakes and marks defining these reserves, with the exception of the stakes on the Great Shuswap and Adams Lakes. These two stakes were placed by Nisquaimlth himself, as he says, in accordance with Mr. Cox's instructions to him.

When in possession of the above information, and such as I gathered from the different letters and papers I enclose, as I found that Mr. Cox's sketches and descriptions did not agree with the position of the marks set up, I was quite at a loss what conclusion to arrive at with regard to them.

As it appeared to me quite out of the question that Governor Sir James Douglas could have given Mr. Cox instructions to make such extensive reservations for a tribe that I should say does not number more than four hundred souls, and have not one hundred acres of land under cultivation, I had various interviews with the Indians, the result being that those settled at Little Shuswap and Adams Lakes wished me to lay off the reserves in the manner I proposed, but the two Chiefs, Nisquaimlth and Petite Louis, both objected to have the lands they claim below the Little Shuswap Lake reduced in extent, giving as one reason that they received considerable sums of money from white men for the use of their grass lands.

I made several efforts to induce these two Chiefs to consent to a reduction of their claims, but without success. They appear to be under the impression that the reservations are more their own and not the general property of the tribe. I explained to the Indians that whatever reservations were made by the Government were for the general benefit of the whole tribe and not of the individual Chiefs;

this appeared to be a popular principle with the majority of the Indians, but was not so with Nisquaimlth, who is not generally liked but is feared by them. I also told them it was my impression the reserves claimed by them, and as they said defined by Mr. Cox, were not laid out in accordance with the intention of Governor Douglas' instructions to him, and if so, that Mr. Cox's grants to them are worthless, as the Governor of the Colony is the only person who can give them a title to any land, and that Mr. Cox had given them what it was not in his power to grant.

Many of the Indians appeared to be of the same opinion, but the immediate followers of the Chiefs always fell back upon their rights to the land as acquired from Mr. Cox, and also from their long residence thereon.

I think by showing the Indians in the first place that their titles from Mr. Cox are of no value, and by a judicious expenditure of a small sum of money, that arrangements can be effected to get the greater portion of these reserves quietly given up. It would be very desirable indeed to get all the lands from the foot of Little Shuswap Lake to Kamloops entirely out of their hands.

As I did not feel myself justified in expending any money then, as the forcible reduction of these reserves by me would have created a bad feeling now, and probably have led to future acts of violence on their part—which ought to be avoided by every possible means, as the Shuswap River is likely to be the principal thoroughfare through the Colony next summer; and as the information in my possession was very meagre, particularly with regard to Governor Douglas' instructions to Mr. Cox, under which he states he acted, I thought it better to postpone any further action in the matter until I could report to you.

Since my arrival here I have endeavoured to find out what records there are in the different Departments relative to these reserves, but have not been able so far to get any information whatever on the subject.

I have, &c.,
(Signed) W. MOBERLY.

The Chief Commisssoner of Lands and Works to the Colonial Secretary.

Land and Works Department,
New Westminster, 5th February, 1866.

SIR,—I have the honour to enclose, for the information of the Officer Administering the Government, a copy of a letter from Mr. Haynes informing me that he had, in compliance with His Excellency's instructions, laid out Indian Reserves at the head and foot of Okanagan Lake, and that sketches of the same would be handed to me by Mr. Turnbull who had assisted in staking them out.

I also enclose copies of a report to me from Mr. Turnbull on the same subject, and of the sketches referred to by Mr. Haynes, which accompanied Mr. Turnbull's report. In reference to Mr. Haynes' suggestion that it should be notified in the *Government Gazette* that the lands around Okanagan Lake heretofore held as Indian Reserves should be declared open to pre-emption, with exception of the tracts staked out by Mr. Turnbull under his (Mr. Haynes') direction, I beg to observe that if the arrangement made by Mr. Haynes is to be considered as a final settlement of the Okanagan Indian Reserve, I am quite of opinion that the suggestion of Mr. Haynes should be adopted, but that, as the question of Indian Reserves in the neighbouring Kamloops and Shuswap Districts is, as I believe, still under discussion, it may be well to defer the publication of any notice on the subject of the Okanagan Indian Reserves until some general decision has been come to in regard to similar reserves throughout that and the neighbouring districts.

I have, &c.,
(Signed) JOSEPH W. TRUTCH.

ENCLOSURES.

Mr. Haynes to the Chief Commissioner of Lands and Works.

Camp, Head of Okanagan Lake,
28th November, 1865.

SIR,—I have the honour to inform you that in compliance with instructions from His Excellency the Governor, contained in a letter of the 9th of last July, I have laid out Indian Reserves at the head and foot of this Lake, sketches of which will be handed to you by the bearer, Mr. Turnbull, who has assisted me in this work.

I think it would be well to notify in the *Government Gazette* that the lands in this vicinity, hitherto looked upon as Indian Reserves, are now open for settlement, except the portion marked on the maps which you will receive.

I have, &c.,
(Signed)   J. C. HAYNES.

Mr. Turnbull's Report.

New Westminster, 17th January, 1866.

SIR,—In compliance with the wishes of Mr. Haynes (Magistrate of the Osoyoos District), I have laid out three Indian Reserves situated on the north and southern extremity of the Okanagan Lake, and I herewith beg to lay before you the enclosed plan, which will show their positions, etc., etc., together with the few following remarks respecting them.

On account of not being provided with chain or suitable instruments I was unable to make surveys sufficiently accurate to answer official purposes. I have, in consequence, merely roughly surveyed as pointed out to me by Mr. Haynes.

Whilst surveying, Mr. Haynes and his Indian, (who is a Chief of the District) accompanied me, the Indian blazing and picketting as I instructed him ; therefore at any furture time either Mr. Haynes or the Indian can point out the boundaries. The boundaries, however, are well defined, being all natural boundaries, as shown on sketch. The first reserve which is situated on the south end of the Okanagan Lake (and known by the Indians as Penticton), is eminently adapted for either stock-raising or agricultural purposes, the altitude above the sea being only 700 feet, abundance of the best feed, good soil and climate, and surrounded by one of the best cattle ranges in the country.

The reserve is bounded on the south by the Lake du Chien; on the east by the Okanagan River ; on the west by the base of the low rolling hills, and terminates about $2\frac{1}{4}$ miles north at the first point, where the hillside and river meets.

The portion unreserved to the east of the river is the most valuable land, being well irrigated by the various streams (which I have shown on sketch). It is more heavily timbered than the portion to the west ; and for that reason (in my opinion) was not selected by the Indians. All the creeks are fringed with a dense growth of tangled bush, such as birch, cottonwood, hazel, thorns, etc.

The next reserve is situated on the west bank of the lake, commencing about $2\frac{3}{4}$ miles from the head, and running south about $3\frac{1}{2}$ miles. It is bounded on the south by the creek (shown on sketch), to the east by the lake, to the west by the hillside, and on the north by the creek running into the lake, about three miles from the head.

This reserve is a level, bunch grass flat with widely scattered trees, the margins of the creeks (as is always the case) covered with a thick growth of birch, hazel, pine, etc. The whole of the flat may be considered eligible for agricultural purposes, as it can be all irrigated with very little trouble ; the feed throughout is of first-class quality; the hillsides to the westward also abound in good feed, and are low and rolling and well suited for cattle range.

The last reserve, which is situated immediately at the head of the lake, is a splendid tract of low bottom land, with dark loamy soil, excellent feed, and surrounded on all sides by low, rolling bunch grass hills and benches. Its boundaries are as follows: To the south by the lake, to the west by the creek, up to the point where the trail crosses it, then by a line running north 60° east by compass for one mile, terminating immediately above the small lake (shown on sketch), next by a line bearing S. 30° East, for 30 chains to the foot of low rolling hill; from latter point by line bearing S. 47° East for about 33 chains, until striking the creek about one mile from the lake; the latter creek there forms its eastern boundary.

Mr. Cox, several years ago, reserved nearly all the agricultural lands situated about the head of the lake, as well as that on the south end, (now reserved under the head of Penticton). The results of this reservation were many men have been prevented from settling on what may be considered the only real agricultural and grazing land in the country. Last winter, a Frenchman brought some one or two hundred head of cattle to Penticton, for the purpose of wintering there. The Indians, who claimed the land, (under the authority of Mr. Cox), ordered him off, or else pay a certain amount per head. The result was the Frenchman left with the whole of his cattle, and wintered at the Mission, where, owing to the scarcity of feed, the hard season, etc., he lost nearly the whole of his stock. Had he been allowed to stop at Penticton, his stock might have survived the winter, as the place is low, well sheltered, and in fact may be considered the best cattle "winter" range in the country.

Mr. Haynes' reservation at Penticton is a great improvement to the last. He has left sufficient unreserved for wintering purposes. At the head of the lake, the next favourite resting place, he has reserved in such a manner so that settlers wintering there run the risk of having to pay the Indians a certain amount per head for the cattle they graze. As this particular portion of the country is in such close proximity to the mines now being discovered in the Big Bend country, and considering it may be termed one of the few safe wintering ranges, I imagine it would have been better had this reserve been done away with, or if reserved at all, reserved under the head of Government Reserve, in which case both white man and Indian would have an equal right.

My reason for expressing these opinions is knowing the difficulties there are in this portion of the country in safely wintering animals.

The reserve at Penticton comprises 842 acres. The one on the west of lake about 1,500 acres, in my opinion more than double the amount necessary to serve the purposes of the Indians settled on the Okanagan.

I have &c.,
(Signed) J. TURNBULL.

The Colonial Secretary to the Chief Commissioner of Lands and Works.

Colonial Secretary's Office,
29th May, 1866.

SIR,—As the settlement of the boundaries of the Indian Reserves about Kamloops and Shuswap will be one of the duties devolving upon you, on your visit to the Kamloops District, the Officer Administering the Government considers it advisable that you should assemble the Chiefs at Kamloops, or other convenient spot, and endeavour to settle amicably and satisfactorily, not only to the chiefs, but to the whole of the families of the tribes, the limits of their reserves.

Should you find any difficulty in curtailing the limits already alleged by the chiefs to have been marked out for them by Mr. Cox, His Honor directs me to inform you that you are authorized to offer a remuneration, either pecuniary or in the shape of presents, to such Indians as feel reluctant or refuse to relinquish any of the land which they imagine they are entitled to as a reserve.

In this arrangement much will be left to your discretion; but His Honor would not wish any expenditure incurred beyond $500, without a previous reference being made to him.

In the settlement of this question, great care must be taken that all the Indian families, who claim any portion of the Indian Reserve, are cognizant of the decreased limits as soon as the negotiations are completed.

I have, &c.,
(Signed)   H. M. BALL.

Mr. Pemberton to the Chief Commissioner of Lands and Works.

Kamloops,
July 26th 1866.

DEAR SIR,—Would you be good enough to tell me in what time the Government intend fixing upon the Indian Reserves in this District, and also when we may expect to see some one up to settle with the Indians and make them understand which land they are to have, and which they are to give up, as under the present circumstances they will not allow anyone to do anything on the land they claim, which is most inconvenient to intending settlers. They prevented us from even cutting down trees, and say they don't want anything to be done until they see you. The chief says he will be quite contented to abide by what you say. The same inconvenience is felt down at Savona's Ferry. The Indians have there driven off the cattle. They are also burning off the grass in every direction, which will make feed very scarce for the hundreds of cattle which winter upon the Thompson; and I am afraid if it be not settled soon it will cause trouble among the Indians, as the other day they prevented some six miners from going up Adams River to prospect; and I really think that you could settle the thing very quickly yourself, as the Indians wish, they say, to see the *Tyhee* himself, and then they will be content. Hoping to hear from you as soon as convenient,

I have, &c.,
(Signed)   A. G. PEMBERTON.

Mr. Howse to Mr. Pemberton.

Lands and Works Department,
New Westminster, 4th August, 1866.

SIR,—I am directed by the Colonial Secretary to inform you that the Chief Commissioner of Lands and Works will shortly visit Kamloops with reference to the subject of your letter dated 26th ultimo.

I have, etc.,
(Signed)   A. R. HOWSE.

Mr. Edgar Dewdney to the Chief Commissioner of Lands and Works.

New Westminster, B. C.,
8th Nov., 1866.

SIR,—I have the honor to forward you the sketches of the several Indian Reserves surveyed by me in the Kamloops, Shuswap, and Adams Lake Districts. The chiefs of the different tribes as well as several of their Indians accompanied me during the progress of the surveys, and made themselves thoroughly acquainted with the boundaries and stakes.

The Reserves are laid out as nearly as possible in accordance with the instructions received on the ground from His Honor the Officer Administering the Government and yourself.

On arriving at Adams Lake, I found that the Indians had several small patches of land cultivated along the shores of the Lake, four of which they wished reserved.

I however gave them the piece of open bunch grass land situated on the South-East end of the Lake, about one and a quarter miles square, that being the only feed they have for their horses and cattle. This I surveyed.

I also gave them fifteen square chains on the West side of the Lake, about 12 miles from the outlet of Adams River.

This I did not survey, but gave them a board 24 inches by 12 inches, marked with marking iron and colored red, "Adams Lake Indian Reserve 15 square chains," with instructions to place this in the centre of the ground they described to me.

I was unable to visit this spot on account of the high wind that prevailed whilst I was there.

The Shuswap and Adams Lake chiefs have each a plan of their respective reserves, but having no paper I was unable to give "Petit Louis" the Kamloops Chief, his; it is now ready for him.

The whole of the Indians appeared perfectly satisfied with their reserves as laid out by me, and I think that no trouble may be apprehended from any of them in future about their land.

I beg to enclose the descriptions of the different reserves. My field notes I will leave at the Lands and Works Office.

I have, etc.,
(Signed) EDGAR DEWDNEY.

Description of Kamloops Indian Reserve.

Commencing at the N. W. stake marked K. I. R., about three miles up the North branch of Thompson River, the West boundary follows the meanderings of the River to its junction with the South branch, at which point a large cottonwood tree is blazed and marked K. I. R., for S. W. corner; for Southern boundary, continue the meanderings up the South branch of Thompson River for a distance of three miles to a group of cottonwood trees, one of which is marked K. I. R. for S. E. corner; from this point the East boundary runs N. 9° E., to a deep gully in the mountain which extends to creek and crosses it at a distance of 2 miles and 10 chains from S. E. corner, at this point several trees are blazed, continue up a deep gully about one mile to a tree blazed and marked K. I. R. for N. E. corner; the North boundary follows along several bunch grass flats to a large bluff of rock from which the line runs S., 76° W. to N. W. corner.

Description of Shuswap Indian Reserve No. 1.

Commencing at the S. E. corner stake marked S. I. R. No. 1. situated at the junction of the North branch of Nesquailmth's Creek with Thompson River, follow the meanderings of the stream to four large cottonwood trees, one of which is broken off half way up, blazed and marked S. I. R. No. 1; cross to South branch of Nesquailmth's Creek N., 81° W., (taking in the Indian potatoe patches), to two large cottonwood trees, one of which is marked S. I. R. No. 1; follow the meanderings of the creek to its outlet from a large Lake, at which point two large fir trees are blazed, and one marked S. I. R. No. 1, for S. W. corner; continue along the meanderings of the East shore of lake to a small creek which feeds it at its Northern end; follow along creek to a tree blazed on its bank for N. W. corner. From this point the Northern boundary runs S., 30° E. to bank of Thompson River 219 chains, where a stake is placed and marked S. I. R. No. 1., for N. E. corner; on the edge of the river, immediately below this stake a large boulder 15 feet square stands immoveable; from this point follow the meanderings of the river to S. E. corner stake at the mouth of Nesquaimlth's Creek.

Description of Shuswap Indian Reserve No. 2.

Commencing at the South-West corner post situated at the base of mountain and marked S. I. R. No. 2, run S. 40° 30′ E., 30 chains to fir tree on edge of little lake blazed and marked S. I. R. No. 2; for South-East corner follow the meanderings of the lake to a large fir tree 5 chains East of Indian burial ground, blazed and marked S. I. R. No. 2; from this point run N. 12° 30′ W. 106 chains, 70 links, to large pine tree, blazed and marked S. I. R. No. 2; and from here run N. 57° 30′ W. 12 chains to round mound. The Western boundary extends along base of mountain from South-West corner stake to stake at base of mound.

Description of Adams Lake Indian Reserve.

Commencing at the North-West corner stake marked A. L. I. R., situated on the East shore of Adams Lake, 97 chains from the outlet of Adams River, follow the meanderings of Lake and Adams River to mouth of small creek, at which point a large cottonwood tree is blazed and marked A. L. I. R., follow the meanderings of creek one mile and a quarter to where it forks. The East boundary runs along the west fork of stream to its rise and across the face of mountain until it cuts the North boundary line, which runs from North-West corner N. 65° 30′ W., and is blazed for some distance up the mountain. The back line was not run owing to its roughness and inaccessibility. Besides the above the Adams Lake tribe have 15 chains square of land situated on the West shore of Lake about 12 miles from the outlet of Adams River.

The Chief Commissioner of Lands and Works to Mr. O'Reilly.

Lands and Works Department,
New Westminster, 16th November, 1866.

Sir,—I have the honour to forward herewith, for your information, a tracing of the map of the Indian Reserves laid out in September last, by authority of the Officer Administering the Government, at Kamloops, and South branch of Thompson River, Little Shuswap Lake, and Adams Lake.

I have, etc.,
(Signed) Joseph W. Trutch.

Mr. McIvor to the Chief Commissioner of Lands and Works.

New Westminster, 8th April, 1867.

Sir,—Having pre-empted one hundred and sixty acres of land in the fall of sixty, on the south bank of Fraser River, nearly opposite the Indian Village of Katzie, and adjoining a small Indian Reserve, I beg to explain that no Indians have lived on or cultivated this reserve within the last six years, and not likely they ever will. Having some cattle on my land, I am anxious to make the creek that runs through the said reserve my upper boundary line, as seen by the annexed sketch, which would answer as a fence and give me high ground for my cattle to run on during high water; without this I am afraid that I will have to abandon the place altogether and lose my six years' toil in that which I was to make my future home. If it is the intention of the Government to keep an Indian Reserve on this side as well as the opposite side of the Fraser, I humbly beg to suggest that said reserve be extended upwards, as the land is equally as good and fully as clear as that on the lower side of the creek, and again, by extending it upwards, there would be no settlers to interfere with.

I have, &c.,
(Signed) JOHN McIVOR.

Mr. McIvor's application to be allowed to purchase a portion of the Indian Reserve opposite Katzie Village.

As Mr. Howse was going to Katzie to survey some Pre-emption Claims in the neighbourhood of the Indian Reserve referred to, I instructed him to enquire into the circumstances of this case, and have awaited his report before forwarding Mr. McIvor's letter for His Excellency's consideration.

Mr. Howse's report is now enclosed herewith, and I fully agree in the opinions expressed by him and by Mr. Brew, that this reserve should not be interfered with, as its extent is not excessive in proportion to the numbers of the tribe; and there is no doubt that portions of the land Mr. McIvor wishes to acquire are cultivated by the Indians as potato gardens.

(Signed) JOSEPH W. TRUTCH.
26th May, 1867.

[Application refused.]

ENCLOSURE.

Mr. Howse's Report.

Lands and Works Department,
New Westminster, 29th May, 1867.

SIR,—I have the honour to inform you that I have seen Michel, the chief of the Katzie Indians, respecting the reserve opposite Katzie Village, laid out by Colonel Moody, R. E., in 1863, for the use of these Indians.

Michel informs me that the Indians have used the land for many years as potato gardens, and that occasionally they have lived there. He wishes to retain the whole of the land allotted to them.

The tribe numbers about one hundred adult Indians, exclusive of females, and the whole of the reserves do not exceed two hundred and sixty acres, which undoubtedly is not too much for their use.

I am informed that the stakes on the west side of the reserve have been taken away without the sanction of Michel.

I have, &c.,
(Signed) A. R. HOWSE.

The Chief Commissioner of Lands and Works to the Acting Colonial Secretary.

Lands and Works Department,
New Westminster, 28th August, 1867.

SIR,—I have the honour to forward herewith enclosed for the consideration of His Excellency the Governor, a report on the subject of the Lower Fraser Indian Reserves which I had drawn up in obedience to His Excellency's minute of the 20th ultimo, before leaving for Cariboo.

I have, &c.,
(Signed) JOSEPH W. TRUTCH.

ENCLOSURE.

Lower Fraser River Indian Reserves.

It is certainly very desirable that the extent of the Indian Reserves along the lower Fraser River should be definitely determined, and the boundary lines thereof surveyed and exactly marked out on the ground as soon as possible, so that the uncertainty now existing as to what lands are to be permanently held by the Indians may be terminated, and the risk of disputes and collisions between the white settlers and the Indians as to their respective land rights be as far as practicable removed.

The subject of reserving lands for the use of the Indian tribes does not appear to have been dealt with on any established system during Sir James Douglas' administration.

The rights of Indians to hold lands were totally undefined, and the whole matter seems to have been kept in abeyance, although the Land Proclamations specially withheld from pre-emption all Indian reserves or settlements.

No reserves of lands specially for Indian purposes were made by official notice in the *Gazette*, and those Indian Reserves which were informally made seem to have been so reserved in furtherance of verbal instructions only from the Governor, as there are no written directions on this subject in the correspondence on record in this office.

In many cases, indeed, lands intended by the Governor to be appropriated to the Indians were set apart for that purpose and made over to them on the ground by himself personally; but these were for the most part of small extent, chiefly potato gardens adjoining the various villages.

Previous to 1864 very few Indian Reserves had been staked off, or in any way exactly defined.

The only Indian Reserves on the lower Fraser actually surveyed off before Colonel Moody left the Colony, as far as I can ascertain, were the following:—

1. Three lots at the mouth of the North Arm of the Fraser:
2. An Island at the mouth of the Coquitlam River:
3. Two lots on the banks of the Coquitlam River:
4. One lot opposite New Westminster:
5. Two lots at Keatsie, one on each side of the River.

In April, 1864, an Indian Reserve of 353 acres in extent was laid off by Mr. McClure, by instructions from Mr. Brew, on the right bank of the Fraser River, opposite Fort Langley.

By letter dated the 6th April, 1864, Mr. Brew directed Mr. McColl to mark out Indian Reserves around the different Indian villages on the Fraser, between New Westminster and Harrison River, wherever reserves had not yet been declared and defined. Also to mark out as Indian Reserves any ground which had been cleared and tilled for years by Indians; all lands claimed by Indians as theirs were to be marked out with corner and intermediate posts, and at all Indian villages where the quantity of land claimed by the Indians was not equal to ten acres for each family, the reserve was to be enlarged to that extent, each grown man to be considered as the head of a family.

Additional verbal instructions were given by Sir James Douglas personally to Mr. McColl, to the effect, as understood by Mr. McColl and subsequently stated in his report to Mr. Brew, dated 16th May, 1864, that all lands claimed by Indians were to be included in their reserves, that the Indians were to have as much land as they wished, and that he was in no case to lay off a reserve under one hundred acres.

Acting on this latter indefinite authority, rather than on the written instructions from Mr. Brew, McColl marked out reserves of most unreasonable extent, amounting, as estimated by himself, to 50, 60, 69, 109, and even to as much in one case as 200 acres for each grown man in the tribe.

The sketch map sent in by McColl with his report is compiled from his own roughly estimated distances alone; no actual survey was made by him. He seems to have merely walked over the ground claimed by the Indians, setting up stakes, at the corners pointed out by them, including the lands they chose to ask for, and then to have estimated the acreage contained therein.

These figures, therefore, cannot be relied on, but it is certain that the extent of some of the reserves staked out by McColl is out of all proportion to the numbers or requirements of the tribes to which they were assigned.

The Indians regard these extensive tracts of land as their individual property; but of by far the greater portion thereof they make no use whatever and are not likely to do so; and thus the land, much of which is either rich pasture or available for cultivation and greatly desired for immediate settlement, remains in an unproductive condition—is of no real value to the Indians and utterly unprofitable to the public interests.

I am, therefore, of opinion that these reserves should, in almost every case, be very materially reduced.

Two methods of effecting this reduction may be suggested—either (1) to disavow absolutely McColl's authority to make these reserves of the extravagant extent laid out by him, and instead to survey off the reserves afresh, either on the basis of Mr. Brew's letter of instructions to McColl, namely, ten acres to each grown man, or of such extent as may, on investigation, be determined to be proportionate to the requirements of each tribe, or—(2) to negotiate with the Indians for the relinquishment of the greater portion of these lands, which they now consider their own, on terms of compensation, in fact to buy the lands back from them.

The former of these systems was carried out last year in the reduction of the Kamloops and Shuswap Indian Reserves, where tracts of land of most unreasonable extent were claimed and held by the local tribes under circumstances nearly parallel to those now under discussion; and I think that a similar course may be very fairly and expediently adopted in this case.

The Indians have really no right to the lands they claim, nor are they of any actual value or utility to them; and I cannot see why they should either retain these lands to the prejudice of the general interests of the Colony, or be allowed to make a market of them either to Government *or to individuals.*

It seems to me, therefore, both just and politic that they should be confirmed in the possession of such extents of lands only as are sufficient for their probable requirements for purposes of cultivation and pasturage, and that the remainder of the land now shut up in these reserves should be thrown open to pre-emption.

But in carrying out such a reduction of these reserves in the manner proposed, very careful management of the dispositions of the Indian claimants would be requisite to prevent serious dissatisfaction; firmness and discretion are equally essential to effect the desired result, to convince the Indians that the Government intend only to deal fairly with them and the whites, who desire to settle on and cultivate the lands which they (the Indians) have really no right to and no use for.

Perhaps the most judicious course would be that some agent of the Government be commissioned to confer with the Indians on each reserve—to ascertain exactly the numbers of each tribe, and the amount of land actually cultivated or used by them as pasturage—to apprise them that their rights to the tracts now held by them are not acknowledged by Government—but that such extents of land will be at once surveyed and confirmed to them, as the Government may determine to be proportionate to their actual requirements—and to report the results in each case, stating the amounts of land that in his opinion should be finally included in each reserve.

The Government would after the receipt of such a report, be in a much better position than at present to take decisive action in the matter.

(Signed)   JOSEPH W. TRUTCH.

28th August, 1867.

Mr. William McColl's Report.

New Westminster,
16th May, 1864.

SIR,—In accordance with Mr. Brew's instructions of the 6th April, I have completed the staking off of the reserves alluded to in that document, (herewith returned).

I beg to inform you that, in addition to the written instructions, I had further verbal orders given to me by Sir James Douglas, to the effect that all lands claimed by the Indians were to be included in the reserve; the Indians were to have as much land as they wished, and in no case to lay off a reserve under 100 acres. The reserves have been laid off accordingly. (See the accompanying diagram).

I also beg to inform you that I have laid off more reserves than what was originally intended when the instructions were written.

List marked A was handed to me by Sir James Douglas, and contained all the names of the reserves that were to be laid off; but afterwards documents B, C, and D were sent, giving a considerable larger amount of work than what was expected at first.

This explanation is given to shew cause why the work was so much longer in hand than what was expected, one month being allowed. The work was one month and eleven days in hand. This I leave for your consideration.

I have, &c.,

(Signed)   WM. McCOLL.

ENCLOSURES.

Instructions to Mr. McColl.

Mr. William McColl will proceed forthwith to mark out Indian Reserves around the different Indian Villages on the Fraser River, between New Westminster and Harrison River, wherever reserves have not yet been declared and defined. He will also mark as Indian Reserves, any ground which has been cleared and tilled for years by the Indians.

Mr. McColl will mark out with corner and intermediate posts, whatsoever land the Indians claim as theirs; and at any Indian Village where the quantity of land demanded by the Indians is not equal to ten acres for each family, Mr. McColl will enlarge the reserve to that extent. Each grown man to be considered the head of a family.

Mr. McColl will be allowed a month to execute this task.

Surveyor General's Office,   (Signed)   C. BREW.
New Westminster, 6th April, 1864.

Surveyor General's Department,
New Westminster, 25th April, 1864.

SIR,—I am directed by Mr. Brew to request that you will upon completion of your present work, proceed to the Harrison River and lay out the Indian Reserves in that locality, irrespective of the claims of settlers.

The quantity of land to be laid off in accordance with your former instructions.

I have, &c.,
(Signed)   A. R. HOWSE.

A.

	Population.
So-why-lee	70
Yuke-you-quay-yoose	70
Iswhya-aayla	65
Iswhy	14
Assaylitch	20
Koqua-pilt	88
Isqwhay	83
Tlalt-whaas	10
Who-nock	33
Saamoqua	20

B.

Government House,
11th April, 1864.

Mr. McColl.

The bearers of this are from the village of Matsqui—a little above Whonock. Please to mark out their boundaries in the same manner as the other villages.

By order of the Governor,
(Signed)   A. T. BUSHBY.

C.

Surveyor General's Department,
New Westminster, 23rd April, 1864.

SIR,—I am directed by Mr. Brew to inform you that the land claimed by the Indians on the North side of the Fraser River, opposite to the Sumass, is to be laid out as a Reserve.

The accompanying sketch will convey to you the position of the land referred to; and if there are any settlers within the space marked on sketch, and lettered A, B, C, and D, you are requested to make a note of them, showing the position of their claims, but not to survey them.

I have, &c.,
(Signed)   A. R. HOWSE.

D.

Mr. McColl may survey the Nicomin Reserve if he has time.

(Signed)   C. BREW.

25th April, 1864.

The Colonial Secretary to the Chief Commissioner of Lands and Works.

Colonial Secretary's Office,
6th November, 1867.

SIR,—The Governor has had under consideration the subject matter of your letter of the 28th of August, last, relative to the extent and boundaries of the Indian Reserves on the lower Fraser.

2. His Excellency considers it very desirable that this question should not be allowed to remain any longer in the indefinite state in which it appears to stand at present; but that these reserves should be defined, so that the Indians may be aware of the exact limits of the ground allotted to them.

3. There is good reason to believe that Mr. McColl very greatly misunderstood the instructions conveyed to him in respect of marking out these reserves in the first instance, and he has in consequence created reserves of land far beyond the wants or expectations of the Indians. The instructions given in Mr. Brew's letter of the 6th of April, 1864, are very simple, viz :—to mark out as reserves any ground which had been *cleared* and *tilled* for years by Indians; and should the ground so circumstanced be not equal to ten acres for each *family*—each *adult male* being considered the head of a family—the reserve was to be enlarged to that extent. As for the verbal instructions which Mr. McColl is said to have received from Governor Douglas—that the Indians were to have as much land as they wished—it is apprehended that Mr. McColl entirely misinterpreted Governor Douglas' wishes, although it is very probable that he was perfectly right in not laying out any Indian Reserve of less extent than 100 acres.

4. The Indians have no power to alienate any portion of their reserves, and no such alienation can be confirmed. The amount of ground reserved should be amply sufficient for all the actual wants and requirements of the tribe for which the reserve may be made; but in no case should it be of such extent as to engender the feeling in the mind of the Indian that the land is of no use to him, and that it will be to his benefit to part with it.

5. All those reserves that have been laid out of excessive extent should be reduced as soon as may be practicable. The Indians have no right to any land beyond what may be necessary for their actual requirements, and all beyond this should be excluded from the boundaries of the reserves. They can have no claim whatever to any compensation for any of the land so excluded, for they really have never actually possessed it, although, perhaps, they may have been led to view such land as a portion of their reserve, through Mr. McColl so loosely reserving such large tracts of land, out of which, at some future day, the various Indian Reserves would have to be accurately defined.

6. His Excellency will be glad if you will, at an early opportunity, make a reconnaissance of the Indian Reserves herein referred to, with the object of enabling you hereafter the more expeditiously and effectually to carry out the work of survey and marking out, and to direct it in such manner as shall avoid any misunderstanding or complications with the Indians.

I have, &c.,
(Signed) WILLIAM A. G. YOUNG.

The Chief Commissioner of Lands and Works to the Colonial Secretary.

Lands and Works Department,
New Westminster, 19th November, 1867.

SIR,—I have the honor to report for the information of the Governor, that in accordance with His Excellency's instructions conveyed to me in your letter of the 6th instant, I have, in company with Captain Ball, the Magistrate of the

District, visited all but four of the Indian Reserves on the Lower Fraser, which were laid out by the late Sergeant McColl, and have conferred with the Chiefs of the various tribes at their respective villages.

The reserves, which from lack of time, we were unable to visit are those laid off on the Upper Chilliwhack for the Scokale and Sowhylee tribes, and those on the right bank of the Fraser, opposite Sumass, reserved for the Flatwhaas and Nickameen tribes, the latter of which, however, we saw from the River extending about four miles along the bank.

I am satisfied, as the result of our reconnaissance, that those reserves are in almost every instance too extensive, and in some cases extravagantly so, but that there will be no practical difficulty in reducing them, with the full concurrence of the Indians themselves, within much narrower limits.

The Indians generally, and indeed without exception as far as we could ascertain, are ready to abide by any decision the Governor may make as to the extent of land to be reserved for their use.

They do not seem opposed to relinquishing portions of the lands which, since McColl's surveys, they have been led to consider as set apart for them. They are only anxious to retain their villages and potato patches and such moderate extents of land around them as may be finally reserved by Government for them.

They express themselves, however, as much aggrieved at the appropriation by white settlers of portions of the lands which they have hitherto considered as intended for the Indians alone, evidently regarding such settlements as unauthorized intrusions on their rights.

I took occasion at each village, to inform the Indians that McColl had no authority for laying off the excessive amounts of land included by him in these reserves, and that his action in this respect was entirely disavowed, but that the Governor would direct that such amounts of land should be secured to the use of each tribe as he should determine to be proportionate to their numbers and requirements, and that next spring these reserves would be definitely staked off, and maps of the same given to each Chief, so that the boundaries thereof should be clearly understood.

I also impressed upon them that such lands would not be their property to sell or convey away in any manner, but would be held in trust by the Government for their use as long as they continued to live upon them, and free from all intrusion either of white people or Indians of other tribes.

I had not time to make such a careful and detailed inspection of these Reserves as would warrant me in recommending what specific tracts of land should be set apart for each tribe. This can be best decided on the ground, the boundaries of each reserve being so arranged as to leave out as far as may be found practicable such lands as have been settled upon, and improved by white persons, retaining always however, for the use of the Indians, the sites of their villages and as much land around them or (as will in some cases be found expedient) both around their villages and at the spots where they have been in the habit of cultivating potatoes, as will amount in the aggregate to ten acres of tillable land to each adult male in the tribe, together with a moderate amount of grazing land for those tribes which possess cattle and horses.

I enclose herewith, a statement of the numbers of each tribe visited by us, and of the cattle, etc., possessed by them, as furnished by the Chiefs at their respective villages.

I have, etc.,
(Signed)   JOSEPH W. TRUTCH.

ENCLOSURE.

Statement of the numbers in the Indian tribes on the Lower Fraser, visited by Mr. Trutch and Captain Ball, on the 11th, 12th, 13th, and 14th November, 1867.

Initial letter on plan	Name of the Tribe.	No. of Acres laid off by Mr. McColl.	No. of men in the tribe.	No. of women in the tribe.	No. of children in the tribe.	Number of cattle, horses, pigs, etc., belonging to the tribe.
A	Whonock	2000	13	14	9	3 cattle, 12 pigs.
B	Saamoqua	500	9	5		6 cattle, 3 horses, 5 pigs.
C	Matzqui	9600	22	25	24	12 pigs.
D	Tlalt-whaas	2000	Not visited.			
E	Sumass (Upper)	1200	8	12	14	21 horses, 12 pigs.
F	Sumass (Lower)	6400	22	39	39	1 cow, 3 horses, 16 pigs.
G	Nickaamen	6400	Not visited.			
H	Iswhy	300	13	11	15	Some pigs.
I	Isquhay	3200	33	23	33	5 cattle and some pigs.
J	Koquaa-plit	400	8	8	7	8 cattle, 1 horse, & some pigs.
K	Iswaya-aayla	1000	11	12	11	9 cattle, 1 horse, & some pigs.
L	Assay-litch	400	4	4	2	Some pigs.
M	Yuke-youqua-yoose-sockale	2500	Not visited.			
N	So-why-lee	4000	Not visited.			

The Colonial Secretary to the Chief Commissioner of Lands and Works.

Colonial Secretary's Office,
4th December, 1867.

Sir,—I duly received and laid before the Governor your letter dated the 19th ultimo, reporting your proceedings in carrying out the instructions conveyed to you by my letter of the 6th November, with regard to adjusting and defining the boundaries of the various Indian Reserves on the Lower Fraser, and I am to acquaint you that His Excellency thinks it desirable that the different reserves should be surveyed and marked off in the Spring, in accordance with the suggestions offered by you. .

I have, &c.,
(Signed)   WILLIAM A. G. YOUNG.

The Rev. Mr. McGucking to the Chief Commissioner of Lands and Works.

St. Joseph's Mission, Williams Lake,
12th May, 1868.

SIR,—I beg leave to enclose you one of the notices that have been posted on the Indian Reserve, Soda Creek, by Mr. John Adams, Mill-owner of same place. These notices have caused considerable excitement and discontent among the Indians.

I have been laboring for the past two years among the Indians of this part of the country, and I must say that I have succeeded beyond even my own expectations in bringing them to habits of morality and industry. But if their reserves are to be interfered with in the manner that Mr. Adams wishes, I would not answer for the consequences. I already see that the Indians of Soda Creek would sooner risk their lives than abandon their native soil. At present I have used my endeavours to pacify them, by assuring them that the Government will protect them.

I shall now take the liberty of giving you some particulars of the Indians of Soda Creek. The *Natives* of *Soda Creek*, counting men, women, and children, number from 80 to 100 persons, and have a reserve extending over 8 miles of the country; but in all this extent there are not more than from 150 to 200 acres of land fit for cultivation. On this plot of good land they have built their church and several dwelling houses, and have other houses in the course of construction. They have it almost all enclosed by a good substantial fence, and a large part of it under cultivation. This spring they have sowed wheat, barley, oats, potatoes, turnips, and garden seeds, in fact, in the course of another year or two, they will have all this good plot of about 200 acres well cultivated. Now it is on this same plot that Mr. Adams has posted his notices, and states that he pre-empted it on the 30th ultimo.

Hoping you will give this matter due consideration, and either through me, or some of the Government Officials, you will take the first opportunity of restoring peace and tranquillity among the Indians of Soda Creek.

I remain, &c.,
(Signed)   JAMES M. MCGUCKING, O.M.I.

ENCLOSURE.

NOTICE.—I have this day pre-empted 336 acres of land, bounded on the North by a line bearing S. 48° East, from this post 60 chains to a post fixed at that distance.

Soda Creek 30th April, 1868.   (Signed)   JOHN R. ADAMS.

The Chief Commissioner of Lands and Works to the Rev. Mr. McGucking.

Lands and Works Department,
Victoria, 30th May, 1868.

SIR,—I have the honour to acknowledge the receipt of your letter of the 12th instant (which however only came to hand three days ago), informing me of Mr. Adams' having posted on the Indian Reserve at Soda Creek certain notices, one of which you forward to me, of his intention to pre-empt a portion of said reserve.

I am unable to ascertain from the records in this office the exact limits of this reserve, in fact, I believe the boundary lines thereof have not yet been surveyed. I will, however, immediately obtain further information on the subject.

In the mean time I may state to you that the Land Ordinance expressly precludes any portion of an Indian Reserve being taken up as a pre-emption claim. If therefore the land on which Mr. Adams has posted his notice is, as you inform me, a part of the Soda Creek Indian Reserve, he can have no right to occupy it.

I will by this mail write to Mr. Brew, the Magistrate of the District in which the reserve in question is included, and will request him to enquire into the matter and to take such steps as he may deem advisable to protect the Indians in the land which has been appropriated for their use. And you may rest assured, at all events, that the land which they have enclosed and cultivated will not be intruded on.

I have, &c.,
(Signed)   JOSEPH W. TRUTCH.

The Chief Commissioner of Lands and Works to Mr. Brew.

Lands and Works Department,
30th May, 1868.

SIR,—I have the honour to enclose, for your information and consideration, a copy of a letter addressed to me by the Rev. James M. McGucking, in charge of St. Joseph's Mission at Williams Lake, stating that Mr. Adams has taken possession of a portion of the Indian Reserve at Soda Creek, and has posted notices on the same of his claim to 336 acres thereof as a pre-emption right.

I am unable to ascertain from the records of this office the exact limits of this reserve, in fact I believe it has not yet been surveyed, nor have I yet learnt by whom it was laid off. I will, however, as soon as possible obtain further information on the subject and again communicate with you regarding it.

In the meantime I have written to Father McGucking, informing him that I would request you to take steps to prevent any intrusion on the lands occupied and cultivated by the Indians at Soda Creek, and that of course no pre-emption right would be accorded to Mr. Adams over any portion of the said reserve.

I shall be obliged by your making such enquiries as you may deem advisable under the circumstances, and furnishing me with any information you may obtain as to this Indian Reserve and Mr. Adams' intrusion thereon, if indeed any such intrusion has taken place.

I have, &c.,
(Signed)   JOSEPH W. TRUTCH.

Mr. O'Reilly to the Chief Commissioner of Lands and Works.

Yale, 19th June, 1868.

SIR,—I have the honour to report for the information of His Excellency the Governor, that since the month of May six pre-emption claims have been recorded in the neighbourhood of Nicola Lake, which is situated in this district, and I have reason to believe that many more applications are about to be made for land in that part of the country.

The Indians have been in the habit of cultivating detached portions of land immediately about the lake, and under these circumstances I would venture to suggest that a survey be made without delay, and the Indian Reserves clearly defined, in order to avoid trouble hereafter.

I have, &c.,
(Signed)   P. O'REILLY.

The Chief Commissioner of Lands and Works to Mr. O'Reilly.

Lands and Works Department,
Victoria, August 5th, 1868.

SIR,—I duly received and laid before the Governor your letter of the 19th June, reporting that a considerable number of pre-emption claims had been taken up this spring in the neighbourhood of Nicola Lake, and recommending that certain lands immediately about the lake, which have for many years been occupied and partly cultivated by Indians, should at once be surveyed off and established as permanent reserves for the use of the Indians resident thereon, so as to prevent collision between them and the white settlers.

I have now to inform you that His Excellency approves of the course recommended by you, and I am directed to instruct you to undertake the adjustment of these reserves at as early a date as you can make it convenient to repair to the spot. I am also to direct you to visit the Bonaparte Indian Reserve, either on your way to or from Nicola Lake, and should you be of opinion that this reserve is, as has been represented, too extensive, you are to reduce it within such limits as you may consider proportionate to the numbers and requirements of the Indians resident thereon.

The extent of land to be included in each of these reservations must be determined by you on the spot, with due regard to the numbers and industrial habits of the Indians permanently living on the land, and to the quality of the land itself, but as a general rule it is considered that an allotment of about ten acres of good land should be made to each family in the tribe.

After a report from you on this subject has been received public notice will be given of any reductions you may make of the extents of these reservations, and a date will be advertised on and after which records of pre-emption claims on the lands so thrown open to pre-emption will be received.

I have instructed Mr. Mohun to go up to Yale by to-morrow's boat and to accompany you thence to the reserves above indicated, for the purpose of surveying the boundary lines thereof under your directions.

I have, &c.,
(Signed)   JOSEPH W. TRUTCH.

The Chief Commissioner of Lands and Works to Mr. O'Reilly.

Lands and Works Office,
Victoria, 6th August, 1868.

SIR,—This will be handed to you by Mr. Edward Mohun, whom I have instructed to place himself under your directions at Yale, to accompany you to Bonaparte and Nicola Lake for the purpose of surveying off the boundary lines of the Indian Reserves at those places, as you may direct.

I have, &c.,
(Signed)   JOSEPH W. TRUTCH.

Mr. O'Reilly to the Chief Commissioner of Lands and Works.

Yale,
29th August, 1868.

SIR,—I have the honor to report for the information of His Excellency the Governor, that in accordance with the instructions contained in your letter of the 6th inst., I have marked off the Indian Reserves on the Bonaparte and at Nicola Lake.

I have also to report that while on my way to Nicola Lake, I was met at Deadman's Creek by the Savona Ferry Indians headed by their Chief, and requested by them to define the boundaries of their land. I thought it advisable to comply with their demand, though the reserve for this tribe was not included in your instructions. I hope that my having done so will be approved of by His Excellency.

Having previously apprised the Indians of my intention to visit them, I was met by the different tribes at the several points indicated by me, and was thus saved much time.

I ascertained from "Ceinshute" their chief, that the whole population of the Bonaparte tribe does not exceed 55 to 60, that they cultivate from 4 to 5 acres, and that their stock consists of 25 horses, and of 9 head of cattle, and that they claimed nearly 7 miles in length of the valley of the Bonaparte, which averages half-a-mile in width.

Having visited this reserve three times, I came to the conclusion that the extent of land claimed by them was out of all proportion to their requirements. With the concurrence of the chief, therefore I staked out about one mile square for their use, within which are situated their houses and all the land they have been in the habit of cultivating.

"Cecinsket" the chief of the Indians who inhabit the country in the neighborhood of Savona's Ferry, informed me that his tribe consists of 62 families, numbering in all 122; their stock consists of 16 head of cattle and 28 horses, and that formerly they claimed, under a promise from Mr. Cox, about 9 miles on both sides of the Thompson River, commencing at the foot of Kamloops Lake, but, a portion of this having been taken possession of by the white settlers, they moved to Deadman's Creek, where they have built a small church and a few houses, and have there been in the habit of cultivating their potatoes. I marked off for their use the whole width of the valley, which averages about half-a-mile, for a distance of two miles; their lower boundary commences about four and a half miles above the waggon road bridge which crosses the creek.

I found that at Nicola Lake the Indians are divided into two tribes, one occupying the Eastern or upper, and the other the Western or lower end of the lake, "Chillihetza" being the chief of the former, and "Nowistican" of the latter.

The tribe under Chillihetza represents a population of 150, owning 20 head of cattle and 130 horses. At their request I marked out a square block of land containing about 800 to a 1000 acres for their use, situated at the mouth of a creek which flows into the lake on the South-East side, about four miles from its head; two and a half miles lower down, on the same side of the lake, I marked out for this tribe a second reserve of about 80 acres, embracing the mouth of another creek, which is particularly valuable to them on account of the fishing.

The tribe under Nowistican consists of about 100, and possess 32 head of cattle and 200 horses. I had considerable difficulty in effecting any arrangement with this tribe, as they claimed a large extent of valuable land, but at last the chief consented that I should mark out about 1000 acres in one block, situated on the Nicola River, commencing nine miles from the foot of the lake.

Mr. Mohun, Civil Engineer, whom you sent up to make the surveys of these reserves, accompanied me, and was present when I made the arrangements with the chiefs of the different tribes; and the boundaries were defined by blazed trees and stakes, so that no misunderstanding can arise, nor do the reserves as laid out interfere with the rights of any of the settlers.

Before leaving Nicola Lake I provided Mr. Mohun with all the assistance he required. The survey of these lands will, I think, occupy him about a month.

The chiefs requested that they might be furnished with a map of their lands, which I promised they should have, and I would suggest that such be sent to them with as little delay as possible.
I have, &c.,
(Signed) P. O'Reilly.

Mr. Mohun to the Chief Commissioner of Lands and Works.

Victoria, 6th October, 1868.

SIR,—I have the honor to inform you that, in accordance with your instructions, I left Victoria on the 7th August, and placed myself at the orders of Mr. O'Reilly, under whose directions and with whom I proceeded to the Bonaparte, Deadman's Creek, and Nicola Lake and River, at each of which places he pointed out to me what he wished done.

Mr. O'Reilly left me on the evening of the 24th August to complete the work, of which I enclose you the field notes and sketches.

The thick smoke overhanging the whole country has been a great hindrance to the work, both in the field and in taking observations; and, in fact, the only one I feel satisfied about is that taken at Deadman's Creek.

Another great drawback has been the scarcity of labour, as it was harvest time, and also the Indian fishing season. On Deadman's Creek, I had to do the whole, and on the Buonaparte, the greater part of the axe work myself.

I completed the work on the 23rd September, having been at work 26 days, and immediately left for Victoria, where I arrived 3rd October.

I have, &c.,
(Signed) EDWARD MOHUN.

Mr. Ball to Governor Seymour.

Yale, October 17th, 1868.

SIR,—I have the honour to report that according to instructions I proceeded in company with Assistant Surveyor-General Pearse, to the Harrison, Chilliwhack, and Sumass Rivers, to define and adjust the Indian Reserves situated in that neighbourhood and some others on the Lower Fraser.

The number of reserves visited amounted in all to fourteen, all of which, with one exception, were reduced, and portions of land (averaging ten acres to each adult) allotted proportioned to the size and requirements of the different Indian villages.

We experienced no trouble with the Indians when the proposal of the reductions was made, and all appeared perfectly satisfied with the reserves laid out for them, as every regard was paid to ensure the enclosure of the ground they had previously cultivated. A great anxiety existed amongst most of the villages to have a final settlement of the limits of their land made, more particularly where the reserves were surrounded by white settlers.

Several hundreds of acres of good agricultural and pasture land have consequently been thrown open for pre-emption, which has hitherto been locked up and unused by white settlers, in consequence of its forming part of the large reserves allotted to the different villages in 1864.

I have, &c.,
(Signed) H. M. BALL.

Mr. Pearse to the Chief Commissioner of Lands and Works.

Lands and Works Department,
21st October, 1868.

SIR,—I have the honour to inform you that in compliance with instructions I proceeded in company with Captain Ball, Stipendiary Magistrate, to define precisely on the ground the limits of the various reserves for the Indians on the Lower Fraser. This was done by marking trees or planting posts on each frontage, and making accurate sketches for the guidance of the surveyor. The chiefs of the various villages were with us in nearly every case, and with one exception (that of Who-nock), expressed themselves thoroughly satisfied with the lands allotted to them. We took great care to include their potatoe grounds in every case. Where doing so would have involved too large an undivided area, we gave them a second lot. The principle kept in view, was to give them from ten to twenty acres for each adult in the tribe, and an extra quantity for those possessing stock or horses. This will throw open about 40,000 acres for settlement by white men. We left Mr. Launders to run the lines and complete the survey of the river line.

In our reconnaissance in the Chilliwhack District we were accompanied by nearly all the settlers, some sixteen in number, who were very useful and obliging in pointing out McColl's and other surveyors' posts. They all seem to be doing well, and thoroughly satisfied with their prospects. There is one point to which I would strongly call the attention of the Government, and that is the necessity of extending the present or an improved "Road Act" to the Chilliwhack and Sumass Districts, the latter containing seven or eight settlers. At present the more energetic men do more or less work on the public trails, whilst those who are less public spirited do nothing. The passage of an Act compelling all to work on the public trails and roads would be a great benefit to these districts. I am aware that the present Act of 1860 is deficient in many respects, but even under it a great deal of valuable work has been done in the Vancouver Island Districts, especially in that of Comox.

         I have, &c.,
          (Signed) B. W. PEARSE.

Mr. Ball to the Chief Commissioner of Lands and Works.

           New Westminster,
            30th October, 1868.

SIR,—I have the honour to enclose a letter received from the Rev. J. B. Good, relative to the survey of some small Indian Reserves on the Fraser River, in the neighbourhood of Lytton.

As the culture of the land in that District is carried on by irrigation, and all the available land eagerly taken up where water can be used for irrigation, I think it would be advisable that in the spring the Indians should have their small plots of land secured to them and surveyed off, together with a certain amount of unappropriated water where required.

         I have, etc.,
          (Signed) H. M. BALL.
[This enclosure cannot be found.]

The Chief Commissioner of Lands and Works to Mr. Ball

          Lands and Works Office,
          Victoria, 20th November, 1868.

SIR,—Having duly submitted for the consideration of His Excellency the Governor, your letter of the 30th ultimo, with enclosure from the Rev. J. B. Good, in reference to the advisability of defining certain pieces of land along the Fraser River in the neighbourhood of Lytton, as reserved for the use of the Indians of that District, I am directed to request that you will inform Mr. Good that it is impracticable to effect any settlement of these reserves at present, and the consideration of the matter is deferred until a more favourable opportunity.

         I have, &c.,
          (Signed) JOSEPH W. TRUTCH.

Mr. Mohun to the Chief Commissioner of Lands and Works.

Victoria, December 3rd, 1868.

SIR,—I have the honour to inform you that in accordance with your instructions, I left Victoria on the 20th November.

In addition to the reserves mentioned in my orders by Mr. Pearse, Captain Ball desired me to lay off one on the south bank of the river at Katzie.

I left New Westminster November 23rd, and stopped at Katzie, where I laid off about 40 acres. On the map furnished me by Captain Ball, the reserve is shown to have a frontage of about 20 chains; the chief claims 40 chains. By the new survey he has a frontage of about 20 chains, which includes all the potato patches, house, &c.

At Whannock I laid off about 100 acres, with which the Indians appear perfectly satisfied.

At Matsqui about 80 acres was laid out, which has caused great dissatisfaction. The chief says it is nearly all swamp; that it cuts off the burial ground and the potato patches, which are to the west on the higher ground; and he wishes his west boundary about 20 chains lower down the river.

I promised to lay his complaint before you, as what he stated is true, and he trusts that you will give directions to have his western boundary removed lower down. The reserve on the Matsqui Prairie contains 52½ acres, of which thirty are grass, the remainder being a rich maple bottom requiring but little clearing; with this they expressed themselves satisfied.

I returned to New Westminster on the 30th November.

I have, &c.,
(Signed)   EDWARD MOHUN.

Mr. J. B. Launders to the Chief Commissioner of Lands and Works.

Victoria, 18th December, 1868.

SIR,—I have the honor to report that having travelled over all the Chilliwhack Indian Reserves with Mr. Pearse, at the same time receiving instructions from him, I was left by him on the 3rd October, and commenced surveying the reserves according to his instructions and diagrams. I shall now write of them as numbered and named on the plans, remarking briefly on the nature of the land, description of timber, and the satisfaction evinced by the Indians.

No. 1, SQUAY-YA A.

This Indian Reserve, commencing at Kipp's Landing, Fraser River, runs S. W. down stream 25 chains; thence up the Ko-qua-pilt Slough about 60 chains; thence due East 68 chains; thence North 40 chains; thence East 20 chains; thence North 8 chains, closing on Squay-ya Slough about 1 mile above Kipp's Landing on Fraser River. The land on this reserve is of excellent quality; timber, maple, cottonwood, pine and alder, some cedar and willow.

No. 2, SQUAY-YA B.

This reserve commences about 80 chains up Squay-ya Slough from Kipp's Landing, Fraser River; it is an Island, and measures by survey traverse exactly 4 miles circuit; the land is mostly subject to floods, but of good quality; timber, pine and cottonwood, willow underwood.

No 3, SQUAY-YA C.

This reserve is about 3 miles up Squay-ya Slough, and on the plan is connected by traverse with the foregoing reserves; it is required by the Indians principally on account of its having for many years been their cemetery; there are also some heavy frames of buildings; it runs S. 59 E. (magnetic bearings) 12 chains; thence N. 31° E. 25 chains; thence N. 59° W. 12 chains, closing on above named slough. Soil first-rate; timber, pine, maple, and alder, crab-apple brush. Indians to which these three reserves belong to were perfectly satisfied.

No. 4, Schuye.

This Indian Reserve is an Island situated on Fraser River between the Chilliwhack River and Ko-qua-pilt Slough (see plan); the greater part of the land is subject to floods, the remainder of middling quality (from limited observation); timber, pine, cedar, and cottonwood, willow brush. There is a town site marked out at S. W. angle of Island, about 5 acres. The Indians displayed no interest in their claims.

No. 5, Ko-qua-pilt.

Reserve commences about 4 chains from Kipp's Farm and runs true East 50 chains; thence up Ko-qua-pilt Slough to its junction with Chilliwhack River; thence following dry slough along Telegraph road to near Kipp's farm. Timber, pine, cedar, and cottonwood, some maple, willow brush, &c.; land of the first quality. Indians, with one unimportant exception, well satisfied.

No. 6, Isqua-ahla.

Reserve commences at the junction of the Chilliwhack River with the Ko-qua-pilt Slough; thence following a dry slough along the Telegraph road about 20 chains to a post marked by me Indian Reserve; thence N. 77° 30' E. (magnetic bearings), 20.70 chains to Duck Slough, along same general direction S.; thence following the Chilliwhack River in its tortuous course to starting point, as above described. Timber, pine, vine-maple, and willows; land partially subject to floods but of good quality. Indians submissively satisfied.

No. 7, Assy-litch.

This reserve commences near the village of the same name and runs magnetic N. 6° 30' E. 15 chains; thence S. 83° 30' W. 30.50 chains; thence S. 6° 30' W. 15 chains; thence N. 83° 30' E. 8 chains; thence N. 82° E. 8 chains; thence S. 74° 20' E. to starting point on Chilliwhack River. This reserve is about 60 chains from the junction of Ko-qua-pilt Slough and Chilliwhack River; it contains a few acres of wet prairie; timber, fir, small cedar, vine-maple, alder and poplar. Indians very well satisfied.

No 8, Sco-kale A.

This reserve is situated about 6 or 7 miles up Chilliwhack River, starting point about 20 chains from Sco-kale village (up stream) N. 26° E. 36.34 chains; thence N. 64° W. 37.20 chains; thence S. 46° W.; thence 4 chains to Chilliwhack River; the boundary then follows the River traversed to starting point. The soil on this Reserve is of the best description; timber, cottonwood, vine-maple, and a few firs, hazel and whitethorn brush. Indians satisfied.

No. 9, Sco-kale B.

Commences opposite the Indian village on last reserve, to which it is drawn on plan in relative position; it runs due West 18.10 chains; thence S. 16 chains; thence E. 22.57 chains to Chilliwhack River.

No. 10, Yuk-yuk-y-yoose.

This reserve commences about 15 chains and extends its frontage up stream on Chilliwhack River; its Eastern boundary runs magnetic N. 6° W. 20 chains; thence S. 84° W. 22 chains; thence to Chilliwhack River S. 6° E. 20 chains. Timber and soil similar in all respects to the Sco-kale Reserves. Indians well satisfied.

No. 11, So-why-lee.

This reserve is probably about 13 or 14 miles from the mouth of Chilliwhack River; starting point about 8 chains from large Indian Ranch on trail, magnetic S. 12° 30′ E. 40.20 chains, planted post; thence S. 79° E. 42.35 chains to base of mountain, planted post; the boundary then follows base of mountain to its spur on Chilliwhack River; this it follows down stream turning up Cultus or Schweltza River, and following the trail past Captain John's house and the village to starting point. Timber, fir, cedar, cottonwood, alder, vine-maple, Oregon grape, and other berry brush. I should think that on this reserve there is the finest maple grove in the Colony; a great part of the land is of a most superior nature, and is fairly cultivated in large, well fenced patches; there is also a trail from Captain John's house to the mountain base, ½ a mile of which is fit for a cart track. Indians thoroughly satisfied.

No. 12, Scow-litz.

Commences about 12 chains above the village near Harrison Mouth, running through wet prairie, magnetic N. 29° 40′ E. 9 chains; thence S. 60° 20′ E. 13 chains to post on trail, which runs North-Easterly from Donnelly's house: the boundary thence follows the trail to Bateson's house on Slough, which it follows to Fraser River, down which to Harrison Mouth, and around past Donnelly's house to starting post; 'there is a small reserve laid out of 2¼ acres for building purposes. Soil excellent where dry; timber, poor fir, small cottonwood and alder. Indians satisfied.

No. 13, Nicomin.

This reserve commences about 8 chains magnetic N. of village, running N. 75° W. 25 chains; thence S. 15° W. 45 chains; thence S. 75° E. 22 chains; thence frontage 45 chains along Nicomin Slough. Soil of fine quality; timber, spruce, fir, cottonwood, maple, and some dogwood and small cedar, willow and hazel underwood. Indians well satisfied.

No. 14, Sque-aam.

This reserve is situated on the Nicomin or Harris's Slough at its junction with a minor slough, which also connects with Fraser River, about a mile below Miller's Landing; it is about 1¾ miles from Fraser River and almost parallel to it; commences about 8 chains down stream from the village and runs S. 50° E. 20 chains; thence N. 40° E. 22.70 chains; thence down small slough to Harris's Slough, along which the boundary runs to starting point; soil in general very good. South, 10 chains wide, very rough; timber spruce, fir, maple, and cottonwood, hazel and thorn brush.

No. 15, Klat-Waas.

This reserve commences about fifteen chains E. of village, on Nicomin or Harris's Slough, about 1½ miles from its flow into Fraser River, running true N. 24 chains; thence West 39 chains; thence 20 chains to McColl's old post, true S.; thence along frontage on Slough to starting point. Soil of the finest quality; timber poor, mostly burned, a few pines, a few maples, small cottonwood, and alder; for the most part this reserve is covered with dense thickets, crab-apple and hazel. There are about 15 acres of prairie, subject to floods, on this reserve. Indians satisfied.

No. 16, Sumass No 1.

Sumass Reserve No. 1 commences about 8 chains magnetic N. E. from village on Fraser River, 20 chains up stream from the mouth of Nicomin or Harris's Slough, running N. 40° W. 21 chains; thence S. 50° W. 15.65 chains; thence S. 40° E. 20.75 chains to post on Fraser River; thence up stream to starting post. Soil of good quality; timber, mostly fir and maple damaged by fire, underbrush of crab-apple thicket, &c. Considerable land has been cultivated on this reserve. Indians satisfied.

No. 17, Sumass No. 2.

Is situated about 20 chains South of Chadsey's Slough on Sumass River; from S. W. post the boundary runs magnetic S. 77° 30′ E. 14 chains; thence N. 12° 3′ E. 30 chains; thence N. 77° 30′ W. 14 chains to post on Sumass River; thence up Sumass River to starting point. This reserve is chiefly wet prairie with a belt of stunted willows along bank of river. The Indians were not well satisfied; they wanted all their original claim.

The reserve which I was directed to survey on the opposite bank of Fraser River was not accepted by the Indians, it was to contain 20 acres, but there is no land above high water mark for 3 miles along the right bank of the river; small patches occur back from the river and extend over $2\frac{1}{2}$ miles of ground, at least 6 or 7 are cultivated by separate families and the largest would not exceed $\frac{1}{2}$ an acre. They wished me to put down 4 stakes at the corners of each of these strips and could not comprehend my non-compliance. After going with or meeting them on the ground twice I had to abandon the hopeless task of giving them satisfaction. I would recommend that some further enquiry be made or something done to secure to them in some way these patches, for they really seem to be the only parcels of land, with the exception of Sumass No. 1, that they seem at all interested in, they displayed considerable apathy about the reserve around their village, which is liable to floods, and would not have it. I therefore did not survey it, but wrote to Mr. Ball and effected an exchange, giving them Sumass No. 2 grass land.

No. 18, Sumass Upper.

This reserve is situated on the Upper Sumass River or Slough, about 2 miles South of the Lake, and commences at a large boulder near a rocky point of the mountain, running S. 54° 30′ (magnetic) 22 chains to slough; thence up the serpentine course of slough by traverse to a clump of pines; thence N 54° 30′, to a post near 3 lone pines; thence ascending to and following the mountain ridge and returning to large boulder at starting point. Timber, pine and maple, belts of crab-apple brush in places along the slough. Three-fourths of this reserve is prairie. Indians well satisfied.

There were 3 other reserves that I should have surveyed, viz: Matsqui, around the village and their potato patches and grass land, about 2 miles back from the Fraser River, somewhere near the telegraph station; the weather being so stormy and promising no abatement, I felt justified, partly on account of swelling expenses by delay, but chiefly on account of ill health, in leaving these for the time, as also the reserve at Wha-nock.

I made a great struggle to complete the work given me to do, and should have finished had not the weather continued so wet. The 3 reserves above named, you are aware, were subsequently surveyed by Mr. Mohun, C. E. I have re-plotted them from his notes and entered them on my plans, as also the Katzie Reserve, and given all the information I can deduce from the notes. See plan, Nos. 19, 20, 21 and 22.

I kept a journal throughout the entire work. It is devoid of detail with the exception of the state of the weather, which was for 5 weeks foggy, and what little information I have made use of in constructing the plans. The lines are well cut and defined, being good trails almost.

The posts deeply scored and put down at the corners or prominent points of each reserve always in the presence of 2 or more Indians. I made it a point to call their united attention to the blazed trees and natural features of the land and timber around their corner posts.

I have, &c.,
(Signed) J. B. Launders.

The Chief Commissioner of Lands and Works to Mr. Sanders.

Lands & Works Office, Victoria,
March 17th, 1869.

SIR,—I have the honour to transmit herewith a tracing of the official plan of the Indian Reserve on Buonaparte River, near Cache Creek, the boundaries of which were defined by Mr. O'Reilly, and surveyed by order of the Governor last year.

I was, until lately, under the erroneous impression that this reserve was in the Lytton District, which will account for my not having sooner sent you a copy of the plans of the definite survey of this reserve. The plan of this reserve, intended to be given to the chief of the tribe for which it is to be held in trust, was handed to Mr. O'Reilly for transmission to the chief.

You will observe by the advertisement in the *Government Gazette*, that the lands hitherto included within the supposed limits of this reserve are open for pre-emption after the 1st instant.

I have. etc.,
(Signed) JOSEPH W. TRUTCH.

The Chief Commissioner of Lands and Works to Mr. Morley.

Lands & Works Office,
April 26th, 1869.

SIR,—The Indians of the several tribes residing in the Cowichan Valley having made complaint to the Governor of the curtailment of their reserves by Mr. Pearse, and especially in reference to the piece of land lately recorded as Mr. Rogers' pre-emption claim; and as it appears there was some misapprehension as to this section being cut off from the Indian Reserve, I think it will be decided to restore the land taken up by Mr. Rogers to the use of the Indians; and although I am not in a position to state this to you officially, I take the earliest opportunity of giving you a hint to this effect, so that you may regulate yourself accordingly, and give some intimation to Mr. Rogers to this effect.

As soon as I am able so to do, I will write you an official communication on this subject; in the meantime, you had better take no decided action in reference to it. The Governor will also, probably, give the Indians assistance, through you, in fencing in their reserves.

Be good enough to write me word, by the return of the "Sir James Douglas," what has taken place, in reference to the dispute between the Indians and Mr. Rogers, since you last reported officially on the subject.

I have, &c.,
(Signed) JOSEPH W. TRUTCH.

Mr. Morley to the Chief Commissioner of Lands and Works.

Maple Bay, April 27th, 1869.

MY DEAR SIR,—In the case of dispute between Mr. Rogers and the Indians, I summoned Te-cha-malt on a charge of trespass, but as I found it was a case of dispute as to the ownership of the land, and on the Indians promising not to interfere until I received further instructions from the Government, Mr. Rogers also agreeing to let the matter stand over, I have taken no further action; since that time all has been quiet.

I still firmly believe the Indian knew the land was open for pre-emption, Lowah, the Comiaken Chief, says he was with Mr. Pearse when he told Te-cha-malt, that the section in dispute was cut off the reserve, and Mr. Pearse showed the Indians where the line ran. I believe it would be advisable not to restore it to the Indians; it will only encourage them to make further demands. I have another case of a similar description in hand. A party of Indians have fenced a good portion of Mr. Munroe's land in, which he paid $5 per acre for.

I really believe the Indian Missions here do a deal to make the Indians dissatisfied. The Catholics appear to have a great influence over them.

Te-cha-malt made use of very improper language, and was very insolent. He said he was the Chief and that the land was his. He also said that Governor Seymour could not take the land from him, that if the Governor sent his gunboat he would fetch his friends from all parts and hold the land against him. He also said the Governor was a liar and had not fulfilled his promise to pay for the land he had taken. And then told me he did not care for me, or the prison either, that I had no power over the Indians, and a good deal more to the same effect.

I remain, &c.,
(Signed) JNO. MORLEY.

ENCLOSURES.

Mr. Lomas to Mr. Morley.

Church of England Mission,
Quamichan, April 30th, 1869.

DEAR SIR,—In accordance with your request I beg to furnish you with a statement of the manner in which the Indian Chief Te-cha-malt and others have taken possession of the section of land outside the reserve.

In February last, Te-cha-malt came to me and asked me to go with him and read to him what was written on a boundary post, as he was going to fence in a piece of land and wished to be sure that it was on the Indian Reserve.

I went and pointed out to him the boundary line. His son See-heel-ton was present and endorsed what I said, as he was with Mr. Pearse when the latter surveyed the land in question. I then accompanied Te-cha-malt to a piece of land *inside the reserve*, which he said he would take up, and the next day he began to fence it in.

About the end of March, when Mr. Rogers first went to take possession of the land in question, there were, I believe, *four Indians* working on it, but the same evening Te-cha-malt came to the Quamichan village and asked all his friends to go with him and work on the section, telling them that if a large number would go they could hold it in spite of the Government. Some went and others refused to go, knowing the land to be outside the boundary lines that Mr. Pearse ran.

At the present time I believe there are twelve or fourteen men working on the said land, including the Chief Te-cha-malt; but from conversation with other Indians I am convinced that all of them knew when they went to work on the land that it was outside the reserve.

There are one or two other items connected with this matter to which I should like to call your attention.

1st. That there are *many hundred acres* of good land in the Cowichan Reserve that are neither cultivated nor occupied.

2nd. That the Chief Te-cha-malt is not an hereditary chief, and has not the slightest influence outside of his family, but was appointed by a Roman Catholic Priest, who some years ago visited Cowichan.

3rd. That Te-cha-malt has for several years conducted himself in an orderly manner, but in this matter, I am persuaded, he is acting under the advice of some white man.

4th. That should the Government deem fit to give up this land to him, other families will expect to be treated with the same favour, especially those occupying Mr. Munroe's land, as they have been squatting on it since last fall. On the other hand should the Government determine to remove the Indians from this section, I would suggest as a peaceable way of doing it, that as they have already planted some of the land, they be allowed to occupy it until next harvest, making them clearly understand that after harvest they must return to the reserve leaving any fences they may have put up.

I remain, &c.,
(Signed)   W. HY. LOMAS.

Mr. Rogers' Statement.

When I first went on to Section 14 there were a few cleared patches upon it. I questioned See-hal-ton as to how many Indians had potatoes there last year, he said there were five old men; I said, how was it they put them on the white man's land; See-hal-ton said the young men understood that it was white man's land, but the old men would not understand it; I then said I did not wish to take the labour of the old men for nothing but would compensate them for the work they had done, See-hal-ton said that was good.

On a subsequent occasion when I went on to the land there were about fifteen Indians gathered there, they were fencing it in all directions, and See-hal-ton then said there were thirty-five men on the land, and that I should not put up a house there nor do any work while they had their hands to prevent me. Te-cha-malt then spoke and said he was Chief and the land was his and he would not let any white men come on to the land. A few days previous to this I had gone on to the land with a man to cut logs for a house. I left the man there and came away; the man had cut several logs, when seven or eight Indians came up and obliged him to leave.

After I received my record paper I went to the land with several men to put up the house. The man was putting up a notice to say I had pre-empted the land, when Te-cha-malt rushed up and tore the notice from his hands and threw it on the ground and said we should not do anything there and we must leave.

Te-cha-malt and his two sons have run a fence across the end of three Sections, viz., 12, 13, 14, correctly on the line Mr. Pearse surveyed as the boundary of the reserve, they will thus have 300 acres fenced in. The Quamichan Indians are generally very much dissatisfied that these three men should have so much land. Te-cha-malt said that when he found I had pre-empted the land he went and got his friends to come and work upon it to keep me off.

The Indians stated first that there were five men on the land, afterwards they said thirty-five; and now they say forty-five.

I have, &c.,
(Signed)   A. W. ROGERS.

The Chief Commissioner of Lands and Works to Mr. Morley

Lands and Works Department,
May 4th, 1869.

SIR,—In reference to the dispute between Mr. Rogers and the Cowichan Indians as to the section of land (Section 14, Range 7) Quamichan District, reported in your letter to me dated April 27th, I have the honour to inform you that this matter had already, before your report was received, been brought under the consideration of His Excellency the Governor on the complaint of the chiefs of the tribes residing on the Cowichan Reserves, that the section of land above named having formerly been part of the land reserved for their use, had been cut off by Mr. Pearse without their concurrence or knowledge.

His Excellency granted these chiefs an opportunity of stating their case at a personal interview with himself, from which statement, corroborated to some extent by the evidence of Mr. Robertson, who was one of Mr. Pearse's surveying party when the reserves were laid out in 1867, it appeared that there must have been a misunderstanding between Mr. Pearse and these Indians as to the exact limits of the lands to be held in reserve for them, and being willing to take a favourable view of the claim of the Indians to the land in dispute, His Excellency has directed me to hold the section of land in question under reserve for their use, and to notify Mr. Rogers that his Pre-emption Record of this land, having been made by me under the mistaken supposition that the said land was open for pre-emption, must be cancelled.

Under further directions from the Governor, I have instructed Mr Mohun, Surveyor, to go up to Cowichan by to-morrow's boat, and under your general directions, and in company with you, to trace on the ground all the boundary lines of this reserve as indicated on the sketch map enclosed herewith. And I am to request that you will take such steps as you may deem advisable, to induce as many as possible of the Indians interested in this reserve to go with you round those boundary lines, and that you will clearly point out the same to them, and give them distinctly to understand that no further alterations of these boundary lines will be made by Government, this being a final settlement of the same.

After Mr. Mohun's return to this office, maps of these reserves will be prepared from his notes and sketches; which maps will be sent to you to be handed to the chiefs of the various tribes resident on these reserves. And I have to request that you will inform the said chiefs, whilst you are pointing out on the ground the boundaries of these reserves, that such plans will be given to them by you; and, further, that the lands so reserved are to be held for the use and benefit of all the Indians residing thereon, and not as the special property of any particular chief or chiefs.

As to the land sold by Government to Mr. Munroe in 1859, viz:—Sections 15 and 16, Range 7, Quamichan District, there can be no question but that these sections were never included in Mr. Pearse's survey, as part of the Indian Reserve, and the Indians must therefore be clearly informed by you that Government will not allow them to trespass on or prefer any claim to these sections, or to any other lands in the Cowichan Valley not included within the boundaries of their reserve as defined on the maps herewith transmitted to you.

I am further to inform you that His Excellency has been pleased to promise aid to the Indians in fencing in these reserves, to be supplied to them through you, in tools, nails, and other materials, in such amounts as you may deem proportionate to their requirements as the work of fencing progresses, to the extent in all of the value of $200 during this summer, for which expenditure you will consider this your sufficient authority.

I have also to request that you will notify Mr. Rogers that the record in his name of Section 14, Range 7, has been cancelled, and that you will ascertain and report to me what amount (in money value) of labour, if any, has been expended by Mr. Rogers on the land pre-empted by him since the date of the pre-emption record of the same in his name, as Government are ready to refund to him any such outlay as he may prove to have been made by him; whilst it is of course open to him to take up another pre-emption claim on any Crown Land not otherwise appropriated.

I have, &c.,
(Signed)   JOSEPH W. TRUTCH.

Mr. Mohun to the Chief Commissioner of Lands and Works.

Victoria, 21st May, 1869.

SIR,—I have the honour to inform you that I have completed the survey of the Cowichan Indian Reserves.

With respect to the difficulty with the Indians while surveying Section 12, Range VIII., Quamichan District, the appearance of Mr. Pemberton was quite sufficient to put an end to the opposition the Chief Te-cha-malt had offered at first.

I have accompanied Mr. Morley over the boundaries, and though we had great difficulty in inducing the Indians to go with us, they all say that they perfectly comprehend the limits of their reserves. In fact, notwithstanding the assertions of the Roman Catholic Priest during his interview with His Excellency the Governor to the contrary, I am persuaded that these boundaries have been well known to most of the Indians since Mr. Pearse's survey two years ago.

Mr. Botterell wishes to obtain a few acres intervening between his west boundary line (Section 13, Range III., Cowichan District), in exchange for a rocky point north of the river, at the north-east corner of his section, now occupied by Indian houses, in order that his cattle may be able to obtain fresh water, as the river is so brackish at its mouth that they will not make use of it.

Messrs. Marriner showed me the piece of land granted them by Governor Douglas, but I estimate it at four and a half acres instead of two. The Comiaken Chief, Low-ha, however expressed himself satisfied that they should retain it, as he said the Indians did not require it. I may add that these gentlemen have, at their own expense, erected a bridge across the Cowichan River at Range line II. and III; and should you feel justified in confirming them in the possession of the land they now hold, I do not think there is any fear of its leading to complications with the Indians, and they are certainly deserving of encouragement.

With respect to Mr. Brennan's 20 acres, I was unable to find the posts. But as it was surveyed by Mr. Patterson and allowed as a Government survey, I wrote to him requesting he would show Mr. Morley and the Indians the boundaries.

With regard to Sections 15 and 16, Range VII., Quamichan District, the Indians have fenced it to a very considerable extent; and in consequence of Mr. Pemberton having promised them Government assistance in removing the rails from Section 12, Range VIII., they afterwards came to me and asked if the Government would also haul the rails from those sections. I told them the Government would not, as they had fenced it in spite of repeated warnings from Mr. Lomas and others, well knowing they were trespassing, and only depending on the inaction of the owner, Mr. Munroe.

I have, &c.,
(Signed)   EDWARD MOHUN.

The Chief Commissioner of Lands and Works to Mr. Morley.

Lands and Works Office,
Victoria, 15th July, 1869.

SIR,—I have the honour to transmit to you herewith six tracings of the map of the lands reserved for the use of the Indians in the Cowichan and Quamichan Districts, as recently surveyed and pointed out on the ground by yourself and Mr. Mohun to the Chiefs and principal men of the tribes interested therein, and I have to request that you will hand one of these tracings to each of the chiefs, viz., to the Chiefs of the Quamichan, Somenos, Comiaken, Kokesailah, and Clanclemaluts tribes, retaining the other for your own information and reference. I have further to request that you will, on handing these tracings to the chiefs, take this opportunity to inform them again that the boundaries of the land to be reserved for the use of themselves and the other members of their tribes, have now been finally settled and that no trespass will, in future, be permitted, either of Indians on lands outside of their reserves, or of white men on the land held by the Government in reserve for the use of the Indians in Cowichan Valley, and that any such trespass will be punished as the law directs.

I have, &c.,
(Signed)   JOSEPH W. TRUTCH.

The Rev. Mr. Tomlinson to the Chief Commissioner of Lands and Works.

Received, 14th June, 1869.

Sir,—A mission has been opened for the benefit of the tribes resident on Naas River, and a mission settlement has been formed and mission buildings erected at Kincolith, which lies at the mouth of Naas River on the northern bank.

As the Missionary in charge of this station I beg to apply for a grant of a piece of ground for building purposes, to be held in trust by the Government for the Church Missionary Society. This piece of ground, on which some mission buildings have already been erected, is triangular. The apex of the triangle is formed by the junction of Kincolith and Naas Rivers. The base by a line drawn from the mission premises on the Naas River so as to form an isosceles triangle. The area of this triangle at low water is about four acres, at high water about three acres.

I also beg to apply for a reserve to be appropriated for the benefit of those Indians who have already, or may hereafter, settle at this Mission Station.

I make this petition on behalf of the Church Missionary Society, because a grant similar to the one prayed for has been accorded to the Mission of the Church Missionary Society situated at Metlakahtlah.

I have, &c.,
(Signed)   Robert Tomlinson.
Missionary, Church Missionary Society.

The Chief Commissioner of Lands and Works to the Rev. Mr. Tomlinson.

26th October, 1869.

Sir,—Your letter handed to me at Kincolith on the 14th June, last, was duly submitted for the consideration of His Excellency the Governor, who has been pleased to authorize me to secure to the Church Missionary Society a right to the use of the piece of ground at Kincolith (about three acres in extent as described in your said letter) for the purpose of a Mission Station. It is not deemed advisable to make any further free grants of land in this Colony for religious bodies, but a lease of the land you apply for will be made to whomsoever may be properly appointed as agent in this Colony for the Church Missionary Society, for a period of seven years, or such further period as the Governor may find himself empowered to grant, at the nominal rent of ten dollars per annum, in trust for the Mission purposes of the society.

The reservation you recommend of land around Kincolith for the use of the Indians resident thereon, has been established by notice in the *Government Gazette,* a copy of which I enclose for your information.

I regret that, having left Victoria with the Governor for the interior of the Colony a few days after the above decision on this matter was communicated to me, I have been unable to write you an earlier reply to your application.

I have now to request you to furnish me with as exact a plan as practicable of the ground you wish conveyed to your society to be appended to the lease, and to inform me to whom, as agent for the society, such lease should be made.

I have, etc.,
(Signed)   Joseph W. Trutch.

The Colonial Secretary to the Chief Commissioner of Lands and Works.

Colonial Secretary's Office,
26th July, 1869.

SIR,—I am directed by the Officer Administering the Government to acquaint you that he has been advised in Council to hand over to the charge of your Department, the management of the Songish Indian Reserve.

This reserve has hitherto been under the management of three Commissioners, who have, however, been formally relieved of any further duties in connection with it, and Mr. Pemberton, the only acting Commissioner of the body, has been directed to hand over to you, on application, all documents, books, and vouchers connected with the matter, together with the balance of money in favor of the reserve fund.

This fund can only be expended on the direct authority of the Government, by whom all checks will have to be countersigned.

Mr. Loewenberg has been for a long time engaged as agent for the reserve, and as he has an extensive knowledge of all previous transactions, it is suggested that you should retain his services, paying him a commission of five per cent. on the transaction.

His Honor requests that on the transfer being completed, you will report accordingly, as well as the steps that you propose to take for the future management of the reserve, the settlement of leases, and the collection of outstanding debts for rent.

His Honor also requests you will furnish a half-yearly report on the condition of the fund, and the general circumstances of the revenue.

I have, &c.,
(Signed)   C. GOOD.

The Chief Commissoiner of Lands and Works to the Colonial Secretary.

30th December, 1869.

SIR,—I have the honour to submit, for the consideration of His Excellency the Governor, the enclosed memorandum, with accompanying documents, showing, as far as I have been able to ascertain after careful enquiry, the past history of the Songish Reserve, especially in reference to the leases of portions thereof which were granted by Commissioners appointed by Governor Douglas for that purpose, and of the present position of affairs in relation thereto, as to which I beg to offer the following remarks:—

2. It is certain that the tract of land known as the Songish Indian Reserve, was formally set apart by the competent authority of the Hudson's Bay Company's Agent, acting on behalf of the Crown, for the perpetual use and benefit of the Indians of that tribe; and that this land is now held in trust by the Crown, acting under a solemn obligation, as guardian of the rights of the Indians in this respect.

3. But it is competent and proper for the Governor of the Colony, as agent of the Crown, to make such disposition of the land in the exercise of this trust as to secure to the Indians the utmost practical benefit therefrom.

4. Governor Douglas' intention to obtain this result by leasing out portions of this reserve and devoting the rent to the improvement of the moral and social condition of the Indians entitled to participate therein was therefore unexceptional; but his measures in carrying this plan into execution are open to objection, inasmuch as it was not competent for him to delegate to others, as was purported to be conveyed in the commission to Messrs. J. D. Pemberton, E. G. Alston, and A. F. Pemberton, the powers of dealing with this land which had been delegated to him as representative of the Crown.

5. The exception in this respect taken against the validity of this commission by Governor Kennedy was well grounded, but it is to be regretted that he did not, as soon as this flaw was brought to his notice, take steps to mend it by confirming by some direct means the then past acts of the Commissioners, and this effected, transfer the charge of the reserve to the Crown Officer whose special duty it is to manage, under the Governor's direction, this and all other Crown lands in the Colony, whether held in trust as Indian Reserves or otherwise.

6. But the commission appears to have been virtually abolished without any means being adopted either to confirm or rescind its acts, or to effect a settlement of the claims arising therefrom, or to substitute for it any other authorized agency for the management of the reserve.

7. The various lessees who were placed by special authorized agents of the Government in possession of portions of this reserve under lease-right, on account of which they have paid considerable sums of money as rent, still hold the lands as leased to them. On the other hand the acts of the Government Agents in granting these leases having been repudiated by a subsequent Government, the lessees might, still holding possession as just stated of the lands leased to them, have refused for years past to pay rent, and some of them have made and still urge claims against Government for damages on account of non-fulfilment of the agreement made with them by these agents of the Government.

8. The whole matter here in fact remained in abeyance since 1865, and now presents a singular complication which presses for solution.

9. To this end, therefore, I beg to suggest that all leases executed by the Commissioners appointed by Sir James Douglas, and all agreements for leases of which written evidence can be produced, as well as all receipts given by the Commissioners or their agents for rents paid on account of such leases, be confirmed by such means as may be deemed sufficient and advisable. That after this has been effected, an agent of the Lands and Works Department make proper applications to each lessee, as far as practicable, for payment to Government of all arrears of rent. In all cases when the lessee shall have paid up such arrears of rent his leasehold shall remain good, with an understanding that the rates of rent will be reduced to such extent as the Government may deem right on each special case; that if payment of such arrears of rent be not made within thirty days from the date of the service of such applications, notice from this Department shall be served on the lessee, or his acknowledged agent, offering to cancel such lease if possession of the leased premises be legally given up within thirty days from the date of such notice; that failing the payment of arrears of rent, or the relinquishment of the premises, an action of ejectment be brought on each such case to recover possession.

10. As it is absolutely necessary that the true legal position of these leases in respect of this reserve should be defined, and all claims against Government on account thereof determined, before any steps can be taken for the further disposal of any portion of the reserve or for the application of the funds now on hand, I refrain from making any suggestions on these latter points at present.

Memorandum as to the Songish Indian Reserve at Victoria.

When the first settlement was made at Victoria by the Hudson's Bay Company, the Songish Indians, composed of many families or septs, possessed by occupation the whole south-eastern portion of Vancouver Island, including Saanich Peninsula, their principal village being at Cadboro Bay; but shortly after Fort Victoria had been established these Indians were induced to remove their chief residence to the point of land in Victoria Harbour, opposite the Fort; and in 1850 the possessory rights of the various families of this tribe in the lands before claimed by them, were purchased by Sir James (then Mr.) Douglas, Governor of the Hudson's Bay Company, at that time lessees of Vancouver Island from the Crown, with full executive powers by written agreement (the original of which is in this office) which sets forth as one of the conditions of the purchase that—" our village sites "and enclosed fields are to be kept for our own use, for the use of our children, and "for those who may follow after us. And these lands shall be properly surveyed "hereafter." Under this condition the tract of land which the Indians had taken up their residence upon opposite Fort Victoria (about 90 acres in extent), as stated in an official return made in 1859 to the House of Assembly, was set apart by the Company's Agent in the Colony for their use and benefit, and has since formally been laid out and established as an Indian Reserve, and so held by the Crown in trust, being styled and known as the Songish Reserve.

In February, 1859, the residence of the Indians on this reserve having become obnoxious to the inhabitants of Victoria, by that time grown into a town of considerable importance, and the land included in the reserve having greatly increased in value, and being much desired for building sites, and especially as affording extended frontage on the harbour, the Legislative Council of Vancouver Island presented an Address to Sir James Douglas, then commissioned by the Imperial Government as Governor of the Colony, enquiring whether the Government had power to remove the Indians from this reserve, and suggesting that if this could be done, the land so held under reservation should be sold and the proceeds devoted to the improvement of the town and harbour of Victoria. To this address Governor Douglas replied that—as this reserve and others had been set apart by solemn engagement entered into by himself, as agent of the Hudson's Bay Company, on behalf of the Crown, specially for the use and benefit of the Indians respectively interested therein, it would be unjust and impolitic to remove the Indians from them summarily; but that he intended to lease portions of the Songish Reserve, and to apply whatever revenue might be obtained from this source to the benefit of the Indians of the Songish Tribe, and particularly to the improvement of their social and moral condition. A copy of this address and reply (marked enclosure A) are forwarded herewith. [This enclosure cannot now be found.]

In accordance with the intention so expressed, a portion of this reserve was leased to Mr. Dougal, who afterwards erected thereon a foundry and machine shop. This lease was executed, on behalf of the Government, by Mr. Donald Fraser, who seems to have been entrusted by Governor Douglas with the management of this reserve, but without any formal commission, as that no written authority to Mr. Fraser to act in that capacity appears to have been ever issued; Governor Douglas having communicated to the Songish Indians his plans for the disposal, under lease, of portions of their reserve, and obtained their consent thereto on the assurance that the funds derived therefrom should be devoted to their benefit.

In August, 1862, however, in order to carry out more fully his views in this matter, he appointed by warrant under the seal of the Colony, Messrs. J. D. Pemberton, at that time Surveyor-General of Vancouver Island, E. G. Alston, Registrar-General, and A. F. Pemberton, Stipendiary Magistrate, Commissioners of this reserve, with general powers of management and leasing under their commission, a copy of which (enclosure B.) is appended hereto. Acting under these powers the Commissioners employed as their agent Mr. John J. Cochrane, a Surveyor and Land Agent, and by him, under their direction, the reserve was laid out into lots and streets according to a plan approved by Governor Douglas, a copy of which (enclosure C.) is also hereto annexed.

On the completion of this survey the Commissioners made known, by advertisement in the public journals, that they were authorized and ready to lease the lots so laid out on terms to be agreed upon; and accordingly many of these lots were applied for and leases thereof executed—which leases were signed, on behalf of the Government, by the Commissioners, or some two of them, under the express authority of their Commission; and the rents of these leased lots were regularly paid, without any expression of dissatisfaction from the tenants, until the arrival of Governor Kennedy in the Colony.

But soon after he assumed the administration of the Government in the early part of 1864, doubts as to the validity of the Commission under which these leases had been executed having been suggested to Governor Kennedy, the Commissioners by his instructions were called upon for a report of their proceedings, which report was accordingly made by them on the 24th May, 1864, and in reply to which a letter was, as I am informed, addressed to the Commissioners by the Colonial Secretary by the Governor's direction, in which they were enjoined not to lease any further portions of the reserve; but the Commissioners appear to have mislaid the original, and no copy can be traced in the Colonial Office.

In consequence, and shortly after the receipt of this communication, Mr. J. D. Pemberton and Mr. E. G. Alston resigned their commissions, and the opinion expressed by the Governor that the leases already executed were not binding on the Crown having been made known, the greater part of the lessees ceased to pay rents for the lots they held, and some of them, especially Dr. Ash and Mr. Wylly, demanded that the rents already paid by them should be refunded, and that they should be compensated for the failure of Government to carry out the engagements contracted with them by its authorized agents. These reclamations were based mainly on alleged assurances stated to have been made to the lessees by Mr. Cochrane, the Government Agent, to the effect that the Indians should be entirely removed from the reserve; that the whole of the reserve should be leased; and that the rents should be expended in improving the property. Dr. Ash still presses his claim on the Government in this respect, although both Governor Kennedy and Governor Seymour have practically declined to entertain it, as will be seen from the correspondence on this subject in the Colonial Office.

Mr. A. F. Pemberton did not, like Mr. Alston or Mr. J. D. Pemberton, resign his connection with this, but continued to act to some extent as manager of the affairs of this reserve, although not exercising the powers conveyed in the commission issued by Sir James Douglas; and in 1865, Mr. Young, then Colonial Secretary, seems to have been appointed, or, at all events, acted as Commissioner of this reserve, but only for the purpose, as far as I can learn, of dealing with the funds of the reserve then deposited in the Bank, and which it appears could not be withdrawn except by the joint cheque of two Commissioners of the reserve.

The management of this reserve, and of the matters connected with the leases executed prior to Governor Kennedy's arrival in the Colony, and of those other leases which it seems had been promised by the Commissioners, appears to have become involved after the powers of the Commissioners were withdrawn, and it is not at all clear from the correspondence on record in the Colonial Office, what the policy of the Government was in respect thereof; in fact the matter seems to have been allowed to remain in abeyance.

The validity of the leases executed by the Commissioners appointed by Sir James Douglas has been called in question, and especially as these leaseholds had already greatly diminished in value since the leases were taken out, the lessees discontinued paying the rents agreed upon, and as the agent could not obtain any authority to support him in enforcing payment of the rents so in arrear, no steps to that end were taken, and such rents have consequently remained until the present time unpaid. And further, in some cases in which the lessees were not unwilling to keep the rents paid up according to the terms of their agreements, the agent was not in a position to give a proper receipt for such rents, and therefore did not collect them. Indeed the condition of the affairs of this reserve has been most unsatisfactory for the last five years, as is testified by all who have been concerned therein; and during that period, more particularly stated in the report (forwarded herewith as enclosure E.) from Mr. Loewenberg, dated July 5th, of the present year, whose services as agent were engaged on Mr. Cochrane's death in the end of the year 1866, which sets forth very clearly the present business position of the reserve, and in which are enclosed a statement of the Songish Indian Reserve Fund Account, showing all the receipts and disbursements from the appointment of the Commissioners in 1862, up to the date of his report, and a return showing what lots in this reserve have been leased and to whom, and from what dates respectively the rents for the same remain unpaid, with remarks on each special case. [The above enclosure cannot now be found.]

It only remains to be stated—by letter from the Colonial Secretary, dated July 26th, 1869, the charge of this reserve was made over to the Lands and Works Department, and that shortly after that date Mr. Pemberton handed over to this Department all the books and papers in his possession connected with this reserve, and the balance of the fund on hand, viz., $1,984 82, which sum was paid into the Treasury on the 3rd September, 1869.

(Signed) JOSEPH W. TRUTCH.
30th December, 1869.

ENCLOSURE B.

[L. S.] JAMES DOUGLAS.

By His Excellency JAMES DOUGLAS, Companion of the most Honourable Order of the Bath, Governor and Commander-in-Chief of the Colony of Vancouver Island and its Dependencies, Vice-Admiral of the same, &c. &c., &c.

To all to whom these presents shall come or whom the same may concern.—GREETING.

KNOW YE that reposing especial confidence in the loyalty, ability, and integrity of Edward Graham Alston, Augustus Frederick Pemberton, and Joseph Despard Pemberton, Esquires, I have nominated and appointed, and by these presents do nominate and appoint them the said Edward Graham Alston, Augustus Frederick Pemberton, and Joseph Despard Pemberton, to be Commissioners for the management of the Indian Reserve at Victoria, in the said Colony; willing and requiring them the said Edward Graham Alston, Augustus Frederick Pemberton, and Joseph Despard Pemberton, to execute and do all such such things pertaining to that office as shall be by proper authority directed and required, especially to grant leases of the said reserve, and recover and receive such rents therefor as to them shall seem expedient; the same to be duly accounted for and paid to the use of Her Majesty, Her heirs and successors, and applied to and for the benefit of the Indians, or for such other purposes as shall be by the authority aforesaid directed in that behalf; and for so doing this shall be their sufficient Warrant.

GIVEN under my hand and seal at Victoria, in the said Colony, this Thirteenth day of August, in the year of our Lord One thousand eight hundred and sixty-two, in the twenty-sixth year of Her Majesty's Reign.

By Command.
(Signed) WILLIAM A. G. YOUNG.

The Chief Commissioner of Lands and Works to Officer Administering the Government.

Lands and Works Office,
Victoria, June 22nd, 1869.

SIR,—In obedience to your request conveyed to me by letter of the 17th inst., from the Private Secretary, I have the honor to lay before you the enclosed Report of the proceedings during the recent visit of His Excellency, the late Governor, to the North-west coast in H.M.S. "Sparrowhawk," and I take this opportunity of submitting the following remarks on that subject.

It is a matter of congratulation that the settlement of the murderous quarrel arried on during the past twelve months between the Naas and Chimpsean tribes, which was the main object of our lamented Governor's visit to this part of the Colony, has been so fully and satisfactorily accomplished. From information obtained from Mr. Duncan, Mr. Tomlinson, and Mr. Cunningham of Fort Simpson, as well as from Indians of the contending tribes, I am satisfied that the killing of the Naas Indian in which this bloody dispute originated was purely accidental.

A Naas Indian, formerly a resident of Metlakahtlah, gave a feast (on the occasion of his marriage to a Chief's daughter) to members of both the Naas and Chimpsean tribes, who up to that time had been living on most friendly terms. For this feast a supply of rum was purchased from the schooner "Nanaimo Packet," and during the drunken orgies which ensued, a Chimpsean Chief, by the accidental discharge of his pistol, killed one of the Naas people. We were fortunate enough to detect the schooner after a twelve-months' immunity, in the act of again dispensing liquor to Indians, amongst whom the quarrel between these tribes originated, and almost at the very place where it arose. Her seizure and condemnation (after due enquiry) had a very salutary and timely effect in showing to the tribes of that neighbourhood that Government are able and determined to punish offenders against the law, whether white people or Indians. In the fight which followed the accidental killing of the Naas Indian, two Chimpsean Chiefs were killed, and in accordance with the savage requirement of Indian Law, the loss of these Chiefs had to be compensated by the slaughter of an equivalent in number and rank of the opposite tribe. Thus murder followed murder in continual succession, with no prospect of complete satisfaction on either side. There was no real ground for the hostility of these tribes towards each other; they were, on the contrary, anxious to be at peace so as to avail themselves of the Spring fishery in the Naas River, which affords the main source of subsistence to all the Indians of this neighbourhood.

Without the interposition of some powerful peace-maker, however, reconciliation was impracticable, and this quarrel might have lasted for years with ever increasing waste of blood, but for the intervention which ensured its complete cessation.

The murder of the three "Kincolith" Indians did not originate in or indicate ill-feeling towards that Mission.

Mr. Tomlinson and his work are held in respect by both contending parties, as well as by the Indians generally along that part of the coast, and there is no reason to suppose that his life was at any time in danger. But the minds of Indians cannot readily admit that members of a tribe with which they are at war can be denationalized and placed out of reach of their savage laws of revenge, by the mere act of residing at the time at a Mission Station, especially a Station situated as "Kilcolith" is, in a most remote part of the Colony and in the midst of a notoriously ferocious race of Indians.

And here it may be observed that however admirable the spirit and intention of such Mission Stations, and however valuable their humanizing influences in many cases on the surrounding savage tribes, tending directly to the discontinuance of barbarous customs such as have given rise to the outrages and disturbances now under reference, it is questionable how far the establishment of such posts should be encouraged in situations so remote from the centre of Government as Kincolith, while a field for missionary labour extending for four hundred miles southward along the coast from Metlakahtlah remains entirely unoccupied.

It would appear more judicious and advisable that Missionary enterprise should radiate gradually from the centre of civilization instead of isolating itself at once in points like Kincolith on the utmost verge of the Colony. So long, however, as that Station is continued it must, most assuredly, be held under the protection of Government, but it is evident that the very remoteness alone of such posts render efficient protection a matter of much practical difficulty, and in many cases entails on the Colonial Government considerable embarrassment and pecuniary outlay.

The mode by which these warring tribes were brought to relinquish their feud, and bound over to live in future according to English Law, appears in happy contrast to the manner in which, by bombardment and burning of Indian villages, canoes, &c., the authority of Government has on some former occasions been enforced, with, perhaps, unnecessary infliction of loss of life and impoverishment, and even, in some cases, destruction of entire tribes.

It may confidently be expected that a more salutary and lasting effect will result from the persuasive but firm course adopted towards the Naas and Chimpseans which was so satisfactorily consummated on board H.M.S. "Sparrowhawk" on the 2nd June, than could have been produced by a more forcible mode of proceeding, and it is a very gratifying reflection in which all who have served under Governor Seymour will, I am sure, fully sympathize that this, his last official act, was in every way so creditable to his administrative ability, and so entirely in consonance with that kindliness of heart which was his peculiar characteristic, and which will long cause his memory to be cherished among us.

It must be borne steadily in mind, however, that as these tribes were specially placed by the direct act of the Head of the Executive under the operation of English Law, that law must in future be enforced among them at whatever cost.

Whilst at Metlakahtlah and Fort Simpson enquiry was made into the merits of the conviction and fine of Mr. Cunningham, the Hudson's Bay Co.'s Trader at Fort Simpson, by Mr. Duncan, acting as Justice of the Peace, on a charge of selling liquor to Indians at the Company's post at Fort Simpson, which conviction had been sustained on appeal before Chief Justice Begbie, but subsequently submitted by Dr. Tolmie, acting for the Hudson's Bay Co., for the Governor's consideration. Upon investigation of the case on the spot, it did not appear that there were any grounds for the Governor's interference with the Magistrate's decision and award.

The Mission Station at Metlakahtlah has been so fully described by others and the benefits conferred directly on the Indians of the neighbouring tribes, and indirectly on the Colony, by Mr. Duncan's labours on the North-west coast are now so generally acknowledged that I need only add an expression of my appreciation of the great importance of the results that have been accomplished by that gentleman's Christian zeal, courage and singular persistence of purpose, combined with remarkable ability and adaptability for this particular work.

The only fear is that should the Mission be deprived of his services, very much of the good work effected by him among the Indians will be undone for lack of his sustaining presence in their midst.

The investigation held at Bella Coola into the complaints of the white settlers at that place as to the behaviour towards them of the Indians amongst whom they reside, leads to the consideration of how far Government are responsible for the protection of settlements isolated as this is at so great a distance from the settled portions of the Colony, and lying so far off any travelled line of communication.

It is impossible to exercise any supervision or control over either Indians or white people at such remote posts;—quarrels arise, the real origin of which it is often impossible to ascertain, and Government are called on to punish the Indians without its being proved that they are actually more blameable than those who accuse them.

As a general deduction from the beneficial results of the late cruise of the "Sparrowhawk" it is apparent how desirable it is that a ship of war should periodically visit the various settlements, missions, stations, and Indian villages along the coast. By this means only can any measure of protection be given to the scattered settlers and Missionaries, and the wild tribes amongst whom they are located, be kept in any control; and by such blows as that inflicted in the confiscation of the "Nanaimo Packet" the sale of liquor to Indians, the cause of nearly all Indian outrages towards white people, as well as among themselves, will be rendered so hazardous a business, that the trade must soon be extinguished in that part of the Colony. Some duly authorized Official Agent of the Colonial Government should be sent in all cases on board of ships engaged in such missions, to share, if not to bear, wholly the responsibility of any extraordinary proceedings that events may necessitate. For officers in command of Her Majesty's Ships, although holding Commissions as Justices of the Peace, may reasonably be supposed to be disinclined to take decisive action in police matters, which can hardly be considered within their proper jurisdiction, and which may involve questions of material importance and great pecuniary interest to the Colony.

I have, &c.,
(Signed) JOSEPH W. TRUTCH.

Rev. Mr. Browning to the Officer Administering the Government.

New Westminster, July 6th, 1869.

SIR,—I beg most respectfully to place before you the following facts:—

1st,—Some months since the Indian lands on the Chilliwhack and Sumass were surveyed and "papers" given to each local Chief by Captain Ball, showing the extent of land to which the several tribes were entitled.

2nd.—Among the Chiefs to whom such "papers" were given are three, who are (if anything) protestants, and who were constantly being threatened by the Catholic Priest to be deprived of their "papers," and the same to be handed over to his own nominees.

3rd.—On the Queen's birthday, or thereabouts, these Indians were induced by the Priest to appear before Captain Ball, who ordered them to deliver up their "papers" to the Priest, or whoever he designated, and furthermore Captain Ball inserted the names of the Priest's nominees in the duly authorized map of the District as the *real* Chiefs, thus at once defacing the map and placing the first named Chiefs in the position of being, in the eyes of the Government, no Chiefs at all.

4th.—The aggrieved Chiefs came to seek my advice and assistance. I went with them to Captain Ball who himself took possession of the "papers," and promised to go up at an early day and investigate matters on the spot.

5th.—Whilst at Chilliwhack, a few weeks since, the Constable (Mr. Greer) informed the Indians in my presence, that Captain Ball had sent him, wishing them to come down to take possession of their "papers" again. They came down repeatedly, but the detention of Captain Ball in Victoria delayed their seeing him.

6th.—At the request of these men I called on Captain Ball after his arrival, to inform him of their answer to his summons, and to send for them whenever he could make it convenient to see them. Imagine my astonishment when I was told that he had sent after *all* of the four so-called Chiefs, intending to give them all "papers," that "I had no right to interfere," was asked "How *often* do you intend to interfere?" was taunted with a desire to "make Chiefs," and finally dismissed with the remark that I might appeal to yourself as soon as I liked.

7th.—The results are—I speak advisedly—the white settlers in the neighbourhood are thoroughly disgusted with the whole proceeding; the Indians are at loggerheads, and may at any moment come to blows. The Chiefs were here on Friday, but seeing how matters stood, declined calling on the Magistrate at all, and the matter as it now stands needs a wiser and a cooler head than Captain Ball's to settle it.

I have, &c.,
(Signed) A. BROWNING.

Mr. Ball to the Colonial Secretary.

New Westminster, July 14th, 1869.

SIR,—I am not aware of the nature of Mr. Browning's complaint with reference to the Indian Reserve at Chilliwhack, but he protested against my giving the map of the Reserve to the Chief who was pointed out to me as the hereditary Chief by the Roman Catholic Priest, because the name of the Indian (who is I believe only the second in authority and who represented himself to me as the Chief) was written on the map.

There is some religious jealousy on the subject between the Roman Catholic Priest and Mr. Browning, the Methodist Parson, as each advocates the rights of his own followers. To solve this difficulty, I have had two maps made of each Reserve, and intend to issue one to each as soon as I can get the four Chiefs together.

I may state that Mr. Browning's interference in the matter has been most objectionable and insulting.

I have, &c.,
(Signed) H. M. BALL.

The Rev. A. Browning to the Chief Commissioner of Lands and Works.

New Westminster, 9th August, 1869.

SIR,—You will remember, in connection with the survey of Indian Reserves on the Chilliwhack, delivering to each local chief a case containing a paper showing the lands reserved for his tribe.

2. At the instigation of the Catholic priest, Captain Ball has taken from two of these chiefs (who happen to be Protestant) the papers given to them by you, and on which their names are inscribed.

3. I have written to the Honorable Administrator of the Government explaining the whole matter, and asking in the name of the two aggrieved chiefs for redress, but no answer has been given me.

4. As the taking of these papers is but part of a system to coerce the Indians into Catholicism, (and the act itself was preceded by threats and followed by boastings of priestly influence with the authorities governing the Colony), I most respectfully request your official interference.

I have, &c.,
(Signed) A. BROWNING.

The Chief Commissioner of Lands and Works to the Rev. A. Browning.

16th August, 1869.

SIR,—Your letter of the 9th inst., was received by me this morning, and I have conferred on the subject matter thereof with the Acting Colonial Secretary, who has informed me that your communication to the Officer Administering Government had been referred to Mr. Ball, who is now at Kootenay, for his remarks, immediately after the receipt of which the matter will be again taken under consideration, and His Honour's decision thereon communicated to you.

The Acting Colonial Secretary did not think it necessary to write to you on this subject as he made you acquainted, at an interview which he had with you at his office here, with the course which had been taken in this matter, and explained to you the reason of a definite reply to your letter to the Officer Administering Government being deferred.

I have, &c.,
(Signed) JOSEPH W. TRUTCH.

The Rev. A. Browning to the Chief Commissioner of Lands and Works.

New Westminster, 18th August, 1869.

SIR,—In answer to yours of the 16th inst, I beg to be allowed to say that the reason assigned by Mr. Good for not acknowledging the communication which I did myself the honor to forward to the Officer Administering the Government, was a press of more important business. He also showed me a letter from Captain Ball in answer to my letter to the Executive, in which he said that he had prepared two other sketches for the case in hand, and should give four papers, one to the original holder at Kutzalla, and one to the original holder at Cultus Lake, and one each to the two men nominated by the Catholic priest. Conceiving this official letter to be a declaration of Captain Ball's action in the matter, I thought it best to appeal unto the head of a Department, from whom, I imagine, should issue all titles to land, whether held by whites or Indians.

It is the first time I have troubled the Government with my complaints, and I beg to apologize for bringing before them privately what others advised me to do more publicly.

It may seem nothing to hon. gentlemen in office that a Catholic priest after many threats succeeds in depriving an Indian Chief of a title to land and acknowledgement of his chieftainship bestowed on him by the Chief Commissioner of Lands and Works, and that simply because he is a Protestant, but there are those at home who, perhaps, will not hesitate in redressing so evident a wrong.

I have, &c.,

(Signed)　　A. BROWNING.

The Private Secretary to Rev. A. Browning.

Victoria, 19th August, 1869.

DEAR SIR,—I am directed by His Honor the Officer Administering the Government to express his regret that any misunderstanding should have arisen concerning a reply being sent to your letter of July 6th. The Acting Colonial Secretary was instructed to acknowledge the receipt of your letter, a copy of which has been forwarded to Captain Ball. Your complaint against that officer will receive due attention, and a reply will be forwarded you as soon as the matter can be investigated.

I have, &c.,

(Signed)　　D. C. MAUNSELL.

Chilliwhack, British Columbia,
November 30th, 1869.

To His Excellency Anthony Musgrave, Governor of British Columbia.

SIR,—We the undersigned settlers of this District, beg to assure your Excellency that the Indians Jim and Captain John, from whom Captain Ball (at the suggestions of the Catholic priest) took the papers given them by the Government, they have always been known by us as the rightful Chiefs of their tribes on the authority of the other Indians. They are also among the best conducted natives in this settlement, and esteemed generally for their honest, energetic qualities. We are apprehensive that unless justice be speedily done serious troubles will arise, involving, perhaps, the whites as well as the Indians, and therefore humbly pray Your Excellency to cause the land titles to be restored at once to their righful owners.

We have, &c.,

(Signed)　　V. VEDDER, and 27 others.

Mr. Ball to the Colonial Secretary.

The two Indians mentioned are both very good Indians, but not the hereditary Chiefs of their tribes, and not the Indians to whom the majority of their respective tribes wish the maps to be given.

All this has been fully shewn in my explanatory letter to the Colonial Secretary with reference to Mr. Browning's letter.

The Indians of each tribe must certainly know who have been the chiefs of their tribes much better than the settlers, who have only been there a few years, and until there was a division of religious feeling amongst the Indians the question of Chiefs was never raised.

I have, etc.,
(Signed)   H. M. BALL, S.M.
December 15th, 1869.

The Rev. Mr. Browning to the Colonial Secretary.

New Westminster, B. C.,
November 10th, 1869.

DEAR SIR,—Will you kindly inform me whether my complaint against Capt. Ball, J.P., has been investigated. In your letter of August 19th, I was led to hope the matter would be speedily adjusted. Its delay is annoying to me and others personally, but worse than this it is having a most pernicious influence on the minds of the Indians.

Hoping the case will receive your kind attention,

I am, &c.,
(Signed)   A. BROWNING.
[No reply to this letter appears to have been sent.]

Mr. Bushby to the Chief Commissioner of Lands and Works.

New Westminster,
30th July, 1869.

SIR,—I have the honour to report that "Snat" and a party of Squamish Indians came to me yesterday to complain that certain white men were intruding upon land on which they were settled, at Burrard Inlet, and on which they have built: they further tell me that they applied at the Lands and Works Office at the Camp, some time back, and that they were told that the Inlet would be visited, their case looked into, and if necessary a "zum" or chart made of their land.

I enclose an extract from a letter I have received from Mr. Brew, of Burrard Inlet, on the subject.

I must confess that I know nothing about the Indian Reserves of the District, and I have not been long enough in charge to have time to make myself aware of the facts; but should there be any truth in the complaint made by the Indians I would respectfully suggest that the matter be sifted, with as little delay as possible.

The Squamish is a troublesome tribe and likely to give the scattered white population of the Inlet a good deal of trouble. The murder of Crosby and the recent murder of Perry will naturally create a very bad feeling between the whites and Indians which any disputes about land will tend to heighten.

I have, etc.,
(Signed)   A. T. BUSHBY.

MEMO.—Deighton's claim is No. 674, and was recorded at N. W. the 22nd May, 1869.
(Initialed)   A. T. B.

ENCLOSURE.

Extract from letter—Mr. Brew to Mr. Bushby, 29th July, 1869.

"Snat" says his people were told by some tyhee at the Camp, "they might settle on the place where Deighton is building; they have no other claim."

The place is a long way from any reserve on the Inlet. The Squamish have built some houses and a church, but have no other claim, unless the priests have pre-empted for them. The Squamish are squatting on every piece of good land about, and disputing with white men who want to settle.

In the case before you "Snat" actually made a man named Cunningham pay rent for living near.

The story of the tyhee at the Camp is told about every other half mile on the Inlet. The Squamish never ventured into Burrard Inlet until 1859 or 1860.

The Chief Commissioner of Lands and Works to Mr. Bushby.

Lands and Works Department,
Victoria, 5th August, 1869.

SIR,—In reply to your letter of the 30th ultimo, respecting the complaints made to you by the Squamish Indian "Snat" and a party of his tribe, of the intrusion of certain white men on the lands upon which these Indians are settled at Burrard Inlet, and on which they have built houses, I have to inform you that the statement made to you by these Indians as detailed in your letter under reply is substantially correct. I enclose for your information a copy of a memorandum addressed by me to the Colonial Secretary for the Governor's consideration, on the 18th February, 1868, and of extracts from a private note to me from Captain Ball, on the subject on which this memorandum was to a certain extent based.

My recommendation that Indian Reserves should be established permanently at False Creek Bay and on the North shore of Burrard Inlet, opposite the V. I. & B. C. saw mills, was not, however, acted upon. No answer was returned to my memorandum, consequently I have never visited the Inlet since, and the reserves have not been surveyed off, as the Indians were led to suppose would be done.

It appears unfortunate, under these circumstances, that Pre-emption No. 674, which seems to intrude on one of these Indian settlements should have been recorded by Mr. Ball, and I should advise that you obtain information as to how far the land claimed under this record was an existing Indian settlement before the date of record, and as such excluded from the operation of the pre-emption right under Clause 12 of the "Land Ordinance, 1865."

I shall hope to hear from you again on this matter, after you have made further enquiries as to how far the claim of Mr. Deighton intrudes on the Indian settlement in question.

I have, &c.,
(Signed)   J. W. TRUTCH.

ENCLOSURES.

Indian Reserves at Burrard Inlet.

Two parties of Indians came to this office yesterday to make application, by Mr. Ball's recommendation, for tracts of land to be reserved for their use around their villages situated respectively on the South shore of False Creek Bay and on the North shore of Burrard Inlet immediately opposite Stamp's Mill.

There are no white settlers on either of these tracts of land. That on False Creek Bay is included within the limits of Captain Stamp's timber cutting license, but I cannot see that its occupation by the Indians would interfere with his use of the timber for logging purposes, or be in any way an infringement of the agreement of the Government with him.

The other piece of land has, I am told by Mr. Ball, been informally appropriated by Mr. Brew as an Indian Reserve. The Indians resident there now, desire that this reserve should be confirmed, as they are about to build a church on it.

I, therefore, beg to recommend that, if on examination of the localities there appear to be no reasons to the contrary, these reserves be established to the extent of not more than ten acres to each family, and that the same be surveyed in the spring and duly notified in the *Gazette* as Indian Reserves.

(Signed)   JOSEPH W. TRUTCH.

To the Colonial Secretary.   18th February, 1868.

Extract from note of Mr. Ball to the Chief Commissioner of Lands and Works.

New Westminster, 15th February, 1866.

*   *   *   *   *   *   *

The bearers are Indians who have had a house on False Creek for several years, and they wish a reserve made in their favour for themselves and families. There are 14 men, 16 women, and 12 children, with potatoe patches for each family.

It appears on the map that the land in question is on a part of the land reserved for Stamp, but as the Company have no interest in the land, a reserve might be marked off for them provided they did not cut the timber required by the Mill Company.

There is also another reserve required to be marked off on the North side of Burrard Inlet. This land was reserved for them by Mr. Brew formerly, and they wish to build a church there in the spring.

*   *   *   *   *   *   *

I have, &c.,

(Signed)   H. M. BALL.

Mr. Bushby to the Chief Commissioner of Lands and Works.

New Westminster, 19th August, 1869.

SIR,—I have the honour to forward for your consideration a Petition from the Indians settled at Burrard Inlet.

Mr. Deighton's claim is the immediate cause of their dissatisfaction, but they also complain of the adjoining pre-emption formerly held by a Mr. Lewis, but whose claim was cancelled by consent on the 20th March, 1869, in favour of Mr. Bridges.

I have, &c.,

(Signed)   A. T. BUSHBY.

ENCLOSURE.

The Memorial of the Indians of Snatt's Village, situated at Burrard Inlet, opposite Stamp's Mill, humbly showeth :—

That before any white people settled at Burrard Inlet, and before Moody's Mill was erected, your Memorialists had their camp at the same place they now occupy. It is true, indeed, they have not resided on the land during the entire year, that is to say the entire of them at the same time, as some were obliged to go from time to time in search of provisions, but, as the Indians do in every village, they always left some of their number to occupy the place. From the time the whites first settled at Burrard Inlet until 1866, none of them came to interfere with the Indians. About that time a white man named Lewis took up a claim near the Indian village, and your Memorialists immediately sent Snatt, their Chief, to complain to Judge Brew, the Stipendiary Magistrate, then residing at New Westminster, that a portion of their land had been taken by Lewis. Judge Brew told Snatt to take away the post, and at same time to notify to Lewis that he had ordered him to do so. Snatt took advantage of the occasion and made application to Judge Brew to have our Reserve surveyed, but this, unfortunately, has not been done up to the present.

Your Memorialists were always most anxious to have the Reserve surveyed, fearing that in the event of a change of Magistrates, another white man might succeed Lewis, and that the new Magistrate might authorize him to take a portion of their Reserve.

In January, 1868, we sent Snatt to beg of Captain Ball, who had replaced Judge Brew as Stipendiary Magistrate, to have our Reserve surveyed; he promised to have it done as soon as the weather would permit.

In the month of March subsequent, Snatt applied a second time to Captain Ball, who gave him a letter to the Chief Commissioner of Lands and Works. Mr. Trutch told Snatt that it would be necessary for him to write to the Governor before marking out the Reserve. After the lapse of a fortnight Snatt waited a second time on Mr. Trutch, who told him he had received no answer from the Governor. A third time the same application was made and the same answer given, and so our Reserve still remains unsurveyed.

Nevertheless we were persuaded and trusted that Her Majesty's Government would guarantee to us the possession of at least the small piece of land we hold and preserve for our children, since we have willingly and cheerfully given up the rest of our land for the use of the white settlers.

About a month ago our hearts were filled with sadness on finding a white man came to establish himself in the midst of our village beside our church, and told us that land was his, that Her Majesty's Government had given it to him, and that we had to permit him to build a house on it. We sent Snatt to make known to Your Honor the cause of our sadness, and to entreat now, at least, to have our Reserve surveyed and marked out. We have not brought our case in vain before you, for the white man who was about to take possession of our land was obliged to desist from his undertaking. But as he is using all his efforts to diminish the extent of our land, which we wish to have and possess, we have deemed it expedient to memorial Your Honor, and most respectfully represent:—

1st.—That the white man who took up the claim near our Reserve and wishes to diminish the frontage of our Reserve adjoining the sea, and which extent of frontage we have always held, has no right whatever to do so now more than in 1867, when by the decision of Judge Brew, orders were sent to have a post that was planted by Lewis already mentioned, for the purpose of diminishing the frontage of our land bordering on the sea removed, and that the more so on account of the frequent applications we have made to the Government to have our Reserve surveyed.

2d.—That we are 50 married men and 16 young men, who have built our church in the midst of our village, and we respectfully demand that there be left for us 200 acres of land having 40 chains of frontage along the sea. Surely 200 acres for 50 families and 16 young men who may hereafter have families, is a very small portion indeed, when compared to 160 acres which the Government allows to each single white family.

3d.—The 40 chains frontage that we demand along the sea should be so marked off that we may have 20 chains each side of our church. The 20 chains at the East or Moody's mill side of our church is absolutely necessary for us to have, for the 20 chains at the opposite or West side, is comparatively useless, or at least very inconvenient to dwell on, on account of the enormous distance of the tide from the land at low water ; consequently it is the 20 chains East (or Moody's

Mill side) that above all we wish to have to build our houses on, &c., &c., because it is the only place we can approach at low water, and this is precisely the portion of land or frontage which the whites, to our very great regret and sadness, wish to have us deprived of.

4th.—An Indian named John built a house on the land that we have always regarded as our Reserve, and which we have always defended against the encroachments of the whites; and, notwithstanding, John has received orders, transmitted to him by an Indian, to remove his house from where it is, and bring it within a few chains of the church. This circumstance appears more strange considering that during the time he was clearing the place and building his house no person told him he was doing so outside our land.

As we hear some white men say that we have no right to the spot we claim and where we have our village and church, because we have another Reserve surveyed at Reaplanon's place, we beg respectfully to represent that the Reserve in question was surveyed for Reaplanon and his people, between whom and your Memorialists there never has been friendly feelings. Moreover that Reserve was intended by the Government for Reaplanon and *his people only*, as evidence of which we have only to refer you to the various responses given by Judge Brew, Captain Ball, and Mr. Trutch, who never even made a remark about the above Reserve, but each of them promised to have our Reserve surveyed at Snatt's village.

Having no other person better acquainted with us and our circumstances than the Rev. Father Dureau, we have requested of him to present this Memorial to Your Honor.

Firmly believing that Your Honor will see the necessity of immediate action in the above matter, your Memorialists will ever pray, &c., &c.

(Signed)   SNATT, and 65 others.

New Westminster, 19th August, 1869.

[This reserve was laid out by the authority of the Governor on the spot.]

Mr. Bushby to the Chief Commissioner of Lands and Works.

New Westminster,
20th August, 1869.

SIR,—I have the honour to inform you that a small party of Indians came to me yesterday in great alarm about some land on which they are settled near Langley. As I could not understand them very well, I directed them to obtain from their priest a written statement of their wants, which he has kindly supplied in the form of a petition, which I have the honour to enclose.

The copy of Mr. Brew's note is correct; the Indians brought me the original. I cannot trace Mr. Brady's claim in the office records.

The Whonock Reserve, I am informed, extended to Brady's claim, but at the time of the actual survey was reduced to its present dimensions. I am also informed that the space the Indians apply for is uncultivated and unoccupied by any others than themselves, and I am not able to trace any record of the land in the Pre-emption Records of this office. If such should be proved to be the case I would respectfully recommend that the land in question be reserved for the Indian applicants.

I have &c.,
(Signed)   A. T. BUSHBY.

ENCLOSURE.

To the Honorable A. T. Bushby, Registrar-General, J. P., &c., &c.

The petition of the Indians living at the entrance of Shelik Creek, on the bank of Fraser River, five miles above Langley, humbly sheweth :—

1. That long before 1862, your petitioners have had their homestead at the entrance of Shelik Creek, on the bank of Fraser River.

2. In 1863, a white man named Cromarty came and took, as his claim, the land upon which our house and gardens were.

3. Having complained to Judge Brew, he gave us, to protect our land against any white man, a note, of which we give a copy underneath.

4. Cromarty left our land and abandoned his claim, but some time after another white man took it, and after him came Mr. Brady, the actual occupant of our land, who assured us that he bought the land and we had no further right on it.

5. Being driven away from our land, we commenced to cultivate a part of the land situated below Brady's claim, but seeing that in spite of the note given us, which we believed would secure our land to us, we have been dispossessed of it, and fearing the same thing may happen us again regarding our present place, and then find ourselves without any land, we humbly pray your Honor to have our new place surveyed and marked out as soon as possible.

6. We would respectfully demand that our reserve be so marked as to extend along the Fraser, from the corner post of Brady's claim to the corner post of the reserve already surveyed for Whonock Indians.

7. The portion of land we now ask for, namely, from corner post of Brady's to the corner post of Whonock Indian Reserve, is unoccupied by any white man. Brady himself has advised us to make application to obtain that land as our reserve, in order to put an end to any future dispute of rights and prevent us hereafter from being overwhelmed with grief and sorrow on seeing ourselves without any land to cultivate.

Firmly believing that your Honor will listen to their request and will cause our reserve to be marked out immediately, your petitioners will ever pray.

(Signed)
{ CHARLES SAL-TEM-TEN,
JULES SKOU-KIATEN,
ADOLPH KOU-KEATEN,
ALICK ———,
2 others who have their gardens there. }

New Westminster, August 20th, 1869.

Copy of Judge Brew's Note.

"The bearer of this, an Indian, complains that Cromarty, near Langley, has taken away his potatoe ground. This is, therefore, to caution Cromarty or any other person against taking or in any way interfering without special authority with any land cultivated by Indians."

(Signed) BREW, C., J.P.

New Westminster, 24th April, 1863.

The Chief Commissioner of Lands and Works to Mr. Bushby.

18th October, 1869.

SIR,—Your letter of the 20th August, forwarding a petition from certain Indians living at the mouth of Shelik Creek for a tract of land to be laid out as a reserve for their use, adjoining the Whonock Indian Reserve, was duly received and forwarded for the Governor's consideration.

I am now directed to state that as the limits of the reserve for the use of the Whonock Indians, to which tribe I understood the petitioners to belong, as well as of reserves for the various other tribes between Langley and Harrison River, were defined last year after careful consideration of each case and consultation with the various tribes on the ground, it is not deemed advisable to alter the arrangements then made and which have been duly advertised in the Government *Gazette*.

The prayer of the petitioners cannot, therefore, be favourably entertained, and I have to request that you will so inform them.

I have, &c.,
(Signed)   JOSEPH W. TRUTCH.

Mr. Michaud to the Chief Commissioner of Lands and Works.

Hope, British Columbia,
15th February, 1870.

SIR,—I have applied to Justice O'Reilly, Magistrate at Yale, in order to pre-empt 160 acres of land east of Fraser River, and immediately above the mouth of the Koquehalla River; having for boundary limits Fraser River to the west, and the Koquehalla to the south, measuring two-thirds from south to north, and one-third from west to east. Justice O'Reilly replied "this land is a part of an Indian Reserve," consequently I am denied even the right of having it registered to my name.

I should not solicit so much if it were not the only land near Hope fit for a farm, and the unfortunate circumstance of having wasted ten years of my life in this place at building houses, erecting fences, and selling fruit trees, on town lots I have bought from the Government, and from which improvements I could derive no profit if I were placed on a farm far away from Hope. Therefore I hope, from your active benevolence and good understanding, the privilege to register in my name the land in question, so that I could erect buildings on it next summer, and then take permanent occupation. I, besides, engage myself to let the Indians living thereupon enjoy peaceably the occupation of their small cabins and little gardens, until the Government think fit to remove them.

Please sir, ponder, consider, and act, still more on account that this would open a way to much more good land back of this reserve, and which remains wild because the Koquehalla and it stands in the way.

I have, &c.,
(Signed)   M. MICHAUD.

The Chief Commissioner of Lands and Works to Mr. Michaud

Lands and Works Department,
21st February, 1870.

SIR,—In reply to your letter of the 15th instant, I have to inform you that on reference to Mr. O'Reilly, I find that the land you applied to him to record as a pre-emption claim in your favour is part of an Indian Reserve, and therefore exempt from the operation of the "Land Ordinance, 1865;" and I regret that under these circumstances, I cannot hold out to you any prospect of your being able to acquire possession of this tract of land.

I have, &c.,
(Signed)   JOSEPH W. TRUTCH.

The Colonial Secretary to the Chief Commissioner of Lands and Works.

Colonial Secretary's Office,
29th April, 1870.

Sir,—With reference to the subject of the survey of the Indian Reserves on the Fraser, I am directed by the Governor to acquaint you that, as has been suggested by you, he approves of the boundaries of all the lands which are to be reserved for the use of the Indians, from Harrison River to Yale, and along the Waggon Road from Yale to Cache Creek, being determined by the local Magistrates, and surveyed under instructions from your Department; the Magistrates personally inspecting such survey.

You will be good enough to give the necessary instructions to the Sub-Commissioners of the District. The surveys in question to be carried out at the earliest possible date.

The sum of $400 is duly authorized to be expended on this service.

I have, &c.,
(Signed)   Philip J. Hankin.

Mr. Brenton to the Chief Commissioner of Lands and Works.

Chemainus, April 30th, 1870.

Dear Sir,—I must apologise for calling your attention to the trouble I have been lately put to with a few of the Chemainus Indians concerning the land I last summer pre-empted in the District of Oyster Bay.

I have been to Mr. Morley, Maple Bay, and have acquainted him of the particulars of the case, and can get no satisfactory arrangement with him. He says he has written to you on the matter, and since then I have heard nothing more about it.

The land, you will find on examination of the sketch map I sent you through Mr. Morley, is situated alout half-way between the two Bays, viz.—Oyster and Chemainus Bays, and about 1¼ miles from the point or termination.

I am given to understand that the Government have never reserved any portion of this land for the use of the Indians, except at the extreme head of Oyster Bay, which, of course, you will better understand. And notwithstanding my repeated cautions to them to keep away, they still persist to come on the land to work, and tell me to keep away, that I have no right there. Despite also Mr. Morley's caution to the same effect, they say (as they always do in such cases) that the land is theirs; that they have used it before for growing potatoes; and that therefore the land belongs to them. They or their ancestors may have used the land before for that purpose, but I candidly confess that there exists no visible signs of their ever having used it; and all they lay claim to is an isolated patch of *fern* containing about 1½ acres, and in or near the centre of my land, and about one mile inland from their ranch.

So soon as they discovered that I had taken up the land, they came and forthwith commenced preparing this piece of land for growing their this season's potatoes; and but for my having taken it up they most assuredly would have never come there. So you will see, sir, from this statement the immediate necessity of attending to this affair, and to get them put off the land without delay, for the longer they are allowed there, the more difficult it will be to rid them.

I have, &c.,
(Signed)   John Brenton.

The Chief Commissioner of Lands and Works to Mr. Brenton.

Lands and Works Department,
May 17th, 1870.

SIR,—In reply to your letter dated 30th ultimo, complaining of the annoyance caused to you by the Chemainus Indians, I have the honour to inform you that I shall take an early opportunity of visiting your locality and defining more exactly on the ground the Indian lands.

I have, &c.,
(Signed) B. W. PEARSE.

Mr. Bushby to the Chief Commissioner of Lands and Works.

New Westminster,
27th May, 1870.

SIR,—I have the honour to inform you that the Chiefs of the Zeluch Tribe of Indians inhabiting a large lodge on the Harrison Rapids, about one mile or so above Harrisonmouth, have applied to have their village and adjoining land surveyed off and constituted a reserve.

The tribe, I am informed, numbers some one hundred and seventy souls.

The Indians seem aware that Mr. Henry Cooper is applying for a lease of land in their vicinity, and they are anxious that he should not clash with them.

I have, &c.,
(Signed) A. T. BUSHBY.

The Chief Commissioner of Lands and Works to Mr. Bushby.

Lands & Works Office, Victoria,
3rd June, 1870.

SIR,—In reply to your letter of the 27th ultimo, I have the honour to inform you, that I shall be prepared to send a surveyor to lay out the Zeluch Indian Reserve so soon as I shall have received replies from Mr. Cooper and other applicants for timber cutting reserves, so that all may be done together. It will be necessary in the case of the Zeluch Reserve, that you go with the Surveyor and arrange the bounds with the chiefs of the tribe, in order that they may be content with the lands as laid out. I should be glad also to have some information from you, at your earliest convenience, as to the number of persons holding pre-empted or purchased lands in your Districts who may wish to have a Government survey of same.

I have, &c.,
(Signed) B. W. PEARSE.

Mr. O'Reilly to the Chief Commissioner of Lands and Works.

Yale, 28th May, 1870.

SIR,—In reply to your letter of the 9th inst., I have the honour to inform you, that after Wednesday, the 1st June, I shall be in readiness to lay out the Indian Reserves on the Fraser River.

Will you have the goodness to inform me at what point on the river I am to commence this work, as I don't know how far above Harrison River the reserves have already been defined.

I have, &c.,
(Signed) P. O'REILLY.

The Chief Commissioner of Lands and Works to Mr. O'Reilly.

Lands and Works Department,
Victoria, 3rd June, 1870.

SIR,—I have the honour to acknowledge the receipt of your letter dated 28th ultimo, and in reply to acquaint you that I have informed Mr. John Trutch, who will be sent up to define the boundaries of the Indian Reserves on Fraser River, and generally in the Yale-Lytton District, that you are now ready to undertake this work. I also transmit herewith three tracings of the Indian Reserves at Hope and Yale, and that at the mouth of Harrison River, beyond which no reserves have been laid out.

I have, &c.,
(Signed) B. W. PEARSE.

The Chief Commissioner of Lands and Works to Mr. John Trutch.

4th June, 1870.

SIR,—I have the honour to instruct you to proceed forthwith to Yale and report yourself to the Magistrate there, with a view to defining, under his immediate supervision and direction, the Indian Reserves on the Fraser River, above Harrison-mouth, as also such surveys as may be required of the pre-empted and purchased lands within the Yale-Lytton Districts. In the latter case only upon due application from the pre-emptor or purchaser for such survey.

These surveys will be executed in accordance with the general instructions to surveyors issued from this office. The field notes will be returned to the office, and the notes will be kept as far as possible on the American plan. You will also keep a diary of your proceedings. Whilst engaged in these surveys you will be remunerated at the rate of $10 per diem, which amount will include all personal allowance for board, etc., excepting only travelling expenses. You will also keep proper vouchers for all expenditures made by you. I append a copy of Messrs. Cornwall's application for a survey of a tract of land, as also a copy of the rough sketch furnished by them.

I have, &c.,
(Signed) B. W. PEARSE.

Mr. Bushby to the Chief Commissioner of Lands and Works.

New Westminster, 28th June, 1870.

SIR,—In the plan of the Scowlitz Indian Reserve, "Culkithl" is mentioned as Chief; this man disclaims that honour. Captain John, or "Scultlaamento" is, I am informed, the rightful Chief. As I shall have occasion to visit their village shortly, am I at liberty to alter the plan and hand it over to Captain John, on being satisfied that he is the actual Chief.

I have, &c.,
(Signed) A. T. BUSHBY.

The Chief Commissioner of Lands and Works to Mr. Bushby.

Lands and Works Office,
Victoria, 30th June, 1870.

SIR,—I have the honour to acknowledge the receipt of your letter, dated 28th inst., informing me of your error in assigning the chieftainship of the Scowlitz Indian Reserve, and asking whether you will be at liberty to alter the plan and hand it over to the rightful Chief, Captain John, upon your being satisfied that he is the rightful claimant. I have to inform you that I think it right that you should do so.

I have, &c.,
(Signed) B. W. PEARSE.

Mr. A. Dods to the Chief Commissioner of Lands and Works.

Cowichan, July 28th, 1870.

SIR,—As you asked me to apply to you in writing for a building site (when I spoke to you at the office) I now do so, as I have made arrangements to go on building provided you see fit to grant the following request: I want about 1½ acres at the corner of west half of Section 11, R. II. It is the only place in the vicinity fit to build a dwelling house on, being convenient to wood and good water. Anywhere on the other half is so cut up with sloughs that it is very hard to get firewood, and the water is brackish, even in the river, about three months in the summer. My neighbours, Marriner and Botterel, have been accorded like privileges. On the other side is a rough sketch of the ground, but I wish you could have seen it. I may mention that the Indians are aware of my intention and are quite satisfied.

I hope you will grant the site as I can't build anywhere else very well, and I am at present putting up at Mrs. Williams'.

I have, etc.,
(Signed) ARCHIBALD DODS.

The Chief Commissioner of Lands and Works to Mr. A. Dods.

Lands and Works Department,
Victoria, 1st August. 1870.

SIR,—I have the honour to acknowledge the receipt of your letter dated 28th ult., applying for a part of S. 11., R II., Cowichan District, for a building site. In reply I have to inform you that the west half of this section was pre-empted by a man named Dan. Campbell, and is not a part of the Indian Reserve at all, so I presume you must have made a mistake in your description. Possibly it is a part of S. 11., R. I., that you seek to acquire.

I have, &c.,
(Signed) B. W. PEARSE.

Mr. Weir to the Chief Commissioner of Lands and Works.

Gordon Bush, Metchosin, August 29th, 1870.

DEAR SIR,—This Indian from Sooke is desirous of purchasing land. The piece he wants is situated on the right side of the entrance to Sooke Harbour opposite the spit, at a place where a small stream flows into the bay. He says he only wants a small piece, but I suppose he can have nothing less than a section; perhaps you would allow him to squat on it if it is not yet surveyed. I have known him for several years for a hard-working and industrious Indian.

I hope you will be kind enough to explain the matter to him as he is rather a deserving character and should be encouraged.

I have, &c.,
(Signed) JOHN WEIR.

The Chief Commissioner of Lands and Works to Mr. Weir.

Lands and Works Department,
Victoria, 10th October, 1870.

SIR,—In reply to your letter dated 29th August, I have the honour to inform you that the Indian "Charley" will be allowed to take up 20 acres of land in Sooke Harbour, opposite the spit, provided he occupy and improve it in good faith.

I have, &c.,
(Signed) B. W. PEARSE.

Mr. Sanders to the Surveyor-General.

Lillooet, 12th September, 1870.

SIR,—Some Indians living between this place and Foster's Bar, midway to Lytton, having expressed to me their earnest desire to have the lands they have so long occupied properly secured to them, I rode down on the 6th inst. and made rough surveys and sketches of the plots claimed. I now beg to forward to you transcripts of the records which have been made in their favour for your information.

I have. etc.,
(Signed)   E. H. SANDERS.

ENCLOSURES.

Tonwick Reservation No. 1.

Recorded this day in favour of a settlement of Indians, a section of land, comprising fifteen acres more or less, situated about eight miles south of Lillooet on the right bank of the Fraser, and adjoining the north line of Won Lin's pre-emption. This reservation is to be known as the "Tonwick Reservation, No. 1." The Indians are to be entitled to fifty inches of water from Tonwick Creek for purposes of irrigation.

Recorded this 12th day of September, 1870.

Tonwick Reservation, No. 2.

Recorded this 12th day of September, in favour of a group of Indians, a section of land on an elevated plateau on the right bank of the Fraser, about seven miles south of Lillooet, to be designated the "Tonwick Reservation, No. 2." This reservation adjoins the pre-emption claim of Ah-Kye, "Side-Hill Farm," abutting on the southern line of said claim, and comprising from ten to twelve acres, more or less. The Indians are to be entitled to fifty inches of unappropriated water, for purposes of irrigation from a creek, "Tonwick Creek," flowing into the Fraser to the southward of this land.

Recorded this 12th day of September, 1870.

Nesekess Reservation.

Registered in favour of the Indians of Nesekess a piece of land containing fifty acres, more or less. The land in question is situated on the right bank of the Fraser, and about fourteen miles and a half from Lillooet; it is to be designated the "Nesekess Reservation." The Indians are to be entitled to the use, for purposes of irrigation, of one hundred inches of water from the first creek below this reserved land.

Recorded this 12th day of September, 1870.

The Chief Commissioner of Lands and Works to Mr. H. M. Ball.

Lands and Works Department,
25th November, 1870.

SIR,—I have the honour to forward herewith, for your information and guidance, plans of the Indian Reserves, two at the north shore of Burrard Inlet and one on the south shore of False Creek, surveyed by Mr. Launders last autumn, and which have been established by notice, of this date, in the *Government Gazette* as reserves for the use of the Indians resident thereon respectively.

I am informed by Mr. Launders that he finds that Reserve No. 3 was wrongly placed by him on the general map of the District belonging to this office, and it seems therefore advisable that you should send down your map by safe hands, so that the position of this reserve should be correctly laid down.

I also forward separate maps of these reserves in tin cases, to be delivered by you to the chiefs or principal men of each tribe for their information and that of the neighbouring settlers.

I have, &c.,
(Signed)   JOSEPH W. TRUTCH.

The Reverend J. B. Good to Governor Musgrave.

St. Paul's, Lytton, British Columbia,
December 19th, 1870.

May it please your Excellency:—

At the earnest request of the Chief of the Nicola Valley, who rode in here on Saturday with the hope of obtaining an interview with the visiting Magistrate, but arrived some hours after Mr. O'Reilly had returned to Yale, I beg respectfully to enclose the accompanying petition for redress of a very crying grievance, which I feel sure will receive from Your Excellency the attentive and kindly consideration the merits of the petitioner and of his appeal crave at your hands.

The circumstances connected with the present case may be briefly stated thus:—

In laying off the reserve at Nicola Valley, between two and three years ago, a piece of land was assigned for the future use of the Indians rendezvousing in this valley, quite apart from either of the three old chief settlements which had previously been the favorite locations of these original possessors of, perhaps, the most favoured valley in this upper country. The names of these Native stations, in the order of their approach from Lytton, are "Nehyig" with its two burial places, two water courses, and long line of Indian potato patches, and situate about a mile inclusive of the new official reserve, a place of remarkable beauty, fertility, and natural attraction; (2.) "To Tulla," some four miles further on where the Nicola River and the fresh-water stream meet, and from whence in turning to the lake we proceed in an easterly direction; and (3) the third is named "Tootch," just at the foot of the lake, where Naweeshistan's elder brother Poash has lived for years past, and from which he has lately been driven in favour of a white settler who has been allowed to pre-empt over his head, and to seize upon his improvements and lands without any compensation being offered him in mitigation of the loss and grief thereby occasioned him.

Naweeshistan from the first was most anxious to retain intact the right of the three spots severally, to which I have directed the attention of Your Excellency, but his heart was specially set upon "Nehyig," his own favorite stopping place and head-quarters. It was here he received a most friendly visit from Your Excellency's predecessor in office, Sir James Douglas, to whom Naweeshistan is well and favourably known. Here, also, the present Chief Justice Begbie called upon him, and left him with assurances of safety and protection of his rights that the old man now regards as standing in imminent jeopardy.

From the first he protested against surrendering "Nehyig," but wished it to be incorporated with the land recently assigned him, but wished in vain. In pursuit of this he made an especial journey to me immediately after the reserve had been laid off, and begged me with many tears to intercede on his behalf. Responding to his anxious wishes and fears, I brought his case under the consideration of the Lands and Works Department before the maps exhibiting the reserve in question had been prepared. I afterwards consulted with Chief Justice Begbie and His Honor Judge Crease, to whose joint opinion I would at this time especially beg Your Excellency to refer, in order that you may arrive at a righteous decision in the matter.

I was advised to refer the matter at once to Your Excellency, but considered it would be most in order previously to write the Magistrate of the District, by whom the Nicola reserve was assigned its present limits.

I understood from him, that he would personally re-visit Nicola and confer with Naweeshistan on the spot. No such visit however has been made, and according to the official announcement, persons may go and pre-empt all lands adjacent to the new reserve, in which case the chief would be turned out of his old homestead and ranch, shut off from his present water privileges, and his whole future life embittered with a sense of injury and wrong that might eventually culminate in rebellion to constituted authority.

A better and more amiable man than this old chief could not well be found. His loyalty and service to the Queen and her representatives have been most conspicuously evinced on all occasions when it has been in his power to exhibit them, or to the interest of the Crown to test them. He and his numerous adherents are prepared in spring to fence in their reserve and concentrate all their energies in its profitable development, if enlarged according to tenor of enclosed appeal. Would it be wise or politic to arrest all this, by denying their present modest and righteous request, and to convert a peace-loving, useful, and improving people into a disaffected, turbulent, and possibly seditious band of men?

The whole course of Your Excellency's Indian policy since assuming the reins of Government here, assures me in believing it impossible that such will be your decision.

I have, etc.,
(Signed) JOHN BOOTH GOOD.

P. S.—If it should be that Your Excellency is disposed to redress the wrong inflicted upon Naweeshistan, in accordance with the request embodied in his address, it will be advisable that special instructions be sent to the office here at once, forbidding pre-emptions to be registered or entertained in connection with the sites now in request, until further notice, by which much trouble and annoyance to all concerned would be avoided.

(Initialed) J. B. G.

PETITION.

Lytton, December, 17th, 1870.

To His Excellency Governor Musgrave, &c., &c., &c.

The humble Petition of Naweeshistan, Indian Chief at Nicola Valley, humbly showeth :—

That the land officially reserved for the use of himself and Indians owning his authority does not meet his and their wants and wishes; but having received it from the beginning under protest, it is still in its present unaltered form, an abiding source of growing discontent and disaffection.

That the said Chief, for himself and people, respectfully prays that the reserve in dispute be laterally extended, so as to embrace on the one side his old location at Nehyig, with the water-courses, burial grounds, and potato gardens thereof, and to the junction of Nicola and fresh-water stream, called "To Tulla," on the other.

That such an amendment of the piece of land secured to him and his numerous adherents would give great satisfaction and quiet their present feeling of having been unfairly dealt with, whilst they never will be reconciled to receive in peace and content the land as now offered for their acceptance and enjoyment.

And he will, as in duty bound, ever pray.

Witness, (Signed) NAWEESHISTAN his x mark.
(Signed) J. B. GOOD.

The Colonial Secretary to the Reverend J. B. Good.

Colonial Secretary's Office,
18th January, 1871.

Sir,—In reply to your letter of the 19th ultimo, enclosing a petition from the Chief of the Nicola Lake Valley in reference to the Indian Reserves in that neighbourhood, I am directed by the Governor to forward you herewith a copy of Mr. O'Reilly's report thereon, and to state that as there seems to be some difference of opinion as to the facts of the case, His Excellency's does not think it advisable at present to make any change in the Indian Reserves already assigned, especially as all Indian affairs will soon be transferred to the jurisdiction of the Canadian Government.

I have, etc.,
(Signed) Philip J. Hankin.

Enclosure.

Victoria, 12th January, 1871.

Sir,—I have the honor to submit the following remarks in reference to Mr. Good's statements regarding the Indian Reserves at Nicola Lake:—

In accordance with instructions received from the Government, I visited the Nicola Lake country in August, 1868, for the purpose of laying out the Indian Reserves, which consist of three blocks (not one as stated by Mr. Good), containing in the aggregate 1,648 acres of the best land in the valley. The Indians of Nicola Lake differ in no way from those of any other part of the country, and when their lands were being defined, they laid claim to small patches scattered over the entire valley, a distance of about fifteen miles. I explained to them that it would be impossible for me to reserve the whole valley for their use, but that I was prepared to mark off, in any place or places they might select, more land than could ever possibly be cultivated by them. The sites of the three reserves were subsequently fixed upon by the Chiefs, and comprise, as I have said before, the richest and best watered tracts in the neighbourhood.

Considering that Mr. Good has never been at Nicola Lake, he has succeeded in drawing an effective description, which however is totally incorrect, and it is to be regretted that he should not have made himself personally acquainted with the locality before submitting such a statement.

About a year since Mr. Good spoke to me about the Indian burial grounds, when I informed him that they are protected by a special Act of the Legislature, and cannot be interfered with by settlement whether included within the Reserves or not; I distinctly told him at the same time that I did not think the boundaries of the reserves could be altered, and that I did not see any good reason for recommending a change, the Indians having already been most liberally dealt with. It is my opinion that but for Mr. Good's interference from time to time the Indians would long since have ceased to consider they had a grievance.

I may add that with regard to the chief's visit to Lytton, it was made at my request, as I was anxious to pay him a sum of money due to him for ranching horses for the Government. I sent him a message to say I should be at Lytton on the 19th December last, and this, I apprehend, was the true cause of his journey there, and not to present the petition drafted by Mr. Good.

I have, etc.,
(Signed) P. O'Reilly, S. M.

The Reverend J. B. Good to the Colonial Secretary.

St. Paul's Mission Parsonage,
Lytton, February 3rd, 1871.

SIR,—I have the honour to acknowledge receipt of your official reply, dated 18th January, to petition from the Chief at Nicola Valley, as forwarded by me, together with copy of Mr. O'Reilly's report, and would in the first place desire to convey to His Excellency my grateful appreciation of the courtesy and attention bestowed on my memorial and representations thus far, in respect to a matter which I most reluctantly venture to obtrude again upon His Excellency's notice. For did I not feel absolutely sure that the case in dispute is one of crying injustice towards a most worthy and deserving chieftain, who looks to me, as one bound by the most sacred ties and obligations, to do all that is in my power to aid and protect him, a case, the merits of which have been most unfairly dealt with by one from whom he might reasonably have expected to receive a very different kind of treatment, and, moreover, just such a wrong as His Excellency in the noble reply he made to our Indian congratulatory address, when he passed through Lytton, declared it was his solemn duty to take in hand and redress upon appeal, I certainly should not have thought it necessary or fit to have troubled the Government with my reflections upon the tone, temper, and animus of the report of Magistrate as enclosed. Most respectfully and earnestly, therefore, do I entreat to be heard a second time on this question and on the opinion and remarks submitted by Mr. O'Reilly for His Excellency's guidance, and then, whatever may be the result, I shall, at the least, have the satisfaction of feeling I have done my duty and discharged my conscience towards all concerned, without partiality, fear, or guile. The fact that the petitioner is an illiterate dependant in this instance upon the Queen's bounty, as exercised by Her Majesty's representative in this Colony, and the one who, as I believe, has so imprudently and unjustifiably limited the display of that bounty as touching the interests of my petitioner when laying off the native reserve at Nicola Valley, is a gentleman of high position with powerful connections will, I feel sure, have no other force or weight with His Excellency than, if at all, to give the benefit of the doubt to the weaker party. Will then Governor Musgrave do me the favour, before proceeding with this statement, to have before him the Government surveys of the Nicola Lake Reservations from the Land Office, together with the Chief Naweeshitan's petition, my letter which accompanied it, and Mr. O'Reilly's report upon both.

Any one reading the latter would imagine that I had been indebted solely to my imagination for the supposed facts supplied through me, that I had no accurate notion concerning the subject matter complained of, and that, but for me, the Nicola Chief would have been content to acquiesce in the allotment already assigned him and his people. How far this is a true statement of the affair, and what reliance His Excellency ought to place upon the accuracy of the Magistrate's report, rather than upon any representation of mine, the sequel will, I hope, abundantly show.

And first, Mr. O'Reilly would lead His Excellency to imagine I was ignorant of the fact that there are three Indian Reservations connected with the Nicola Lake and Valley, and stated there was only one, whereas I knew to the contrary as well as himself. But Mr. O'R. knows also that No. I. and II. on the south side of Nicola Lake belong to the Chief "Chilehascut," who ranges between Nicola Lake and that of Okanagan, and that so far as Chief "Naweeshistan" is interested or concerned they might as well be placed on the other side of the Rocky Mountains. *It is with Reservation No. III. of 920 acres my remarks were wholly connected, and it was in reference to the limitation and character of this the petition alone refers.* Now, whilst I never thought of denying the two former to be well watered and satisfactory to all concerned, I do again most emphatically assert that No. III. is not so, and that if "Nehyig," Naweeshistan's camping grounds, burial places, two water courses, with long line of continuous potato patches, are still to be shut out and left open to pre-emption at any hour, *this reserve is practically useless, and will never be accepted as a central home for Naweeshistan and his numerous increasing people.* The Chief, moreover, says distinctly that he begged that Nehyig might be included (a matter of only one-half mile extension northwards), and was told " he was too covetous."

Secondly, Mr. O'R. informs His Excellency, with most astonishing assurance, I have never been to Nicola Lake and Valley. I beg to say I have been to both. I spent a Sunday within a mile of the lake (about two years since), and had Naweeshistan with me all the time to explain, on the spot, the whole of his troubles.

Thirdly, in relation to the burial grounds, Mr. O'R. on my earnest expostulation; and in the presence of Naweeshistan and many others at the Court House, distinctly promised to visit Nicola and lay off so many acres, encircling these places of sepulchre, and at the same time re-examine the limitation of Naweeshistan's Reserve, *but never went*, notwithstanding the Indians put themselves greatly about to stay at home in order to meet him at the time announced for his visit.

Lastly, I am charged with inciting the chief to consider himself aggrieved, who would otherwise have remained quiescent. In answer to this, I have to say that the Chief, as soon as he realized his condition, hastened to me, so long ago as the fall of 1868, and with bitter tears and lamentation besought my interference, saying the loss of Nehyig would break his heart, and also, he feared, *drive his followers into commission of acts of disaffection, violence, and rebellion against authority.* And again and again he has renewed the theme. In his behalf, and in the absence of Mr. O'Reilly at Kootenay, I represented the matter to the Lands and Works Department, subsequently to the two Judges, and Mr. O'Reilly, and now lastly the appeal is made to the highest authority. In my eager desire to honour and obey the Queen, and to behold my flock walking in all due subjection to authority, and maintaining peaceful relations with the European population settling in their midst, I write thus at length, and would respectfully suggest *that if the matter cannot at present be adjusted satisfactorily, at least an order should be sent up prohibiting any one from pre-empting Nehyig, or, which would be better, forbidding the officer in charge here from entertaining the preliminary notice of pre-emption, and also that the same caution should be published in the Government Gazette.* Query—might not the chief himself pre-empt it ? *or nominally lease the whole ?*

I have, &c.,

(Signed) JOHN B. GOOD.

P.S.—Further reflection confirms me in the conviction, that to give to the chief *a lease of Nehyig in perpetuity*, at a nominal rental, would meet the difficulty, and allow Reservation No. III. to remain undisturbed. This lease should include the right to the water courses by which alone the aforesaid reservation can be irrigated. And until the lease was executed, a prohibition to pre-empt the land in dispute would avoid all complication in the matter.

(Initialed) J. B. G.

The Colonial Secretary to the Reverend J. B. Good.

Colonial Secretary's Office,
13th March, 1871.

REV. SIR,—I am directed by the Governor, in reply to your letter of the 3rd ultimo, on the subject of the Indian Reserves at Nicola Lake, to forward copy of a report from Mr. O'Reilly; and letter from Mr. Mohun, who surveyed the land in question, and to remark that His Excellency thinks you are mistaken in supposing the Reservation No. 3 is not well watered.

There would appear to be no reason why the Indian burial grounds should not be fenced in, and as Nehyig is, as His Excellency is informed, a barren undesirable spot, the Indians are not likely to be disturbed in their use of it as a camping ground.

I have, &c.,

(Signed) PHILIP J HANKIN.

ENCLOSURE No. 1.

Victoria,
4th March, 1871.

SIR,—With regard to the Rev. Mr. Good's letter of the 8th ultimo, relating to the Indian Reserves at Nicola Lake, I regret that I can see no good reason advanced by him for altering the opinion I have already expressed concerning these lands.

In my former letters I have replied to the various points urged by Mr. Good, and I have now, therefore, only to deal with the following paragraph which I copy from his letter:—"*It is with Reservation No. III. of 920 acres, my remarks are "wholly connected, and it was in reference to the limitations and character of this, the "petition alone refers. Now whilst I never thought of denying the two former to be well "watered, and satisfactory to all concerned, I do again most emphatically assert that No. "III. is not so.*" In answer to this, I have to append the report of Mr. Mohun who surveyed the reserve in question, from which it is apparent that the statement made by Mr. Good, viz: that reserve No. III. is not well watered, and is in consequence useless, is incorrect. I can only infer that Mr. Good is personally unacquainted with the situation of this particular land, and the singular advantages it possesses in the very respect in which he professes to take exception.

My instructions in laying out these reserves were to deal liberally with the Indians, and I have done so, as will be seen by reference to the maps, to the utmost extent which I considered justifiable in the public interest, and far more so than with their present limited and apparently decreasing numbers the Indians there can ever really require. I considered it indispensable that the reserves should be well supplied with wood and water, and I affirm that the one in question is so, and that it is, both in extent and situation, indeed in all respects, admirably adapted for an Indian Reservation. I cannot, therefore, recommend any further extension of the present reserve.

With regard to the burial grounds, although they are already protected by a special act of the Legislature, under heavy penalties, there can be no objection, but the contrary, to their being fenced in by the Indians.

I have, etc.,
(Signed) P. O'REILLY, S. M.

ENCLOSURE No. 2.

Victoria, B. C.,
24th February, 1871.

SIR:—In answer to your enquiry as to the supply of water on Indian Reserve No. 3., situated on the Nicola River, and surveyed by me in the latter end of August, 1868, I have the honour to inform you that I consider the above reserve to be exceptionally well watered.

In the first place, the Nicola River, a stream of considerable size, flows through it, with a sufficient fall for purposes of irrigation; and in the second, there is a never failing spring, from which an abundant supply of water may be procured in the height of summer.

As you are aware I was there at the driest time of a very dry season, when the settlers in the valley were complaining of the scarcity of water, yet, even then, the flow from that spring was sufficient to cause a reed swamp of two or three acres in extent and six or eight inches deep in mud.

You will doubtless remember that, had you not decided on laying out that portion as an Indian Reserve, there was a settler who was eager to take up that very piece of land, simply because it was so well watered.

I have, &c.,
(Signed). EDWARD MOHUN.

Mr. Bushby to the Chief Commissioner of Lands and Works.

New Westminster,
1st February, 1871.

Sir,—I have the honour to inform you that the Lachouwa, a small band of Indians residing at the Sumass, near Miller's Landing, have complained to me that their land promised to them in a letter from the Colonial Secretary, dated 26th May, 1870, and addressed to Father Durieu, has not yet been surveyed, and that certain white men are molesting them.

I enclose a note from Father Durieu on the subject, and trust that the survey may be made as soon as possible.

I have, &c.,
(Signed)   A. T. Bushby.

The Chief Commissioner of Lands and Works to Mr. Bushby.

Lands and Works Office,
February 6th, 1871.

Sir,—I have the honour to acknowledge the receipt of your letter dated the 1st instant, enclosing a letter from Father Durieu on the subject of the Indian Reserves near Miller's Landing. I have no copy of the letter from the Colonial Secretary to Father Durieu; but if it should appear to you to be strictly right, I shall be obliged if you will employ the first Government Surveyor who may be in your neighbourhood to make the necessary survey.

I return, herewith, Father Durieu's letter.

I have, &c.,
(Signed)   B. W. Pearse.

Mr. Bushby to the Chief Commissioner of Lands and Works.

New Westminster;
20th February, 1871.

Sir,—Referring to a report from Mr. Justice Crease, and my remarks thereon, respecting the Sowassen Indians at Point Roberts, and forwarded to you some short time back, I would wish to know whether it is the intention to lay them out a reserve this summer. I have to visit them to explain the Fence Ordinance, under which they are now included, and I should like, at the same time, to be able to give them a satisfactory assurance as to their reserve.

I have, etc.,
(Signed)   A. T. Bushby, S. M.

The Chief Commissioner of Lands and Works to Mr. Bushby.

Lands and Works Department,
Victoria, 27th February, 1871.

Sir,—I have the honor to acknowledge the receipt of your letter, dated the 20th instant, asking whether it is designed to lay out the Sowassen Indian Reservation during this summer. In reply I have to inform you that a surveyor will be sent into your neighborhood very shortly and that you can then instruct him to make the necessary survey.

I shall also be glad if you will, at your earliest possible convenience, inform me what number of applications for survey have been made, and generally the locality of such applicants.

I have &c.,
(Signed)   P. W. Pearse.

The Chief Commissioner of Lands and Works to Mr. Mohun.

Victoria, 27th March, 1871.

Sir,—I have the honor to instruct you to proceed to Fraser River, and place yourself under the orders of the Assistant Commissioner of Lands and Works at New Westminster, in order that you may carry out the various surveys of pre-emption and pre-emption purchase claims, Indian Reserves, etc., in that District.

Your instructions of last year will hold good this year, and your rate of remuneration will be the same.

I have, &c.,
(Signed)   B. W. PEARSE.

The Chief Commissioner of Lands and Works to Mr. O'Reilly.

Victoria, B. C.,
26th April, 1871.

Sir,—I have the honor to transmit herewith twenty-four tracings of all the recent surveys of the Indian Reserves in the Yale-Lytton District.

The tracings for the Indians are complete, and packed in separate tin cases, which will be sent to you, in spring, for distribution.

I have, etc.,
(Signed)   B. W. PEARSE.

Mr. Mohun to the Surveyor-General.

New Westminster, 9th June, 1871.

Sir,—I have the honour to forward you herewith the field notes and sketches of two Indian Reserves surveyed by me, in accordance with instructions received from the Assistant Commissioner of Lands and Works at New Westminster.

One at Sumass adjoining David Miller's pre-emption claim and containing about thirty-five acres; the other at Tsow-wassen, English Bluff, and containing about four hundred acres.

I have, &c.,
(Signed)   EDWARD MOHUN.

Mr. Haynes to the Chief Commissioner of Lands and Works.

Custom House, Ossoyoos Lake,
1st May, 1871.

Sir,—I have the honor to inform you that, at the request of Mr. O'Reilly, I have laid out as an Indian Reservation a piece of land called "Ashtuolan," or "Ashnola," on the Similkameen River.

I have also marked out as an Indian Reservation a piece of land near the head of Ossoyoos Lake, which the natives of that vicinity have tilled for several years.

Mr. Lowe, the officer in charge of this station, will point out these lands for survey.

I have, etc.,
(Signed)   J. C. HAYNES.

Mr. Morley to the Chief Commissioner of Lands and Works.

Maple Bay,
28th May, 1871.

Dear Sir,—The Indians, the bearers of this note appear to have some difficulty about a road at Chemainus with Mr. Thomas. I believe you laid the road out when you were last there. Please send me word where the road should go, and I will see that it is carried out.

I am, etc.,
(Signed) JOHN MORLEY.

P. S.—I have not quite finished my report upon Salt Spring Island, but will send it down next opportunity.

The Chief Commissioner of Lands and Works to Mr. Morley.

Lands and Works Office,
Victoria, 26th May, 1871.

Dear Sir,—I send you herewith a rough sketch of the south part of the Indian Reserve at Chemainus, showing the proposed bridge and approaches thereto on both sides. Mr. Thomas has no power to interfere with the Indians or with their reserve. If you find any further difficulty with him or them write to me fully at once. I think with the sketch to refer to you will have no difficulty in the matter.

I have, etc.,
(Signed) B. W. PEARSE.

Mr. R. White to the Chief Commissioner of Lands and Works.

Cowichan, B. C.,
June 22, 1871.

SIR,—I have the honor to apply for permission to lease a certain lot of land, portion of the Indian Reserve, Comiaken, indicated in the sketch attached hereto, and marked red, containing three acres, more or less. I at present occupy a section adjoining the piece I desire to lease, some of my buildings which, located on the river?s bank, are yearly threatened with destruction by the river displacing the banks during freshets, etc.; my object in leasing the above land being to enable me to take steps to protect my property from destruction as described, by driving piles on the river's bank, which, at this particular point, is much exposed to wear. I have the permission of the Indians to occupy this small portion of their reserve, and pray for the consent of the Government. I shall be perfectly willing to pay a nominal rent of $5 per annum, and would wish to have the lease for a period of not less than ten years.

I have, etc.,
(Signed) R. WHITE.

The Chief Commissioner of Lands and Works to Mr. R. White.

Victoria, B. C.,
5th July, 1871.

SIR,—I have the honor to acknowledge the receipt of your letter, dated 22d ultimo, applying for a lease of a portion of the Comiaken Indian Reservation, being about three acres, and informing me that the Indians have no objection to such a lease being granted. In reply I have to inform you that I am authorized, in view of the facts stated in your letter, to grant you a lease of this small piece of ground at a rental of $5 per annum, for ten years, provided you can show to my satisfaction that the Indians are consenting parties thereto.

I have, etc.,
(Signed) B. W. PEARSE.

Mr. Claudet to the Chief Commissioner of Lands and Works.

New Westminster,
28th August, 1871.

Sir,—I have the honour to inform you that the Coquitlam Indians have applied to me for a map of their reserve, which they are anxious to get on account of the neighbouring settlers having frightened them by threatening to have them removed. I shall feel obliged by your forwarding one to me as soon as convenient.

I have, &c.,
(Signed)   F. G. Claudet.

The Chief Commissioner of Lands and Works to Mr. Claudet.

Lands and Works Department,
Victoria, 15th September, 1871.

Sir,—In reference to your letter on the subject of the reserves for the use of the Coquitlam Indians, dated 20th ult., I have the honour to inform you that their reserves have been surveyed and marked out on the ground, in accordance with the sketch appended hereto. If you find any white men encroaching on either of these reserves it will be necessary to warn them that they are doing wrong, and that all Indian Reserves are specially exempted from pre-emption.

I have, &c.,
(Signed)   B. W. Pearse.

Mr. O'Reilly to the Chief Commissioner of Lands and Works.

Germansen Creek, Omineca,
October 21st, 1871.

Sir,—I have the honour to enclose herewith, a rough description of the Indian Reserves which I have marked off in the District of Omineca up to this date.

I also enclose a description of two Government Reserves which I have marked off on Babine Lake, one at the terminus of the trail from the Forks of Skeena, and the other at the commencement of the trail from Babine Lake to Lake Trembleur.

I have, &c.,
(Signed)   P. O'Reilly.

Enclosures.

Grande Rapide Indian Reserve, situated on the right bank of Thatchy River, about six miles from Lake Trembleur.

Chief's name, Nah-ky-ley.   Population, sixteen.

Boundaries of Reserve.—Commencing at a post marked "Indian Reserve," planted about four hundred yards above the Grande Rapide, on the right bank of the river, and running up stream five hundred yards to a post similarly marked; thence running back to the base of the mountain, forming a block of land about one quarter of a mile square.

Thatchy Indian Reserve, situated on the North-East bank of Stuart's Lake, and the left bank of Thatchy River.

Name of Chief, Ah-dec-chas.   Population, twenty-five.

Boundaries of Reserve.—Commencing at a stake marked Indian Reserve, near the mouth of Thatchy River on the left bank, and running up stream nine hundred yards to a similar post; thence running back a distance of one half mile; thence a line parallel to the frontage until it strikes the margin of Stuart's Lake.

NECOSLIE VILLAGE, situated on Stuart's Lake, immediately below Fort St. James.

Prince, Chief. Twenty families. Total population, one hundred and twenty.

Boundaries.—Commencing at a post on the bank of the Lake, one hundred and eighty-six feet from the Hudson Bay Company's Post, and extending three hundred yards towards the mouth of Stuart's River, and two hundred yards back towards the base of the mountain.

Omineca, October 20th, 1871.

LOWER FISHERY VILLAGE, situated on Babine River, about seven miles from its mouth.

Zaneane, Chief. Population, one hundred and fifty.

Boundaries.—Commencing at a post fifty yards below the lower fishery, and running up stream about half a mile, including both fishing lodges, to a point fifty yards above the upper fishery, and one quarter of a mile on either side of the river.

NAYAU VILLAGE, fishing station situated on Babine River, about one mile from its mouth.

Nayau, Chief. Population, sixty.

Boundaries.—Commencing at a post about fifty yards above the small island on which the fishing lodges are placed, and running up stream to a post twenty yards above the Hudson's Bay Co.'s store, one quarter of a mile on either side of the river.

BABINE LAKE winter village, situated on Babine Lake near its mouth.

Nayau, Chief. Population, fifty.

Boundaries.—Commencing at a point about two hundred and fifty yards below the burial ground, and running up about four hundred yards to the foot of the lake, and back towards the mountain two hundred yards.

LATACULSA VILLAGE, situated on Babine Lake, adjoining the Hudson's Bay Co.'s store.

Nastell, Chief. Seventy families. Population, two hundred and fifty.

Boundaries.—Commencing at the Hudson's Bay Co.'s boundary line, and running down stream along the bank of the lake four thousand feet, and running back towards the mountain four hundred yards.

PINCHIE VILLAGE, situated on the north-east bank of Stuart's Lake, about twelve miles above Fort St. James.

Yabee, Chief. Twelve families. Total population, Sixty.

Boundaries.—Commencing at a blazed tree at a bluff below the mouth of Pinchie River, and running along the shore of the lake thirty-two hundred yards to a post marked "Indian Reserve, September 5th, 1871," thence running back to the base of Pinchie Mountain, thence following the base of the mountain to starting point.

CORRESPONDENCE BETWEEN THE SECRETARY OF STATE FOR THE PROVINCES AND THE LIEUTENANT-GOVERNOR.

The Secretary of State for the Provinces to the Lieutenant-Governor.

Ottawa, 21st July, 1871:

SIR,—I have the honour to transmit to you herewith, a copy of a letter addressed by the Bishop of Columbia to the Secretary of State for the Colonies, and by him communicated to His Excellency the Governor-General, respecting the educational condition and wants of the Indian population of British Columbia.

May I request that you will bring this document under the early notice of your Government, and communicate to me, for the information of His Excellency the Governor-General, their views on the important subject therein referred to.

I have, &c.,
(Signed) JOSEPH HOWE.

ENCLOSURE.

70, Upper Berkeley Street, London, W.,
27th May, 1871.

MY LORD,—I have the honour to ask your kind attention to the subject of the welfare of the Native Race of British Columbia, who number some 50,000, and live in villages scattered throughout the Colony.

For some years the Church of England has carried on Missions amongst them, expending annually about £2,000 in four chief centres, in each of which two Missionaries are at work. These chief centres are—

    1st.—The Chymseans and Nishtacks:
    2nd.—The Tahkats:
    3rd.—The Cowichans:
    4th.—The Fraser and Thompson River Tribes.

The first of these is supported by the Church Missionary Society, the three latter in part by that for the Propagation of the Gospel.

The result of this work is, that some 5,000 Natives are under instruction, and many more ask for teachers. Industrial improvement is promoted, and some 300 gardens are a witness to considerable progress.

We have hitherto received no assistance from the Government, upon which point I beg to quote the remarks of the Archdeacon of Vancouver. He says in a letter to the New England Company, published in the Columbia Report for 1870:—
"The Government of this Colony has hitherto had no definite or tangible policy "with regard to the Native Indian Tribes. They have preserved for them Crown "Lands under the name of Indian Reserves; they have prevented their lands being "encroached upon; they have in existence a Liquor Law, with penal clauses "stringent and severe, but honored more in the breach than in observance. Beyond "this they have done nothing so far as I know. There does not exist an Indian "Hospital in the Colony to ameliorate the evils which contact with a too advanced "stage of civilization has brought upon its unprepared victims. There may be "insuperable obstacles in the way of any definite policy of preservation and develop-"ment being adopted. I am bound to suppose that such obstacles do exist, other-"wise such negligence would make the very stones cry out for redress against

"wrongs of suffering humanity. Some such obstacles assuredly must exist, other-
"wise what is known here would scarcely be credited elsewhere. I have before
"me as I write, the Colonial Estimates for 1869. The estimated expenditure of the
"Government for that year is £122,250, and in that amount this item occurs—
"'Expenses connected with the Indian Tribes £100,' the Indians in the Colony
"being estimated by some at over 50,000, who pay duty on every article that they
"consume, if it has been imported into the Colony. I do not wish to say more on
"this point, neither have I said this by way of complaint; but I could scarcely
"have said less to make the New England Society realize the fact that little or
"nothing is done for the moral and social benefit of the North American Indians on
"this Coast, outside the circle of efforts of the various religious societies."

It has been computed that the Native Race contributes at least a fourth of the revenue of the Colony, and it would appear to be only just, as well as politic, that they should share with the Europeans in the Educational Grant. It will be of advantage to the Colony if, before the influx of Emigrants which is expected in connection with the Pacific Railroad, the Indian Tribes shall have been trained in Christian principles and the arts of peace.

I would respectfully suggest that a grant be made for Indian improvement, and dispensed through Missionary Societies under a Superintendent of Indian Affairs to be appointed by the Government. I quote a precedent for this from the last annual Message of President Grant, delivered to Congress in December last. He says—
"Reform in the management of Indian affairs has received the special attention of
"the Administration from its inauguration to the present day. The experiment of
"making it a Missionary work was tried with a few agencies given to the denom-
"ination of Friends, and has been found to work most advantageously. All agencies
"and superintendencies not so disposed of were given to Officers of the Army.
"The Acts of Congress reducing the Army, renders Army Officers ineligible for
"civil positions. Indian Agencies being Civil Offices, I determined to give all
"the Agencies to such religious denominations as had heretofore established
"Missionaries among the Indians, and perhaps to some other denominations who
"would undertake the work on the same terms, i. e., as a Missionary work. The
"Societies selected are allowed to name their own agents, subject to the approval
"of the Executive, and are expected to watch over them and aid them as Mission-
"aries to christianize and civilize the Indian and to train him in the arts of peace.
"The Government watches over the official acts of these agents, and requires of
"them as strict an accountability as if they were appointed in any other manner.
"I entertain the confident hope that the policy now pursued will, in a few years,
"bring all the Indians upon reservations, where they will live in houses, have
"school-houses and churches, and will be pursuing peaceful and self sustaining
"avocations, and where they may be visited by the law-abiding white man with the
"same impunity that he now visits the civilized white settlements. I call your
"special attention to the Report of the Commissioner of Indian Affairs for full in-
"formation on this subject."

I am sorry to say that without Government assistance we shall be compelled to break up some of our Mission work. Having been in England some months incessantly labouring to obtain support, I have only partially succeeded, and am about to return under the painful necessity of contracting instead of enlarging, as I had hoped, the important work of Native improvements.

         I have, &c.,
          (Signed) G. COLUMBIA.

The Lieutenant-Governor to the Secretary of State for the Provinces.

Government House,
26th September, 1871.

Sir,—Having laid before my Executive Council your Despatch of the 21st July, last, and the copy therewith transmitted of a letter addressed by the Bishop of Columbia to the Secretary of State for the Colonies, respecting the educational condition and wants of the Indians of this Province, and in accordance with your request invited the expressions of their views thereon, I have now the honour to forward herewith enclosed the minutes, which I have just received, conveying the opinions and remarks of my Council on the matters referred to in the Bishop's letter.

2. I regard the charge of the Indians in this Province as among the most critical and direct responsibilities, as well as among the foremost and most pressing duties of the Dominion, as it has been of the Colonial Government; and I rejoice in the hope and confident expectation that the increased financial means which it may be anticipated will now be appropriated for the improvement of the condition of our Indian population, may be so applied as to promote in reality their welfare, spiritual and temporal.

3. But I cannot advise that the Federal Government should delegate to any other body or bodies, whether religious or lay, the responsibility in this matter, which is so especially its own. The success or failure of the endeavours which may be made to ameliorate the social status of the Indian Tribes here, will depend most materially, if not entirely, on the careful and wise selection by Government of its Agent for the disbursement of the funds that may be set apart for this purpose, rather than on the amount of such funds; and whilst I fully admit that it may be advisable in some instances for Government to aid pecuniarily, and in other ways, the educational work already commenced by Missionary Clergymen, or even to employ such reverend gentlemen as special agents, yet I should deem the duty but ill fulfilled if its efforts in favour of our Indian population be restricted to the subsidizing of the Missionary Churches, of whatever denomination, now established in the Province.

4. All must acknowledge, as I do with thankful appreciation, the benefits conferred on the Indians—and which are reflected indirectly on the white population—by the good work done among them at some Missionary Stations in British Columbia, and most specially at two points with which I am well acquainted, viz:—Metlahkatlah on the North-west Coast, and at St. Mary's on Fraser River. But the civilizing and moralizing results attained at one at least of these places, I know to be directly attributable—and I believe this remark is equally true in the other instance above named by me—to the special fitness of the Missionary for the work he has devoted himself to; to his courage, moral and physical, his zeal, self-denial, and great administrative ability.

But, on the other hand, I cannot conceal from myself, and feel bound to state without particularizing, that the instances of entire failure of Mission Stations to produce any good results in their neighbourhood, have been as notable, and unhappily far more numerous, than the success we have to rejoice in.

5. As to the Indian policy hitherto of the Government of British Columbia, for, although not a written code based on legislation, the policy of the Government in Indian affairs has been "definite and tangible"—a well considered system, ably devised by experienced men specially interested in favour of the Indians, to suit the circumstances of this Country, and consistently carried out so far as the pecuniary means at command would admit of, (as proof of which I need only point to the remarkable freedom from Indian disturbances, few in number as we have been, scattered through this immense territory among some fifty thousand Indians). I would observe, that in direct contrast with the Indian system of the United States, as stated by President Grant, as the quotation from his Message contained in the Bishop of Columbia's letter, that adopted in this Province does not appear to me to require

reform, but greater development. We need funds to provide tuition for our Indians in the pursuits of civilized life, as well as in school-book education; and we still more need special officers to superintend the expenditure of these funds; to take charge of, and apportion out under careful regulation, the lands which have been or may be set apart as Indian Reserves, or to sell or rent them for the benefit of the tribes for whom they were reserved, and to act both as the defenders and representatives of the Indians in all matters between them and the white population, and as conservators of peace and order by the Indians among themselves and towards the rest of our people. And, as much as, if not more than all else, we require the means of carrying the Indian Liquor Law into effect, which can only be done by providing a special preventive police for the purpose.

6. I deny that Archdeacon Reece's allegations quoted by the Bishop of Columbia are well founded. With the highest respect for that gentleman's ecclesiastical position, I must say that I cannot so highly estimate either the trustworthiness of his statement, or the soundness of the deductions he draws therefrom; and although the passage cited from his letter to the New England Society may have been well adapted to attract sympathy to the cause of the Indians in our country, and thus to secure, as I trust it may have done, a full measure of material aid to our Indian Mission Fund, I regret that it should have been brought so prominently before me as to compel distinct confutation from me.

7. Similar imputations against the Government of British Columbia have been advanced on previous occasions, and most particularly by Mr. W. S. Sebright Green, by whom charges more exaggerated in degree, and far more objectionable in the manner of their preferment, were made in a letter to the "Aborigines Protection Society," which was transmitted by the Secretary of State to Governor Musgrave for his remarks, and on which I made a report by the Governor's request. A copy of this report which was printed in the "Colonial Intelligencer" in reply to Mr. Green's accusations previously inserted in that publication, and of the correspondence on which it was based, is forwarded herewith*, as it conveys information on several matters connected with the Indian affairs of British Columbia, and expresses my opinion thereon in direct contravention of the Archdeacon of Vancouver's allegations and of the inferences he makes. I will only add further, in reference to the Archdeacon's criticism as to the remissness of the Government to provide that the Indians who contribute so largely to our revenue should participate in the benefits derived by the population from the expenditures—in support of which he cites that only the insignificant sum of one hundred pounds appeared in the "Estimates for the year 1869," as appropriated for expenses connected with the Indian Tribes—that both that Reverend gentleman and his Lordship the Bishop seem to have omitted from consideration, that, although from the pecuniary inability of the Colony in the past no such appropriations have been made as could have been wished, for the special purpose of promoting the well-being of our Indian population, they have yet partaken on equal, and in some cases on more than equal, terms with our white people in all the advantages of civilization which we have brought to them, in the use of the roads and trails throughout the country, which have cost us the whole of our public debt, free of the tolls imposed in most cases on white people, cheapening food to them, and bringing to their hands implements of husbandry and agriculture, the chase and fishing, &c., which before they were without; and more especially in the blessings which result from the preservation of law and order throughout the country, instead of those scenes of bloodshed and robbery which prevailed formerly among them, and amidst which their lives were passed in a state of constant dread and uncertainty of life or property; nor again, is there at this moment any bar whatever, that I am aware of, to their sharing in the sum voted in aid of Education in the Province.

8. The strongest motives of duty and interest combined to press upon the Government, as upon each honest individual member of our community, the urgency

---

* See Appendix B. to Report of the Government of British Columbia, page 10.

of our striving by every means in our power, to advance the material and moral condition of our Indian population. By such influences may we hope so to change their habit of mind, that in a following generation they may become susceptible of appreciating the truths of revealed religion; although, and I state it most regretfully, in my twenty years' experience among the Aborigines of this Coast, I have not yet met with a single Indian of pure blood whom I consider to have attained to even the most glimmering perception of the christian creed. In fact the idiosyncrasy of the Indians of this country appears to incapacitate them from appreciating any abstract idea, nor do their languages contain words by which such a conception could be expressed.

9. But I contend that the policy which has prevailed in British Columbia since its settlement by Europeans, has been essentially benevolent towards the Indians; that the degree of civilization which we have introduced into their country has in fact conferred infinite benefits upon them, although bringing with it all the evils incidental to its vices; and that this system needs not change or reform, but only increased means to bring out its real merits and capabilities. And chiefly I urge that the grave responsibility which the Government of the Dominion has undertaken towards these Indians and to the people of the Province in general respecting them, should not be devolved on others from any consideration whatever.

I have, &c.,
(Signed) JOSEPH W. TRUTCH.

The Lieutenant-Governor to the Secretary of State for the Provinces.

Government House,
5th October, 1871.

SIR,—Acknowledging the receipt of your Despatch of the 19th August, asking to be supplied with certain statistics on Indian matters in this Province, and with maps of the various tracts of land held under reserve by Government for the use and benefit of the Indians, I have the honour to acquaint you that the information you desire is now being prepared in the Lands and Works Office, under the direction of the Chief Commissioner, as far as it is practicable to furnish it from the office records, and will be transmitted to you as soon as completed, which however will not be for some considerable time yet, as the copying of the maps of Indian Reserves is a lengthly undertaking.

I have, &c.,
(Signed) JOSEPH W. TRUTCH.

The Lieutenant-Governor to the Secretary of State for the Provinces.

Government House,
3rd November, 1871.

SIR,—I have now the honour to transmit herewith a copy of a letter, and accompanying tracings, from the Chief Commissioner of Lands and Works to the Colonial Secretary, conveying, as far as it can be furnished from the Lands and Works records, the information applied for in your Despatch of the 19th August, the receipt whereof was acknowledged by me on the 5th ultimo.

2. I am not aware that any expenses have been incurred by the Lands and Works Department in complying with your request in this matter, but should any such expenses be charged in connection with the copying of the maps of Indian Reserves I will defray any such reasonable charges from Dominion funds and acquaint you thereof, in order that you may obtain the vouchers for the same, which will be forwarded from the Bank of British Columbia, and bring the amount to account in whatever manner you may deem fit.

3. As to the title by which the various Indian Reservations in this Province are held, I may add to Mr. Pearse's letter that all these lands have been severally set apart at various times for the use and benefit of the Indians resident thereon, or who, being members of the particular tribe for which any such reservation was created are entitled to participate therein, by order of the Governor, publicly notified in the Government *Gazette*, or in such manner as was held to be sufficient advertisement of such notice previous to the establishment of the Government *Gazette*.

4. The authority of the Governor for creating such reservations was based up to 1865, on the mainland portion of British Columbia, and up to 1870, in Vancouver Island, on the power conferred on him, to this effect, by his Commission and the Royal instructions, and since those dates on the provisions of the Land Ordinances, 1865 and 1870, respectively.

5. As I have already in my despatch to you, No. 20, of 26th September, treated of Indian affairs at some length I will not at present enter into any further remarks on this subject.

I have, &c.,
(Signed)   JOSEPH W. TRUTCH.

ENCLOSURES.

The Chief Commissioner of Lands and Works to the Colonial Secretary.

Lands and Works Office,
Victoria, 16th October, 1871.

SIR,—I have the honour to acknowledge the receipt of your Instructions under date of 5th September, to prepare tracings of the Indian Reserves existing in this Province, together with statistics of the Natives generally.

I have now to transmit herewith a series of tracings lettered A to Q inclusive, showing all the Indian Reserves which have been surveyed, together with a Schedule showing the locality, number of section, general description, acreage, name of tribe in whose favour each reserve has been made, also an Appendix one, (1) showing what portions of any particular reserve have been leased to white men, together with the terms of lease. Parts of the Songish Indian Reserve, opposite to Victoria, have been so leased by Commissioners appointed by Sir James Douglas. These leases have all expired or been cancelled,

A certain sum of money, Nineteen hundred and eighty-four dollars and eighty-two cents, is now lying in the Treasury to the credit of this Reserve, and is constantly increasing.

The leases shown in the Appendix were executed by me, in virtue of the authority of the late Governor, and are only binding so far as the Government may have the power. The rents shown in the Appendix are due from the date of each respective lease. I have no statistics as to the number of Indians in each tribe, and have no means of obtaining them. It would cost a great deal of time and money, and would involve a visit to each Indian Village throughout the Province. There are, especially in Vancouver Island, a great many tribes which have no Reserves marked out either on plan or on the ground.

The "Land Ordinance, 1870," under which alone lands can be acquired by intending settlers, especially exempts all Indian lands and settlements from its operation. It has generally been the practice to lay out on the ground the Indian Reserves synchronously with the settlement of the district by the whites. This system has been found effectual and far less costly than that of surveying the reserve all together, as they are naturally scattered and often at great distances apart. In the latter case the posts and marks on the ground might become obliterated before the white men advanced, as the Indians, though tenacious of their rights in the lands when once surveyed, will not take the trouble to perpetuate these posts and marks, or to preserve them in any way.

Appendix two (2) shows the position of land included in the Quamichan District (sheet B) which have been promised to certain settlers in the District with the consent of the Natives.

There are various Missions established in different parts of the Province, but as they are chiefly located on lands taken up under the Pre-emption Laws, I have not reported them as existing, inasmuch as the Indians have no direct interest in the land.

The Metlakahtlah Mission on the North-west Coast of the Province, is established on land specially reserved by the Government for the purposes and uses of the Mission.

Other reserves can be made from time to time as may be found necessary.

No titles to lands held by the Indians have been issued.

The Executive has always exercised a general control and supervision over the Indians and their lands, and has always prevented them from alienating in any way any portion of their reserves.

No Indian Reserves have been laid out on Vancouver Island on the west side, and none beyond Comox on the east side. No Indian Reserves have been laid out on the coast of the Mainland beyond Burrard Inlet.

The total area of land laid out on the ground for the use of the Natives is 28,437 acres.

I have, &c.,
(Signed)   B. W. PEARSE.

SCHEDULE of all INDIAN RESERVES (surveyed) in the PROVINCE of BRITISH COLUMBIA.

Sheet.	Locality and short description of Reserve.	Range.	Section.	Acreage.	Tribe to which Natives belong.	Remarks.
	Vancouver Island Districts.					
A.	Esquimalt District (Esquimalt Harbour)		XXV.	47	Songish	Part of this Reserve has been leased to white men. See Appendix 1.
	Do. do. (Victoria Harbour)		CXIX.	112	Songish	
	Sooke District (Mouth of Sooke River, left bank)		VIII.	60	Sooke	
	North Saanich District		15 N.	69	Tsaikum.	
	Do.	I. W.	4 & 5 N.	315.02		
	South Saanich District	I. & II. W.	7, 8, & 9 S.	*494	Chawilp.	
	Do.	I. & II. W.	6, 7, & 8 S.	*727	Tsaihit.	
	Do.	IV., V., & VI. E.				
B.	Cowichan District	I.	11 to 17 inclusive		Quamichan.	Vide Appendix 2.
	Do.	II.	12 to 16 inclusive		Clemclemaluts	
	Do.	III.	14, 15, & 16, excluding 20 ac.'P. Brennan		Comiaken & Karmutzen.	
	Quamichan District	V.	15 & 16	2675	} Somenos.	
	Do.	VI.	15 & 16			
	Do.	VII.	N. E.½ portion of 10, E. portion of 11, & sec.14 N. ½ Sec. 10, 11, & 13 to 17 inclusive.		Quamichan, (part of).	
	Do.	VIII.	5	100	Kokesailah.] Halalts.	
	Chemainis District	VII.	E. part of 6	30	} Penalahuts.	
	Do.	VIII.		139		
	Nanaimo District (Reserve W. side of Harbour)			40		Indian Schools and Missions on this Reserve, of all Denominations.
	Do. (mouth of Nanaimo R., W. side)	VI.	Sec. 1, part E. of River.	131	Nanaimo.	
	Do. do. do. E. side)	VII.		273		
	Cranberry District	VII.	19 and 20, East of River			
	New Westminster District.					
C.	Burrard Inlet, Junction of 1st Narrows and Kapilano Creek			165		
D.	Do.			112.46		
	Do.			37.45		
E.	North side of Fraser River, near mouth of Coquitlam River			37		
	Next Reserve, further up Coquitlam River			1		
F.	Coquitlam River, 200 yards from Fraser River			18.40*		
G.	North Arm of Fraser River			6.50		
	West bank of Harrison River			342	Musqueam.	
H.	Left bank of Fraser River, 1½ miles from Harrison River			626	Chehalis.	
I.	Right bank of Fraser River			658	Whanock.	
	Left bank do.			92	Matsqui.	
				96		

	Location		Number	Tribe
I.	Left bank of Fraser River		52	Matsqui.
	Do. do.		108	Katzie.
	Sumass River, near Chadsey's Slough		43	} Sumass.
	Upper Sumass River		440	
	Right bank of Fraser River, near junction with Nicoamen Slough		32	Clatwass.
	Nicoamen Slough		86	Scowlitz.
	Junction of Harrison and Fraser Rivers		330	Nicoamen.
	Right bank of Nicoamen Slough		109	Squeeam.
	Left bank of do. at junction with Small Slough		73	
	Yale District.			
J.	Left bank of Fraser River, about 10 miles below Hope		488.50	Ohanuil.
	Do. do. 20 do.		375	Cheeam.
	Do. do. 18 do.		369	Popkum.
	Do. do. 13 do.		380	Squatits.
K.	Greenwood Island, opposite Hope		10	
L.	Left bank of Thompson River, at junction with Fraser, just outside of Lytton		14	
	South-east of Lytton		12	
	Left bank of Fraser River, 2 miles north of Lytton		18	
M.	Right bank do. 20 miles above Lytton		111	Nickelpalm.
	Do. do. 5 do.		297	Stryem.
	Between 35 and 36 mile-post, on Waggon Road (Boothroyd's Flat)		204.50	Shoo-ok.
	Left bank of Fraser River, between 42 and 43 mile-post, on Waggon Road		40	Sta-uja-hamig.
	Right bank do. 1¼ miles below Lytton		100	Macaiya.
	Do. do. 1½ ,, above ,,		30	Nohomeen.
	Do. do. Waggon Road		58	Skopah.
	Right bank do. Yankee Flat, 2¼ miles above Boston Bar		205	Kopachicken.
	Left bank do. Junction of Anderson River, 24 mile-post		82	
	Do. do. between 16 and 17 mile-post, Waggon Road		81	
	Do. do. about ¾ mile below Alexandra Bridge, and same distance inland		19	
	Right bank do. between 9 and 10 mile post, Waggon Road		110	Spuzzem.
	Left bank do. 2 miles below Alexandra Bridge, about 1 mile inland		51	
	Right bank of Similkameen River, Vermillion Forks		21	
N.	Left bank do.		342	
O.	Right bank of Fraser River, 4 miles below Yale (Albert Flat)		1028	
	Do. do. about half-way between Princeton and Keremeoos		163.50	Skowall.
	Do. do. 7 ,, Hope		135	
	Small ralley, about 1 mile from Spellumcheen River		200	} Spellumcheen.
	Left bank of Spellumcheen River		18.50	Nicola.
	Junction of Nicola and Thompson Rivers		30.50	Nicoamen.
	Left bank of Fraser River, between 67 and 6¾ mile-post, Waggon Road		61	
P.	Deadman's Creek		575	
	Nicola River, junction of Trail from Cook's Ferry to Savona's Ferry		918	
	Bonaparte River, between 113 and 114 mile-post, Waggon Road		471	Bonaparte.
	Nicola Lake, east bank		670	
	Do. Lagoon, east side		60	
Q.	Right bank of Thompson River, extending back to Lake		3112	} Shuswap.
	North-west side of Little Lake, on trail to Adam's Lake		abt. 1900	Adam's Lake } These Indians have also 15½ chns. sq. on W. side of lake.
	East side of Adam's Lake, mouth of Adam's River		,, 1000	Kamloops
	Junction of North and South Branch of Thompson River		6000	

APPENDIX 1.

SCHEDULE OF LEASES granted of portions of SONGISH INDIAN RESERVE, ESQUIMALT DISTRICT.

Date.	Name of Lessees.	Description of Property.	Term.	Rental.	How payable.	Remarks.
6th July, 1871	Jane Sophia Bales	Lots 6 and 7, 5.34 acres	7 years	$75 per annum	Half-yearly	
” ”	William Dalby	Lot 13, 1.52 acres	” ”	40 ”	”	
30th June, 1871	Patrick Everett	Lot 4A, 1 acre	” ”	25 ”	”	
” ”	Jeremiah Nagle	Lot 5, 3.08 acres	” ”	77 ”	”	
28th April, 1864	The Bishop of Columbia	Lot 51	21 ”	5	Yearly	Indian Mission, in connection with Church of England.

MEMORANDUM.—Dr. Ash held a Lease, formerly, of a Lot on this Reserve. He is now applying to the Government of the Dominion for another, or a renewal of the old one, which was forfeited for non-payment of the Rent.

APPENDIX 2.

SCHEDULE OF LEASES PROMISED (being parts of the INDIAN RESERVE at COWICHAN).

Date.	To whom Promised.	Description of Property.	Remarks.
7th August, 1871	Mrs. Williams (by authority of the Governor)	East part of Section 11, Range II., Cowichan District	Contents : 500x2000 links, 10 acres.
	Harry Marriner	Lease of a portion of Cowichan Reserve, of no use to Indians.	
5th July, 1871	R. White	East part of Section 13, Range II., Cowichan District	10 years, at $5 per annum.

CORRESPONDENCE BETWEEN THE PROVINCIAL GOVERNMENT AND THE SUPERINTENDENT OF INDIAN AFFAIRS.

The Superintendent of Indian Affairs to the Chief Commissioner of Lands and Works.

Victoria, October 28th, 1872.

Sir,—I have the honour to request that you will furnish me, for the information of the Dominion Government, with a statement or record of all the lands held or reserved for Indians of this Province by the Local Government; the extent, area, and location of these lands; upon what terms held; and for the benefit of what particular tribes.

I should feel obliged, if in your power, to send me a map or general plan of these lands, together with such other particulars in respect to the same, or other Indian matters, as may be in the possession of your Department.

I have, &c.,
(Signed)   I. W. POWELL.

The Chief Commissioner of Lands and Works to the Superintendent of Indian Affairs.

Lands and Works Department,
Victoria, Oct. 31st, 1872.

Sir,—I have the honour to acknowledge the receipt of your letter of the 28th inst., asking for full information—including tracings or plans—respecting the Indian Reserves of this Province. Upon enquiry, I find that plans, together with a schedule of all the reserves, and a full statement of the policy pursued with regard to the Indians, were forwarded to the Honorable the Secretary of State for the Provinces some time last fall.

I shall, however, have much pleasure in showing you the different plans of the reserves in my office; and any gentleman whom you may appoint for the purpose can make tracings of them here.

I have, &c.,
(Signed)   GEO. A. WALKEM.

The Superintendent of Indian Affairs to the Provincial Secretary.

Victoria, October 28th 1872.

Sir,—I had the honour to-day of addressing a letter to the Hon. Chief Commissioner of Lands and Works, with a view of obtaining as soon as possible, for the information of the Dominion Government, all particulars in respect to lands, &c., reserved for the use and benefit of Indians in the Province by the Local Government.

May I beg of you, for the same reason, that I may be furnished with a statement of any and all matters appertaining to the past and present treatment of Indians by the Provincial Government in possession of your Department. Can I be supplied with any statistics as to the number and character of tribes and Indians? Have treaties been made with any of the tribes, and if so, can I be furnished with copies of the same? Has any encouragement been given to the establishment of Indian Schools? What has been the general policy of the Government in the treatment of Indians? Have any grants of money, periodical or otherwise, been made by the Government? Have presents been made to tribes or chiefs? Has any system of medical treatment been carried out with Indians?

As it is the intention of the Dominion Government to establish, with as little delay as possible, a branch in this Province of the Indian Department at Ottawa, you will, I trust, perceive the great importance of supplying me with the fullest particulars at your command, as soon as convenience will permit.

      I have, &c.,
        (Signed) I. W. POWELL.

The Provincial Secretary to the Superintendent of Indian Affairs.

          Provincial Secretary's Office,
            November 4th, 1872.

SIR,—I am directed by the Lieutenant-Governor to acquaint you, in reply to your communication of the 28th ultimo, requesting to be furnished with certain information respecting the Indians of this Province, that maps of the Indian Reserves are now in the hands of the Department at Ottawa, and that a Despatch from His Excellency, dated January, 1872, is in the hands of the Secretary of State for the Provinces, conveying full information on most of the topics alluded to in your letter.

    I have, &c.,
      (Signed) A. R. ROBERTSON.

The Superintendent of Indian Affairs to the Provincial Secretary.

         Victoria, November 5th, 1872.

SIR,—I have the honour to acknowledge your letter of the 4th inst., in answer to my communication of the 28th ultimo, in respect to certain matters connected with the Indians of this Province, in which you state that a Despatch from His Excellency, dated January, 1872, is in the hands of the Secretary of State for the Provinces conveying full information of the topics alluded to in my letter.

As I am instructed to report upon the information referred to, with such additional statistics as may be in my power to obtain previous to the coming session of the Dominion Parliament; and as the limited time at my command will not allow of my obtaining His Excellency's Despatch from the Secretary of State for the Provinces, may I beg of you to be kind enough to furnish me with a copy of the same at your earliest convenience.

       I have, &c.,
        (Signed) I. W. POWELL.

The Provincial Secretary to the Superintendent of Indian Affairs.

          Provincial Secretary's Office,
            6th November, 1872.

SIR,—In reply to your letter of yesterday's date, requesting that you may be furnished with a copy of the Lieutenant-Governor's Despatch to the Secretary of State for the Provinces, in relation to Indian affairs of British Columbia, I have the honour to acquaint you that I have no access to His Excellency's Despatch, and would therefore suggest that you should make application to the Governor direct for the information you require.

    I have, &c.,
      (Signed) A. R. ROBERTSON.

The Superintendent of Indian Affairs to the Lieutenant-Governor.

Victoria, November 7th, 1872.

Sir,—Having been instructed by the Indian Department of the Dominion Government, to report "with as little delay as possible" upon the Indian tribes of British Columbia, and especially to acquire from the Local Government information as to the nature of any grants (if any) hitherto made to Indians, the number and extent of reservations, and for the benefit of what particular tribes, together with such other matters as may appertain to the past treatment of Indians by the Colonial Government,"

I addressed the Honorable the Chief Commissioner of Lands and Works and the Honorable the Provincial Secretary on the 28th ult., with a view to obtaining the same.

I am duly acquainted in their respective replies "that a full statement of the policy of the Government towards Indians with such other information" as I had the honour to request, was forwarded by your Excellency in a Despatch, dated January, 1872, to the Honorable the Secretary of State for the Provinces.

As my instructions were to obtain the information above referred to, for the purpose of reporting upon it without delay, I again addressed the Hon. Provincial Secretary requesting to be furnished with a copy of your Excellency's Despatch, and he suggested in his further reply " having no access to it," that application should be made direct to your Excellency.

I should feel greatly obliged, therefore, if consistent with official duty, your Excellency could provide me with the required information as contained in the despatch alluded to.

No doubt there may be much of additional import among the Government archives, respecting past Indian difficulties, consequent treaties and other matters connected with the administration of Indian affairs by former Colonial Governments.

I need not add how desirable such archives would be, in compiling reliable statistics of Indian matters in this Province, nor how much I should be obligated by any additional information which your Excellency's long official connection in British Columbia may enable you to give.

(Signed)   I. W. Powell.

The Private Secretary to the Superintendent of Indian Affairs.

Government House, B. C.,
8th November, 1872.

Sir,—The Lieutenant-Governor directs me to acknowledge the receipt of your letter to him of yesterday's date, and to state to you in reference thereto, that he is assured by the Provincial Secretary and Chief Commissioner of Lands and Works that they will most readily afford you access to the documents recorded in their respective departments, from which you may obtain all the statistical information on the subject of the past treatment of the Indians of British Columbia by the late Colonial Government, which it is in the power of the Provincial Government to furnish, including particularly details of the several tracts of land held under reservation for the use and benefit of various tribes throughout the Province, but that as the charge of the Indians is not among the functions of the local Government no policy respecting their treatment has been adopted by that Government since the union of the Province with the Dominion of Canada, all matters connected with Indian affairs having been directed by the Lieutenant-Governor, so far as any action has been taken, as the Agent of the Indian Department of the Dominion Government. His Honor's despatch to which the Provincial Secretary refers in the letter which you mention having received from him does not, therefore, contain any statement of the policy practised by the present Government of the Province towards Indians, nor does it embody any such statistical details on the subject of Indian affairs on the past as you may readily obtain from the offices of the local departments above referred to, but is mainly taken up with a presentment of His Honor's individual opinions on the character of our Indian population on the system of past Governments towards them, with comments on certain suggestions for the alteration of the system which has been submitted for the consideration of this Government, and these views His Honor will be happy to convey to you should you deem them worthy of your attention, if you will do him the pleasure of calling upon him at any time to-morrow or Monday morning that may be convenient.

I have, &c.,
(Signed)   ARTHUR PINDER.

The Chief Commissioner of Lands and Works to the Superintendent of Indian Affairs.

Lands and Works Department,
Victoria, November 22nd, 1872.

SIR,—I have the honour to forward to you, for the use of the Indian Department, all the plans, books, and papers connected with the Indian Reservations of Vancouver Island now in this Office.

You will be good enough to sign the enclosed receipt for the same.

I have, &c.,
(Signed)   GEO. A. WALKEM.

The Chief Commissioner of Lands and Works to the Superintendent of Indian Affairs.

Lands and Works Office,
Victoria, December 5th, 1872.

SIR,—Shortly after your appointment as Superintendent of Indian Affairs in November last, I had the honour of drawing your attention to the position of the Chilcotin Reserve, and the desirableness of some steps being at once taken to map out the Indian Reservations, and throw the country open to intending settlers.

On the 20th August, last, Mr. O'Reilly reported to His Excellency the Lieutenant-Governor the result of his conference with the three principal Chilcotin Chiefs. They were then assured of protection, and that their tribes would not be disturbed in the possession of their homes, and their hunting and fishing grounds; and that the Dominion Government would provide them with the means of education, and assist them in their agricultural pursuits. The nature, also, of the Railway Survey, then initiated, was explained to them, and they were told that they need not apprehend any loss as the result of such survey.

The Indians and one John Salmon had had a quarrel, which Mr. O'Reilly investigated—Salmon having recently pre-empted land in their midst. Mr. O'Reilly then strongly advised this Government to reserve the District from further pre-emption, lest collisions of a more serious character should occur between the Indians and intending settlers, and in order that the Dominion Government might have a fair opportunity of specifying, by application, the tracts of land they required for Indians.

On the 26th August, a Despatch was forwarded to the Dominion Government urging immediate action, and the appointment of a Superintendent with instructions to define the reservations necessary. It was also stated that all the lands had been reserved for this purpose. No reply to this Despatch has been received, though nearly four months must have elapsed since its probable receipt at Ottawa.

I understood from you in our last conversation upon this subject, that you had written to the head of your Department for instructions; but I would take the liberty of suggesting that you might, with advantage, authorize some person to proceed to the Chilcotin country at once, and lay off, in a rough form, such reserves as may be required until a survey can be made and these lines be more clearly defined.

I have, at considerable trouble, gathered such information respecting the country lying between Bute Inlet and Alexandria, as Mr. G. B. Wright, Mr. Smith, Mr. O'Reilly, and other gentlemen could give me. They differ, however, materially as to the wants of the Indians; and Mr. O'Reilly suggests that without a more specific knowledge of the subject, it would be unadvisable to lay out reserves which might be inappropriate and useless.

As you must be aware, it is highly undesirable that intending settlers should be longer excluded from the District. I am therefore anxious for information as to the extent and locality of the lands which your Department may require.

Permit me, therefore, to press upon your attention the suggestion which I have made.

I have, &c.,
(Signed) GEO. A. WALKEM.

The Superintendent of Indian Affairs to the Chief Commissioner of Lands and Works.

Office of the Superintendent of Indian Affairs,
Victoria, December 6th 1872.

SIR,—I have the honour to acknowledge the receipt of your letter of the 5th instant, in respect to the desirability of laying off, without delay, a reservation of land for the use of the Chilcotin Tribe of Indians, and suggesting "that I might, with advantage, authorize some person to proceed at once to the Chilcotin Country for that purpose," &c., &c.

In reply to the above, I beg to state that as yet I have received no instructions in respect to the active duties of my office, and am therefore not in a position to act definitely in regard to the subjects alluded to in your letter.

Appreciating, however, the great importance, not only to the future condition of these Indians, but to the safety of the white settlers in that country, I should not hesitate to take the responsibility of adopting your suggestions if it were possible to do so at this season of the year with satisfaction. I am informed by parties acquainted with the District, that at the present time the ground is covered with snow, and that it would be impossible to take up land for reservation, or indeed any other purpose, unless it had been previously sketched. I shall, however, take the liberty of forwarding a copy of your letter to Ottawa for definite instruction in respect to it, and shall be prepared to carry out your wishes, which I most fully reciprocate, at the earliest practicable moment.

I have, &c.,
(Signed) I. W. POWELL.

The Chief Commissioner of Lands and Works to the Superintendent of Indian Affairs.

Lands and Works Department,
Victoria, 15th January, 1873.

SIR,—I have the honour to inform you that the Government propose taking off the reservation in the Chilcotin Valley, and desire that you will acquaint them officially with your views as to the reservations you may consider should be made in that section for Indian purposes, and at your earliest convenience.

I have, etc.,
(Signed) ROBERT BEAVEN.

The Superintendent of Indian Affairs to the Chief Commissioner of Lands and Works.

Victoria, January 15th, 1873.

SIR,—I have the honour to acknowledge the receipt of your letter of this date, acquainting me with the desire of the Government "to take off the present reservation in the Chilcotin Valley, and requesting my views as to the reservation I may consider should be made in that section, for Indian purposes."

In reply I beg to state that I consider *the removal of the whole of the present reservation* would prove a fruitful source of Indian difficulty, were no special Reserve provided for the Native Tribes, and of danger to the white settler who might be sufficiently courageous to take up land in their country previous to such Reserve being made.

From the best information at my command, however, I think the present Reserve might be taken off that portion of the District extending from the mouth of the Chilcotin on the Fraser River, to a point within (say) five miles of Alexis Creek on the said Chilcotin River, excluding from the right of pre-emption any Indian settlement which may exist between these points, (I am not aware of any). Should the Government adopt this suggestion a large portion of the most fertile part of the District in question, would be thrown open (I think without danger) to white settlement. From the part still reserved, I will endeavour as soon as practicable, to select the quantity of land necessary for a Chilcotin Indian Reservation and for which I have now the honor of making application.

I have, etc.,
(Signed)   I. W. POWELL.

The Superintendent of Indian Affairs to the Provincial Secretary.

Victoria, February 4th, 1873.

SIR,—On the 7th of January, I had the honour of addressing a letter to his Excellency the Lieut.-Governor, in respect to the moneys which have accrued from the Songish Indian Reserve, and was informed in reply, "that the Honorable the Provincial Secretary would furnish me with the information desired."

I perceive, by reference to the reserve books, that on the 3rd of September, 1869, the sum of $1,984 82 was paid by the Commissioners of Reserve to the Hon. J. W. Trutch, C. C. L. & W., which amount I presume was then paid into the Colonial Treasury.

As I have no account of the further disposition of this sum nor of the moneys collected since 1869, may I beg that you will have the goodness to acquaint me with the same, for the information of the Indian Department in the matter referred to.

I have, &c.,
(Signed)   I. W. POWELL,

The Provincial Secretary to the Superintendent of Indian Affairs.

Provincial Secretary's Office,
5th February, 1873.

SIR,—I have the honour to acknowledge your letter of the 4th inst., referring to the moneys which have accrued from the Songish Indian Reserve.

In reply, I have to inform you that no money has been paid into the Provincial Treasury since Confederation, on account of the said reserve, and that you have been rightly informed as to the disposition of the balance of $1,984.82 paid on the 3rd September, 1869, by the Commissioners of Reserve to the Chief Commissioner of Lands and Works. This sum was paid into the Colonial Treasury, formed part of the assets of the Colony at the date of Confederation, and was taken over by the Dominion Government.

I have, &c.,
(Signed)   JOHN ASH.

The Superintendent of Indian Affairs to the Provincial Secretary.

Indian Department,
Victoria, February 7th, 1873.

Sir,—I have the honour to acknowledge the receipt of your letter of the 5th inst., informing me that the Indian Reserve Fund of $1,984 82 paid into the Colonial Treasury in Sept. 1869, "formed part of the Provincial assets at the date of Confederation, and was taken over by the Dominion Government."

In justice to the Indians the amount could not, in my opinion, be considered as Provincial revenue nor assets, but belonged to the Songish tribe of Indians, and formed a special deposit in the Treasury—merely for safe keeping.

I should be glad if you will kindly acquaint me, if this sum has special mention in the schedule of assets, or by whom it was taken over for the Dominion Government, as I shall be thereby enabled to have the amount placed to the credit of the Indian Department of this Province.

I may further add that the remainder of this fund collected by Mr. Pearse and myself has been so deposited.

I have, &c.,
(Signed)   I. W. Powell.

The Provincial Secretary to the Superintendent of Indian Affairs.

Provincial Secretary's Office,
26th February, 1873.

Sir,—I have the honour to acknowledge the receipt of your letter of the 7th inst., respecting the Indian Reserve Fund.

In reply, I have to inform you that I can find no evidence of any special mention having been made in reference to the specific sum of $1,984, which was the balance of Songish Indian Reserve Fund, 1869, nor of any action in regard thereto having been taken to distinguish it from the ordinary Revenue, when it was paid into the Colonial account with the Bank of British Columbia.

I have, &c.,
(Signed)   John Ash.

The Chief Commissioner of Lands and Works to the Superintendent of Indian Affairs.

Lands and Works Department,
Victoria, 16th April, 1873.

Sir,—I have the honour to inform you that constant complaints are being made to me by parties desirous of pre-empting land at Alberni, that the Indians in that locality claim the lands as their property, and threaten to molest parties occupying said land. Now it is almost impossible to prevent some parties going in there, and I have therefore to call your attention to the imperative necessity of at once having all Indian land claims settled, not only at Alberni, but in other parts of the Province. There are at present numerous parties desirous of settling in British Columbia, but the fact of Indians being located in almost every District where white settlers would wish to locate is preventing many from doing so, and is consequently retarding the settlement of the Province. I must therefore, most respectfully but urgently, request your earliest attention to this subject, as delay at this juncture may be a very serious matter to this Province.

I have, etc.,
(Signed)   Robert Beaven.

The Superintendent of Indian Affairs to the Chief Commissioner of Lands and Works.

Department of Indian Affairs,
Victoria, April 17th, 1873.

SIR,—I have the honour to acknowledge your letter of the 16th inst., in respect to apprehended trouble at Alberni with Indians, and the wish of the Government to have *all* Indian land Reserves made with the least possible delay, etc., etc.

In reply I have the honour to enclose excerpts from a Copy of an Order in Council just received by me, and I shall be glad to confer with you in regard to the subject of your letter whenever convenient to yourself.

I have, etc.,
(Signed)   I. W. POWELL.

ENCLOSURE.

Excerpts from Copy of a Report of the Honorable the Privy Council approved by His Excellency the Governor-General in Council on the 21st of March, 1873.

The Committee have had before them a Memorandum from the Deputy Superintendent General of Indian Affairs, submitting a letter from I. W. Powell, Esq., local Superintendent in British Columbia, relative to apprehended difficulties with Indians at Alberni, etc., etc., etc.

The Deputy Superintendent General accordingly suggests that each family be assigned a location of 80 acres of land of average quality, which shall remain permanently the property of the family for whose benefit it is allotted.

That it is a matter of urgent importance to convince the Indians of that Province that the Dominion Government will do full justice to the rights of the Indian population, and thus remove any spirit of discontent which in various quarters appears to prevail.

That authority be at once given to Mr. Powell to confer with the Local Government in regard to Indian Reserves already set apart, which may require to be extended and the outlines marked out in survey, also for setting apart such additional reserves, as in his judgment he may deem to be important, for the purpose of fulfilling the just expectations of those Indians, etc., etc., etc.

Certified,
(Signed)   W. A. HIMSWORTH.

The Chief Commissioner of Lands and Works to the Superintendent of Indian Affairs.

Lands and Works Office,
Victoria, April 18th, 1873.

SIR,—I have the honour to request that you will furnish me with a return showing the name and number of individuals and families in every Indian Tribe, and the total Indian population and number of families in each District in the Province; specifying also the name and locality of all Indian Reservations, and the acreage of such reservation claimed by you on behalf of the various tribes; distinguishing (in the manner requested above) Indians whose present abode is on land other than known Indian Reservations, and the acreage desired for them.

I have, &c.,
(Signed)   ROBERT BEAVEN.

The Superintendent of Indian Affairs to the Chief Commissioner of Lands and Works.

Department of Indian Affairs,
Victoria, April 19th, 1873.

Sir,—I have the honour to acknowledge the receipt of your letter of the 18th instant, requesting "that I will furnish you with a return showing the name and number of individuals and families in every Indian Tribe, and the total Indian population and number of families in each District in this Province; specifying the name and locality of all Indian Reservations claimed by me on behalf of the various tribes," &c. &c., &c.

In reply, I beg to state that a return showing the names of the individual population of Indians in this Province is quite unattainable, except under the most extraordinary circumstances—certainly not now at my command.

"A return showing the number of families in every tribe," and the name of each head of every family who would have the right to a certain portion of reservation land, can only be known after the Indian Department has been fully established in this Province by Statute, and by means of local agencies, &c., becomes possessed of the means of securing a correct and reliable census in this respect. With the crude information in my possession at present, I estimate the total Indian population of the Province to be 28,500—possibly an accurate enumeration may hereafter prove even this number to be too large an estimate.

In regard to a "return showing the names and locality of all Indian Reservations, and the acreage of each claimed by me," I beg to refer you to a schedule (furnished me by your predecessor) and maps at present in the Land Office, a copy of which I have in my possession.

I have, &c.,
(Signed)   I. W. POWELL.

The Chief Commissioner of Lands and Works to the Superintendent of Indian Affairs.

Lands and Works Office,
Victoria, 19th April, 1873.

Sir,—Complaint has been made to me by Mr. Edward Marriner, of Cowichan, that some of the Clemclemalut Indians are fencing in about 5 acres of his land which is included in his Crown Grant. He asserts that the Indians are well aware that it is his (Marriner's land), but that they state that they require it for the use of their cattle.

I have, &c.,
(Signed)   ROBERT BEAVEN.

The Chief Commissioner of Lands and Works to the Superintendent of Indian Affairs.

Lands and Works Office,
Victoria, 30th April, 1873.

Sir,—I have the honour to acknowledge the receipt of your letter of the 17th instant, with enclosures. In regard to the suggestion shall " each family be assigned a location of 80 acres of land," it will be found in the first place necessary to define the number as applied to the term "family," and would suggest that we adopt the rule in use in the North-West Territory, viz:—" six" as applied to that term; but in doing so, consider that 80 acres is far too large an average for each family of six.

The reservations so far in this Province have averaged about six acres to each family—taking the population at your figures and the acreage of present reserves.

I have, &c.,
(Signed)   ROBERT BEAVEN.

The Superintendent of Indian Affairs to the Chief Commissioner of Lands and Works.
Department of Indian Affairs,
Victoria, May 12th, 1873.

SIR,—As the possession of field notes of the various lands reserved for Indians would greatly facilitate defining the boundaries and regulating the same, may I beg that you will kindly furnish me with copies of those in the Lands and Works Office.
I have, &c.,
(Signed) I. W. POWELL.

The Chief Commissioner of Lands and Works to the Superintendent of Indian Affairs.
Lands and Works Department,
Victoria, May 14th, 1873.

SIR,—I have the honour to acknowledge the receipt of your letter of the 12th instant, and find upon investigation that much delay will take place if you are obliged to wait for the field notes referred to, until they can be made by our present staff in the Land Office—their time being fully occupied with other work; and as no doubt you are anxious that as little delay as possible should take place, in order to assist you I shall be happy to place a desk in the office at the disposal of any gentleman you may authorize to take copies of the said field notes.
I return copy of Indian Reserves.
I have, &c.,
(Signed) ROBERT BEAVEN.

The Superintendent of Indian Affairs to the Lieutenant-Governor.
DEPARTMENT OF INDIAN AFFAIRS,
June 21st, 1873.

SIR,—I have to address Your Honour in respect to the urgent necessity of adjusting existing Indian Reserves—extending them where required, and of setting apart Indian lands for tribes not now provided for—and should the arrangements proposed by the Dominion Government be satisfactory to the Government of the Province, that I am now ready to proceed with the necessary surveys.

I am informed at different places, just visited by me, that in some instances great injustice has been done the Indians in not reserving sufficient land for their use, and in some cases, such as Comox, Chemainus, &c., land actually occupied by Indians, as potatoe patches, &c., has been pre-empted by white settlers and certificates granted.

From these causes abundant discontent prevails among Indians, both on the Island and Mainland, and I regard it as a matter of urgent and paramount importance, not only to the future peaceful settlement of the Province by whites, but as a matter of justice to the Indians themselves, that their complaints should be adjusted and reserves also made for them in those parts of the Province where they do not at present exist.

I have also the honour to enclose a copy of an Order in Council relating to these Indian Lands, empowering me to confer with the Local Government, and I shall be glad if Your Honour will take such steps in regard to the same as may be deemed expedient.

I beg further to enclose a letter received by me from Mr. Ld. Loewenberg, who has been acting as agent and collector for the Songish Reserve, and shall feel obliged if Your Honour will cause the same to be transmitted to the Honourable the Provincial Secretary, with a view to my obtaining the papers in queston, or any others in possession of the Government relating to the Indian affairs of the Province.
I am, &c.,
(Signed) I. W. POWELL.

Enclosure No. 1.

Excerpt from a Copy of the Report of a Committee of the Honorable the Privy Council, approved by His Excellency the Governor-General in Council, on the 21st March, 1873.

The Committee have had before them a memorandum from the Deputy Superintendent-General of Indian Affairs, submitting a letter from I. W. Powell, Esquire, Commissioner at Victoria, British Columbia, relative to difficulties apprehended with Indians at Alberni.

The Deputy Superintendent states that the apprehended trouble appears to arise (as shown by correspondence, copies of which the Superintendent has furnished) in consequence of the sale of lands in that locality having been made by the Local Government to Messieurs Anderson & Company, and a contention on the part of two settlers who had attempted to pre-empt land at that place.

That it would seem no reservation for the Indians had been made there, nor other satisfactory arrangements entered into with them, &c., &c., &c.

That this and other communications transmitted by Mr. Superintendent Powell prove the absolute necessity of his being empowered to confer with the Local Government, with a view to sufficient reserves on a liberal and just scale being set apart and marked off in survey for the various bands of the Province.

The Deputy Superintendent-General submits, therefore, that authority be at once given to Mr. Powell, to confer with the Local Government in regard to Indian Reserves already set apart which may require to be extended and the outlines marked out in survey. Also for the setting apart such additional reserves as in his judgment he may deem to be important, for the purpose of fulfilling the just expectations of those Indians; and he accordingly suggests that each family be assigned a location of eighty acres of land of average quality, which shall remain permanently the property of the family for whose benefit it is allotted.

On the recommendation of the Honourable the Secretary of State for the Provinces, the Committee advise that the suggestions submitted in the foregoing memorandum of the Deputy Superintendent be approved and acted upon.

Certified,
(Signed)   W. A. HIMSWORTH.
Clerk, Privy Council

Enclosure No. 2.

Mr. Ld. Loewenberg to the Superintendent of Indian Affairs.

Victoria, B. C.,
June 20th, 1873.

Sir,—Amongst the papers which you hold in the affairs of the Indian Reserve are certain documents and correspondence missing, which are necessary for you to have in order to find out on whom notices were served for the surrender and renewal of leases to the said reserve. These notices were served at the time when His Excellency the Governor was yet Commissioner of Lands and Works, and I have no copies thereof and am without data. I have reason to believe that those papers are in the Office of Lands and Works. It is necessary for me, in order to make arrangements with the applicant for a lease to a part of the Indian Reserve, to have these papers, and especially the list of the parties to whom notices had been served.

I have, &c.,
(Signed)   LD. LOEWENBERG.

The Provincial Secretary to the Superintendent of Indian Affairs.
Provincial Secretary's Office,
15th July, 1873.

SIR,—I have the honour to forward herewith for your information, copy of a complaint made by "Gustinama," a Kootenay Chief, before Mr. Booth, from which you will perceive that he claims the whole of that District. It would, therefore, appear desirable that the rights of the Indians in that quarter should be defined.

As disputes have already arisen between the whites and Indians at Kootenay, the case is an urgent one, and I am directed to express a hope that you will be enabled to visit the locality at an early date.

I have, &c.,
(Signed) JOHN ASH.

The Superintendent of Indian Affairs to the Provincial Secretary.
Department of Indian Affairs,
Victoria, July 16th, 1873.

SIR,—I have the honour to acknowledge the receipt of your letter of the 15th inst., enclosing a copy of complaint made by a Kootenay Chief, and expressing the desirableness of having the rights of Indians defined and the consequent urgency of a visit to the locality, etc.

In reply, I have to state that application has been made by me, some little time since, for the allotment of lands by the Provincial Government for Indian purposes customary in other parts of the Dominion. I am of opinion, therefore, that until a satisfactory arrangement has been arrived at by the Local Executive, little can be done in the way of defining rights to which you allude, nor can I think that in the meantime any further official visitations to Indian tribes with a view to the settlement of land disputes would be advisable.

I have, &c.,
(Signed) I. W. POWELL.

The Superintendent of Indian Affairs to the Provincial Secretary.
Department of Indian Affairs,
Victoria, July 22nd, 1873.

SIR,—I have the honour to enclose a letter from the Rev. Father McGucking, relative to an Indian murder said to have been committed at Bella Coola.

Should the Government deem it a matter for police enquiry, I shall be glad to give any assistance in my power, though I may add that during my recent official visit to the Bella Coola Indians, I heard nothing whatever of the occurrence alluded to.

I have, &c.,
(Signed) I. W. POWELL.

Copy of a Report of a Committee of the Honourable the Executive Council, approved by His Excellency the Lieutenant-Governor, on the 25th day of July, 1873.

The Committee have had under consideration the letter of I. W. Powell, Esquire, Superintendent of Indian affairs in this Province, dated 21st June, 1873, and covering an excerpt from an Order in Council of the Dominion Government, which matters have been referred to them by Your Excellency.

The letter of the Superintendent of Indian Affairs urges the adjustment of existing Indian Reserves, their extension where requisite, and the setting apart of

Indian lands for tribes not now provided for. The Order in Council of the Dominion Government authorizes the Superintendent to make the application, and specifies that it is advisable that to each Indian family should be assigned a location of eighty acres of land of average quality.

The Committee remark that this quantity is greatly in excess of the grants considered sufficient by previous Governments of British Columbia, and recommend that throughout the Province Indian Reserves should not exceed a quantity of twenty acres of land for each head of a family of five persons.

Certified,
(Signed)   W. J. ARMSTRONG,
Clerk. Executive Council.

The Provincial Secretary to the Superintendent of Indian Affairs.

Provincial Secretary's Office,
28th July, 1873.

Sir,—I am directed to acknowledge the receipt of your letter of the 21st June, addressed to the Lieutenant-Governor on the subject of Indian Reserves, and with reference to that part which more particularly refers to the acreage allowed to each family, I am to acquaint you that the Provincial Government is unable to concur in the views expressed in the Order in Council, of which you enclose a copy, to the effect that 80 acres should be assigned to each family. This quantity is greatly in excess of what has been found to be sufficient by previous Governments, and the Government has decided that throughout the Province the land to be reserved for Indians should not exceed 20 acres of land for each head of a family of five persons.

I have the honour, therefore, to notify you that all future reserves for Indians will be adjusted on the basis of twenty acres of land for each head of a family of five persons.

I have &c.,
(Signed)   JOHN ASH.

The Superintendent of Indian Affairs to the Provincial Secretary.

Department of Indian Affairs,
Victoria, July 29th, 1873.

Sir,—I have the honour to acknowledge the receipt of your letter of the 28th inst., acquainting me with the desire of the Provincial Government that all future Reserves for Indians should be " adjusted on the basis of twenty acres of land to each head of a family of five persons."

I am not aware that any restriction of the kind is customary in the other provinces of the Dominion, and, before communicating the same to the Department at Ottawa, may I beg of you to inform me as to whether it is intended to restrict the proposed grant of twenty acres of land to a family " of five persons " and, if so, the particular quantity of land which may be reserved for a family of two, three, four, six or more persons.

I have &c.,
(Signed)   I. W. POWELL.

The Provincial Secretary to the Superintendent of Indian Affairs.

Provincial Secretary's Office,
1st August, 1873.

SIR,—In reply to your letter of the 29th ultimo, requesting that you might be informed as to whether it is intended to restrict the proposed grant of twenty acres to a family of five persons (the decision of the Provincial Government as to the extent of Indian Reserves, as communicated to you in a letter from this Department of the 28th ultimo), and, if so, the particular quantity of land which may be reserved for a family of two, three, four, six or more persons, I am directed to acquaint you that the intention of the Government in regard to Indian Reserves is as follows : That to each five persons there shall be allotted twenty acres of land.

       I have, &c.,
          (Signed) JOHN ASH.

  The Superintendent of Indian Affairs to the Provincial Secretary.
         Department of Indian Affairs,
           Victoria, August 23rd, 1873.

  SIR,—Referring to your letter of the 28th July, I have the honour to state that I am authorized to accept the proposition of the Government to make the quantity of land to be hereafter reserved for each Indian family in the Province *twenty acres*. As the restriction of twenty acres to each family of *five* persons, besides being quite unusual in other Provinces of the Dominion, would tend much to complicate matters in connection with Indian lands, I am to express the hope that the Government will not insist upon the acreage referred to being confined to any specified number of persons in a family, and should be glad to have your early reply in regard to the same.

       I remain, &c.,
         (Signed) I. W. POWELL.

  The Provincial Secretary to the Superintendent of Indian Affairs.
         Provincial Secretary's Office,
           27th August, 1873.

  SIR,—With reference to your letter of the 23rd instant, on the subject of the amount to be allotted as Indian Reserves, I have the honour to acquaint you that the matter will receive attention and a reply be conveyed to you immediately on the return of the Lieutenant-Governor.

       I have, &c.,
         (Signed) JOHN ASH.

  The Superintendent of Indian Affairs to the Lieutenant-Governor.
         Department of Indian Affairs,
          Victoria, 27th October, 1873.

  SIR,—I have the honour to enclose a copy of a letter received from the Honourable the Minister of the Interior, respecting the Songish Indian Reserve.

  May I beg that your Honour will have the goodness to take such steps in the matter as may enable me to carry out the request contained therein.
         (Signed) I. W. POWELL.

       ENCLOSURE.
  The Deputy Minister of the Interior to the Superintendent of Indian Affairs
        Ottawa, 29th September, 1873.

  SIR,—Referring to your letter of the 27th ultimo, calling attention to your former letter of the 28th February last, on the subject of certain moneys belonging to the Songish Indian Reserve, I have the honour to enclose a copy of a communication received to-day from the Department of the Minister of Finance, showing that, in accordance with your request, the amounts remitted in your letters above referred to have been placed to the credit of the British Columbia Indian Funds.

The Superintendent-General directs me to add that he entirely coincides with you in thinking that it would be desirable, in the interest of the Indians and of the public generally, that the Songish Reserve in the neighbourhood of Victoria should be leased, or otherwise disposed of, for the benefit of the Songish, and another Reserve secured for them more suitable for agricultural purposes. The Superintendent-General does not think that the new Reserve should be, as you seem in your printed report to suggest, in the neighbourhood of Victoria, but would prefer it some distance from the city, with a view to avoid the very serious evils to which the proximity to the city of the present Reserve has given rise.

The Superintendent-General would be glad that you should consult the wishes of the Lieutenant-Governor and the Local Government on this whole question, and he will be prepared to consider carefully any scheme which you may submit after such consultation.

You will, of course, report as to the superficial extent, the position and character of the soil of the Reserve to which you would propose to transfer the Soughees.

I have, &c.,
(Signed)   E. A. MEREDITH.

The Attorney-General to the Superintendent of Indian Affairs.

Executive Council Chambers,
November 5th, 1873.

SIR,—His Honour the Lieutenant-Governor has referred your letter of the 27th ult., with its enclosure, to the Executive Council for consideration.

Will you favour me with information upon the following points as soon as convenient :—

What is the strength of the Songish tribe ? distinguishing the sexes, and adults and children.

What is the area of their reserve ?

Where do you propose to locate the tribe if the reserve at Victoria be sold or leased ?

Would it be advisable, if their reserve be sold, to purchase land partially cultivated or wild land ?

Where would the Indians visiting Victoria with furs, etc., from the north encamp should the present reserve be sold ?

Do you propose to provide for such visiting tribes ?

I have, &c.,
(Signed)   GEO. A. WALKEM.

The Superintendent of Indian Affairs to the Attorney-General.

Department of Indian Affairs,
Victoria, November 6th, 1873.

SIR,—I have the honour to acknowledge the receipt of your letter of the 5th instant, respecting the Songish Indians, and requesting, on behalf of the Honourable the Executive Council, information upon the following points :—

1st.—What is the strength of the Songish Tribe ? distinguishing sexes, adults, and children.

2nd.—What is the area of the reserve ?

3rd.—Where do you propose to locate the tribe, if the reserve at Victoria should be sold or leased ?

4th.—Would it be advisable, if their reserve be sold, to purchase land partially cultivated, or wild land?

5th.—Where would the Indians visiting Victoria with furs, &c., from the North, encamp should this reserve be sold? Do you propose to provide for such visiting tribes?

In reply to the above, I have the honour to state—

1st.—The strength of the Songish Tribe is about 120—45 men, 45 women, and 30 children.

2nd.—The reserve contains about 112 acres (much of which of course is unfit for cultivation).

3rd.—I think the purchase of partially cultivated land preferable, or what is still better, one of the outlying Islands, where buildings might be erected for them. The sale or lease of their present reserve would justify, in my opinion, the expenditure of any sum deemed necessary for their permanent improvement and comfort.

4th.— *Very few* of the Northern Indians *comparatively* now bring down furs, &c., to Victoria—especially those from Queen Charlotte's Island—of whom we have the greatest number making regular sojourns here. *Invariably* (as I learned by personal inspection of their camp during the past summer) they bring down their young women only, many of them girls from 10 to 14 years of age, for the purposes of prostitution—the men remaining here for some three or four months simply as procurers or pimps. I do not hesitate to add, that two-thirds, if not more, of the Indian retail traders in Victoria depend for support upon the open prostitution carried on within the confines of the City. *All* the Indian liquor manufactured and sold in Victoria is purchased with means derived from the same source. Next to the *City itself*, where there is no Municipal regulation preventing or controlling the vice alluded to, the present Songish Reserve is the greatest depot for its encouragement and continuance.

5th.—In case of the sale or lease of the present reserve, I should recommend that a small portion somewhere near the entrance to the Harbour should be, for the present, retained. This would be kept in the care and under the control of the Indian Department; and besides being available for the *legitimate* camping visits of *all* tribes, would be serviceable for an Indian Hospital or House of Refuge so desirable here. I have, &c.,

(Signed) I. W. POWELL.

The Chief Commissioner of Lands and Works to the Superintendent of Indian Affairs.

Lands and Works Office,
Victoria, 14th Dec., 1873.

SIR,—I have the honour to point out to you that certain Indians in Cowichan District have threatened to shoot a respectable settler, Mr. A. Dods, in consequence of his residing upon Section 2, Range 2, Cowichan District, and to suggest to you whether it would not be advisable to prevent a recurrence.

I have, etc.,

(Signed) ROBERT BEAVEN.

The Superintendent of Indian Affairs to the Chief Commissioner of Lands and Works.

Department of Indian Affairs,
Victoria, 15th December, 1873.

SIR,—I have the honour to acknowledge the receipt of your letter of the 12th inst., acquainting me of threats made upon the life of a settler at Cowichan by Indians in that District.

In reply, I beg to state that it is my intention to proceed to Cowichan at an early date, when I hope to settle the difficulty you refer to amicably to all parties.

(Signed) I. W. POWELL.

Attorney-General Walkem to the Superintendent of Indian Affairs.
Attorney-General's Office.
26th December, 1873.

SIR,—As I am aware that your attention has been drawn to the Cache Creek telegram, reported in the *Dominion Herald*, stating that the Indians had assumed a hostile attitude to the whites, I need not of course further refer to its substance.

I feel it my duty, however, to state that the matter is of a character too serious to be overlooked. From enquiries I have made, I find that one Mr. Ranald McDonald, who lives near Cache Creek, has informed Mr. Barnston by letter that the real cause of the discontent is the fact that you have not paid them a visit, and that they feel that they have been neglected by the Indian Department. Coming from such a source, I believe the information to be correct, and, under the circumstances, permit me to say that an immediate personal visit by you is due to the whites as well as to the Indians, as the threatened danger may thus be easily averted, without expense or—the still more serious contingency—loss of life. I take the liberty of pressing the suggestion upon your attention at once, as the prevention by such simple means is far more desirable than any future remedy which may be devised to meet losses which it may be beyond human power to repair or redress.
I have, &c.
(Signed)   GEO. A. WALKEM.

The Superintendent of Indian Affairs to the Attorney-General.
Indian Office, Victoria,
29th December, 1873.

SIR,—I have the honour to acknowledge your letter of the 26th instant, respecting threatened Indian troubles at Cache Creek, and calling my attention to a letter received by Mr. Barnston from one Ranald McDonald. In reply I have to state that it is my intention to proceed to New Westminster to-morrow morning (should I receive no telegram to the contrary during the day), and, if upon further enquiry, I find that the report has any reliable basis, my journey will be extended to Cache Creek at once. At the same time, you will permit me to doubt the correctness of the authority you quote, especially since there are so many gentlemen lately from the district in question, at present in this city, who can give more valued evidence. From all I can learn, the fear that they will lose their land and not be sufficiently provided for in this respect, is the real cause of disturbance if, indeed, there be any among the Indians.

May I beg to bring to your notice a letter addressed by me to the Honourable Provincial Secretary on Saturday, on the subject of these lands, and to solicit the action of the Government thereon, if possible, at once. Again I have to express the hope that no extensive leases of grazing lands in the vicinity of Indian habitations, will be given by the Government until their reserves are fixed, and, I assure you, the most fruitful source of anxiety or fear of injustice on their part will be avoided.
I have, &c.,
(Signed)   I. W. POWELL.

The Superintendent of Indian Affairs to the Attorney-General.
Indian Office, Victoria,
26th December, 1873.

SIR,—I have the honour to request that you will allow the Superintendent of Police to proceed to Cowichan for the purpose of ejecting two or three Indians who are trespassing upon the lands of white settlers—Messrs. Dods and Munro.

I propose that Mr. Sullivan may act in the matter in connection with the local Magistrate, (Mr. Morley), and I may add that any expenses incurred by the Superintendent will be borne by this Department.
(Signed)   I. W. POWELL.

The Superintendent of Indian Affairs to the Provincial Secretary.

Indian Office, Victoria,
27th December, 1873.

SIR,—In view of a possible visit to Cache Creek and other Indians, among whom there are rumours which have reached me of threatened trouble, I have the honour to request that the quantity of land to be reserved for Indians east of the Cascades should be forty acres for each Indian family, instead of twenty, as agreed upon.

My reason for applying for the increased quantity is, that the interior Indians are nearly all possessed of horses and cattle, and I am convinced that twenty acres would not be found to be sufficient.

Should a personal inspection prove the correctness of my impression on this matter, it would be both highly important and practical in quieting all their fears of future injustice, if I could promise that an additional quantity of land would be laid aside for the grazing purposes of each tribe.

I might remind you that this principle is recognized in the present pre-emption law for white settlers, where 320 acres are allowed each individual east of the Cascades and 160 acres west of the same.

I have, &c.,
(Signed) I. W. POWELL.

The Provincial Secretary to the Superintendent of Indian Affairs.

Provincial Secretary's Office,
29th December, 1873.

SIR,—I have the honor to acquaint you with reference to your letter of the 27th inst., conveying a suggestion that the grant to a native family should be increased on the east side of the Cascade Range to from twenty to forty acres of land, that large reserves of land have already been made in these districts.

The subject, however, will receive the mature consideration of the Government, meanwhile I have to request you will be good enough to confer with the Attorney-General on the subject.

I have, etc.,
(Signed) JOHN ASH.

The Attorney-General to the Superintendent of Indian Affairs.

Attorney-General's Office,
December 29th, 1873.

SIR,—Your letter of the 27th inst., to the Honourable Provincial Secretary, asking on behalf of the Indians east of the Cascade Range, for tracts of forty instead of twenty acres of land as a bonus to each family, has been referred to me with instructions from the Committee in Council to confer with you upon the subject.

I called at your office and at your dwelling about 2½ p. m. to-day, but was not fortunate enough to find you.

I have since received your letter of this date, informing me of your determination to proceed to-morrow by steamer to New Westminster, and thence to Cache Creek (should you receive no replies to your telegrams), to confer with the Indians of the interior. Permit me to say that I feel convinced that you have acted wisely in this serious matter. I would, however, suggest that no matter what peaceful assurances you may receive by telegraph, that it would be better to pay the Indians a visit than to stop short at New Westminster.

The Indians are certainly entitled to such a small piece of attention, accomplished too at such small expense, though it must be admitted that you cannot but encounter personal discomfort by reason of the inclemency of the weather.

As to the extra twenty acres asked for by you, as above stated, I have the honour to draw your attention to the list of, really in some instances, enormous, and in all cases, sufficient reserves, already laid aside for the Indians residing near Cache Creek, Kamloops, Okanagan, Shuswap, and other places. They cannot be, and as I have been credibly informed are not, dissatisfied with the amount of land allotted to them. On the contrary you will, after looking at your plans copied from the official records, agree with me that many of the reserves must be cut down, being out of all proportion to the strength of the tribes to which they have been respectively granted in days gone by, when land in the vicinity referred to seems to have been considered of little value.

When the reserves near Cache Creek, and some of the other places mentioned, were set apart, a conference was held with each of the Chiefs before any decision was arrived at. Their views were ascertained and their wishes were fully consulted. A parchment sketch of each reserve, enclosed in a tin case, was handed to them, and they expressed themselves entirely satisfied. The tribes now dread the idea of being placed upon and confined to these reserves, as they have ascertained that the Indian Department intend, if possible, to carry out such a course.

The Indians speak freely upon the subject, and intimate their intention of resisting such a step. This is the cause of their dissatisfaction, and they wish to see you about it.

They are fully aware of your appointment and position, and to my personal knowledge they have expected a visit from you for nearly eight months back.

They, moreover, expect the usual presents from you as the representative of the great Chief, and in this I would respectfully suggest that you do not disappoint them. A few hundred dollars' worth of blankets, clothing, food, &c., would be well laid out if given to them.

I trust that you will excuse me for thus trespassing upon questions of an official character, of which you must necessarily possess a more intimate knowledge than I do. It is only a suggestion which I venture to make, as it might be overlooked in the hurry of an unexpected visit. I consider that whether the Indians are peaceably disposed or not that presents should be given, especially as the conference proposed by you is the first of its kind, and is one which they should always recollect with pleasure.

I have, &c.,
(Signed)   GEO. A. WALKEM.

P. S.—Having seen you upon the subject of the foregoing, and as Mr. DeCosmos stated that there would be no difficulty in granting any extra lands to the Indians if absolutely necessary, and as your views and mine coincide as to a just treatment of the Indians, I take the responsibility of stating that you may tell the Indians that where the lands occupied by them are only suitable for grazing purposes and are inadequate to meet their wants, that twenty acres more than the twenty now conceded, should be given to each Indian family requiring them for pastoral use, regard, of course, being had in the disposition of the lands to the average acreage per family of all the reserves hitherto granted or hereafter added.

The Superintendent of Indian Affairs to the Attorney-General.

Indian Office,
Victoria, 12th January, 1874.

SIR,—I have the honour to inform you that owing to further telegrams which have been transmitted through the press, respecting the rumour of threatened Indian attacks upon the white settlers of the interior and your own wishes in regard to the same, I have determined upon proceeding at once to Cache Creek and Kamloops for the purpose of instituting personal inquiry into alleged grievances of the Natives, and if possible to allay for the present any hostile feeling existing on account of them. In addition to my own opinions upon this subject, as conveyed in my letter of the 27th ult., and which you were good enough to consider favourably for the purpose intended, I feel it my duty to report to you that among the assigned causes of discontent of the Indians, is the driving their cattle off unfenced lands or those held under pastoral lease. One case has been reported to me of a judicial decision, in which an Indian was mulcted in comparatively large damages for alleged trespass upon lands which were not fenced, but held under a lease from the Government for pastoral purposes, a case which I am told has been taken up by many other Indians, and is said to form one of the prominent grievances for adjustment now. It would, perhaps, be invidious for me to reflect upon what certainly seems an injustice, but you will, I am sure, agree with me as to the necessity of ascertaining your opinion regarding the legality of such an issue, or in other words, whether cattle grazing upon unfenced lands, belonging to other than the holder thereof, can be subject to the penalty of trespass?

If these instances of grievance are correct, it is highly important in undertaking what may be a most grave and responsible mission, that I should be fortified by correct information upon all points likely to arise in the settlement of any complaint made by Indians. If, on the other hand, the leaseholder of an extensive tract of land is justified by law in driving Indian cattle off any unfenced portion and having the owner fined for damages, I fail at present to see how lasting disaffection is to be prevented, unless indeed, a far more liberal treatment is pursued towards them than the terms of Confederation would seem to justify on the part of the Dominion Government, or by the immediate passage or enactment of some local Statute which would modify, if not change altogether, the existing pastoral land law which permits such apparent injustice. As I intend leaving early on Wednesday morning may I beg that you will be good enough to favour me with a reply some time to-morrow.

I have, etc.,
(Signed) I. W. POWELL.

Telegram.

Clinton, January 9.—From Mr. Vasey, who lives on the Bonaparte, we learn that on Thursday last he was told by Father Grandidier, who was at Kamloops a few days previous, that, in a Council of Chiefs in that vicinity lately, seven were for war and two opposed. He (the Father) gave it as his opinion that the Indians were liable to commence hostilities at any moment.

A late decision of the County Court, whereby an Indian was compelled to pay damages for trespass of his stock (the Indians claim, unjustly,) has considerably agitated them. The leasing of large tracts of their grazing lands, and the non-arrival of the Indian Commissioner, as was promised them, adds to their agitation. By these last reports, the excitement which prevailed among the settlers lately is again revived stronger than ever, and a general feeling of insecurity prevails. The Indians here who have been questioned regarding the matter deny all knowledge of it.

The Attorney-General to the Superintendent of Indian Affairs.

Attorney-General's Office,
January 13th, 1874.

SIR,—I have the honour to acknowledge the receipt of your letter of yesterday, informing me that you intended to proceed to Cache Creek and Kamloops to investigate the causes of the Indian disturbance in that vicinity.

In reply to your query as to whether a stranger who permits his cattle to run upon pastoral lands under lease is liable to the lessee as a trespasser, I have to refer you to Section 38 of the "Land Ordinance, 1870," which lays down the proposition as law that any lessee from the Crown can maintain ejectment or trespass in the same manner as if he were owner of the land referred to, and "either party "may refer the cause of action to the Stipendiary Magistrate of the District wherein "the land lies, who may proceed summarily," &c.

No Justice of the Peace or Magistrate, except he be of the Stipendiary class, has power to deal with such cases.

By the Common Law of England, which is in force here, the proprietors or occupiers of land are not obliged to fence their lands. The owners of cattle or other animals are, by the same law, bound to see that they do no damage and that they commit no trespass.

Indians are subject to the same laws as whites. Your observations upon the subject will, I need hardly assure you, receive the attention of the Government.

Will you be good enough to take a note of and report all matters of grievance which may be brought under your notice in the upper country.

I have, &c.,
(Signed)   GEO. A. WALKEM.

The Provincial Secretary to the Superintendent of Indian Affairs.

Provincial Secretary's Office,
30th January, 1874.

SIR,—The Lieutenant-Governor in Council has had under consideration your letter of the 12th instant, forwarding copy of telegrams having reference to the alleged disaffection of the Indians in the interior; a verbal answer was given to you before your departure, but I hasten on your return from the interior to acquaint you that the Provincial Government is of opinion that an Indian outbreak is highly improbable, and that they did not at the time of the receipt of your letter, and do not now, consider it necessary to offer you any advice on the subject.

I have, &c.,
(Signed)   JOHN ASH.

The Superintendent of Indian Affairs to the Lieutenant-Governor.

Indian Office, Victoria,
16th February, 1874.

SIR,—I have the honour to solicit the attention of your Honour to my letter of 27th October, 1873, respecting the Songish Reserve, further referred to in my letter (reply) of 6th November, to the Honorable the Attorney-General. I should be glad if your Honour would have the goodness to inform me, if it is proposed to take any action towards meeting the wishes of the Honorable the Minister of the Interior as conveyed in the letter above alluded to.

(Signed)   I. W. POWELL.

The Provincial Secretary to the Superintendent of Indian Affairs.

Provincial Secretary's Office,
23rd February, 1874.

SIR,—I am instructed by His Excellency the Lieutenant-Governor to inform you in reply to your letter of the 24th October last, on the subject of a proposal to remove the Indians from the Songish Reserve, and to deal with the said reserve by selling or leasing the same, that it is deemed by the Provincial Government unadvisable to interfere in any manner with the duties assumed by the Dominion Government under the Terms of Union.

I have, &c.,
(Signed)   JOHN ASH.

The Attorney-General to the Superintendent of Indian Affairs.

Attorney General's Office,
26th February, 1874.

SIR,—I have the honour to forward copies of two letters respecting the Indian disturbance at Cowichan; from them it will appear that the Indians emboldened by the failure of your negotiations, have assumed an attitude of aggression. As you are about to start for Ottawa, the opportunity will prove favourable for laying this matter before the Indian Department. Neglect of the Dominion Government to organize the Department upon a proper footing here, and the more than probable mischievous results which may thence ensue, ought, permit me to say, to be strongly impressed upon them. Loss of lives of white settlers, as you are aware, is not at all an impossible contingency. I have therefore the honour to request you to take such immediate steps as will lead to the settlement of these and other Indian difficulties.

I have, &c.,
(Signed) GEO. A. WALKEM.

ENCLOSURES.

Mr. Dods to the Attorney-General.

Cowichan, February 20th, 1874.

SIR,—I herewith transmit for your consideration a concise statement of a grievance I have:—

Last April I pre-empted, and in November purchased a piece of land, but I cannot get the use of it. The Indians who have been allowed to use it will not go off or allow me to go on it to clear or fence. I lost the use of it last year from this cause. They have threatened me repeatedly with personal violence if I attempt to prosecute my claim further. I cannot of course take the law into my own hands while the country has a Government, but the Indians can and have done so with impunity. Owing to the inaction of the Indian Commissioner a very bad feeling prevails among them. I have applied to Mr. Morley for redress, but he is unable, for want of a sufficient force, to arrest the five or six principal offenders. It is needless to dilate on the state of affairs; I hope you will see your way to an immediate remedy.

I have, &c.,
(Signed) A. DODS.

Mr. Morley to the Attorney-General.

Maple Bay, February 20th, 1874.

SIR,—I have the honour to inform you that Mr. Archibald Dods, of Cowichan, has been to complain that the Indians will not allow him to go on to the land he has purchased from the Government. On Wednesday the 18th a party came to him whilst he was working and compelled him to leave. What steps shall I take in the matter? Mr. Dods wishes to cultivate the land. On a former occasion I issued a summons and bound the Indian over to keep the peace; other Indians continue to annoy him.

I am, etc.,
(Signed) JOHN MORLEY.

The Deputy Indian Commissioner to the Attorney-General.

Indian Office, Victoria,
February 26th, 1874.

Sir,—I have the honour to acknowledge the receipt of your letter of this date. In reply I am directed by the Indian Commissioner to forward for your information a copy of his last communication, of February 14th, to Mr. A. Dods, and to express his opinion that if Mr. D. has been threatened with aggressive measures by the Indians, it is altogether attributable to the complete absence of a conciliatory spirit towards the Indians on the part of that gentleman. Mr. Dods *refused* to follow the advice of the Commissioner, or, in his opinion, the matter would soon be settled, hence the only course left open to him is to have recourse to the law against trespass, as in such cases provided.

The subject, however, will no doubt come up in the discussion of kindred subjects during his visit at Ottawa, when your letter will be laid before the Minister of the Interior.

(Signed)   H. MOFFATT.

ENCLOSURE.

The Indian Commissioner to Mr. A. Dods.

Indian Office, Victoria,
14th February, 1874.

Sir,—I have the honour to acknowledge your letter of the 12th inst., referring to the Indians trespassing on your land' and advising that decisive action be taken at once to have the matters complained of set right, etc.

In reply, I have to remind you that former Colonial Governments have always considered and treated Indians as British subjects, and consequently they have always been amenable to the same laws.

Should an Indian, therefore, trespass upon your property there is a law which you can appeal to and obtain, without fail, just redress.

Mr. Superintendent Sullivan was not sent to Cowichan to interfere with or *advise* the Indians in any way, but solely to carry out the *instructions of the Magistrate*, Mr. Morley, to whom your complaint ought to have been preferred at the time. I am persuaded that the legal manner of settling any dispute is far better than incurring the risk, as you add, of your own life and that of your neighbours by taking aggressive measures into your own hands. I regret that my own visit to Cowichan does not appear to have met with your approval.

I think now, however, as I thought then, that a little patience and forbearance on your part would be beneficial in your matter, but should you still have a different opinion, the proper and therefore the advisable course is that which the law always affords you.

I have, &c.,
(Signed)   I. W. POWELL.

The Superintendent of Indian Affairs to the Provincial Secretary.

British Columbia,
Indian Office, Victoria, May 15th, 1874.

Sir,—I have the honour to enclose for the information of His Honor the Lieutenant-Governor in Council a copy of an Order in Council, dated March 1st, 1874, respecting the Indian Reserves of this Province.

With a view of carrying out the instructions conveyed in the said Order with as little delay as possible, and especially taking advantage of the present season for surveying the proposed allotment of Indian Reserves, I shall be glad if the same could be submitted at once to the consideration of the Government.

The vastly increased expense of dividing a Reserve into *four* acre allotments, in addition to the great difficulty of satisfying the just requirements of the Indians by alloting "twenty acres to each five persons," strongly urges me to hope that the wish expressed in the eighth Section of the enclosed Order in Council, may meet with and have the favorable consideration of the Government. Again, I do not think that the granting of twenty acres to *each head* of an Indian family will make any perceptible difference in the *aggregate* quantity of land reserved for the whole Indian population.

I have the honor, also, to recall attention to your letter of the 29th December, and to the correspondence which subsequently followed between the Honorable the Attorney-General and myself.

I propose to proceed at once to Kamloops ; and, if the agreement between the Attorney-General and myself in making the grant East of the Cascades forty acres instead of twenty could be adopted by the Government, I feel sure of making my intended visit to this lately disturbed district not only one of great satisfaction to the Indians themselves, but to the settlers, in assuring them of future peace and protection.

I have, &c.,
(Signed) I. W. POWELL,
Indian Commissioner.

Copy of a Report of a Committee of the Honorable the Privy Council, approved by His Excellency the Governor-General in Council on the 24th April, 1874.

The Committee of Council have had under consideration the Memorandum, dated 1st April, 1874, from the Honorable the Minister of the Interior, having reference to the Order in Council of the 21st March, 1873, and the correspondence arising out of that Order, respecting the Indian Reserves in British Columbia, and they respectfully submit their concurrence in the several recommendations submitted in the said Memorandum, and advise that the same be approved and adopted.
Certified,
(Signed) W. HIMSWORTH.

British Columbia Reserves.
Department of the Interior,
March 1st, 1874.

The undersigned has had under his consideration the Order of His Excellency the Governor-General in Council, under date the 21st March, 1873, and the subsequent correspondence arising out of that Order in reference to the Indian Reserves in British Columbia.

By the 13th Article of the Terms of Union, between Canada and British Columbia, the Indian Reserves in British Columbia were transferred to the Dominion Government and are now under the control of this Department.

From the official and other information in possession of the undersigned, it is clear that the dissatisfaction now existing among the Indians in British Columbia arises, to a great extent, out of the present state of the Reserves, and if prompt measures be taken to satisfy the requirements of the Indians on this head a fruitful source of dissatisfaction will have been removed. By the Order in Council above to, it is provided, among other things, that each Indian family shall be assigned 80 acres of land of average quality, to remain permanently the property of such family.

The local Government of British Columbia has positively declined to grant such an extent of land for the use of the Indians, as being far in excess of the quantity previously allowed the Indians by the local Government, and under the Terms of Union the local Government are only bound "to give tracts of land of such extent "as had hitherto been the practice of the local Government to appropriate for that "purpose,"—ten acres for every family of five persons. The Government of British Columbia, however, on the representation of Mr. Commissioner Powell, consented to double this amount and to appropriate twenty acres of land to every five persons. This offer Mr. Powell was authorized to accept, while at the same time he was urged to obtain, if possible, double that quantity for the Indians East of the Cascade Range, in accordance with the general usage in British Columbia of granting a double allowance to the white settlers East of the said range.

In view of the foregoing circumstances it is recommended :—

1st. That the paragraph in the Order in Council above referred to, appropriating 80 acres of land to each Indian family of five persons be rescinded, and that it be provided that only 20 acres be allotted to five persons.

2nd. That, whenever it is so desired by a majority of Indians at any Reserve, such Reserve shall be divided into suitable allotments on the basis of 20 acres to each five persons in the said band, and the holder of every such allotment shall be placed in possession thereof, by some formal instrument to be given him by the Commissioner.

3rd. Whenever any Reserve does not contain sufficient land to give 20 acres to each five in the band of Indians to which such Reserve has been apportioned, then land in the immediate vicinity, or as near thereto as possible, should be obtained from the local Government for the individual not so provided for.

4th. Whenever, in any part of the Province, no Reserves of land have been made for the Indians, and there are any white settlers or any immediate prospect of such, application should be made to the local Government, for the required number of acres to be there reserved for the Indians.

5th. Great care should be taken that the Indians, especially those inhabiting the Coast, should not be disturbed in the enjoyment of their customary fishing grounds, which should be reserved for them previous to white settlement in the immediate vicinity of such localities.

6th. The Commissioner should be instructed to suggest such measures as he may think necessary to prevent difficulties among the Indians resident in pastoral districts, arising from the unfenced condition of extensive lands leased to white men for grazing purposes.

*

8th. In view of the difficulty and expense of making the allotment of the surveys on the basis of twenty acres to each five persons, and taking into consideration the very large and unlooked for expenditure which the general administration of Indian Affairs in British Columbia is about to entail upon the Dominion Government, the undersigned would recommend that the Indian Commissioner be authorized to press strongly upon the Local Government the duty of co-operating in every way with the Dominion Government in pacifying the Indian population of the Province, and satisfying their reasonable demands ; and as the amount of land which they now propose to allot to the Indians is very small, that he be particularly requested to urge the Local Government to allocate twenty acres of land to every Indian, *being a head of a family*, without reference to the number of persons in the family.

(Signed)   D. LAIRD.

*MEMO—Clause 7 refers to amount of money granted for immediate prosecution of proposed surveys.   (Initialed)   I.W.P.

The Provincial Secretary to the Superintendent of Indian Affairs.

Provincial Secretary's Office,
22nd May, 1874.

Sir,—I have the honour to acquaint you that your letter of the 15th instant, on the subject of Indian lands, is still under the consideration of the Government; an answer will, however, be forwarded to you at the earliest possible opportunity.

I have, &c.,
(Signed) JOHN ASH.

The Attorney-General to the Superintendent of Indian Affairs.

Attorney General's Office,
15th June, 1874.

Sir,—I have the honour to forward you copy of a letter from Mr. A. Dods, relating to a matter of grave importance.

I wrote Mr. Dods on the 3rd instant informing him that by your direction the Surveyors would lay out the reserve in six weeks.

I have, &c.,
(Signed) GEO. A. WALKEM.

ENCLOSURES.

Mr. Dods to the Attorney-General.

Cowichan,
June 11th, 1874.

DEAR SIR,—I intended to have requested you to be kind enough to give a little attention to the case of the Indians trespassing on my land. It becomes now doubly imperative, as I have heard this evening that they have broken out at last as I was almost certain they would, from this policy of dallying with them. One of them stopped Lomas, took hold of his horse's head, and told him that he (the Indian) intended to kill some white man, and he would do so. Lomas got disengaged, went home, got his gun, and started out to look for the Indian. The latter, as Lomas afterwards heard, had got his gun also, and lay in ambush, watching for Lomas. The Indian fired three times at Lomas, the cap snapping each time, this, of course, saving his life. Lomas heard the click of the caps, but did not put it down to that cause. They had some of them promised him that they would shoot him, the same as they have me. Drink, I believe, was the immediate cause. Where they get it I don't know, but they seem to get any amount. They are all gone to Nanaimo to a big potlatch.

They affect to hold in contempt all the "wa-wa" of Dr. Powell. What he said to them has also been misinterpreted, or else they have misunderstood it. They evidently think that they may stop on my land if they like, their going depending upon whether they are put on a piece that will suit them better or not. They will not voluntarily look for a piece. I and a good many others look upon the way I have been treated as one of the greatest outrages that can be perpetrated in a civilized community. It is not a matter of indifference to me. The fact is, that the only little source of income we have is cut off. I can't milk my cows, because those that are away cannot get home on account of the fences ; and those that are at home get nothing to eat, from the same cause. What open space there is between fences is eaten down by everybody's cattle and pigs. I have lost (stolen by Indians) pigs that would be worth every cent of $100 now, from not being able to fence in my land, although posts and timber are lying all ready. They have fenced in portions of my ground for hay to feed their cattle, while I have not enough for myself. I cannot get wood off my own land, except by a sort of permission. I cannot build as I intended to do. Everybody says, "sure what the devil is the good of a Government that can't put a few siwashes off a man's land." I said, always, "I'm waiting for Powell." Now, Powell has not fixed it, nor is there even a probability that he can or will. You see, he won't even hear the case stated before you. The idea that I have had, from first to last, in this affair, is, that you must make the Indians respect your power. They have a hundred times more respect for a gunboat than all the talk in creation. Now, I don't want to oust the Indians if inconvenient, but I do want some guarantee that I shall have the land to use and to build on, that they shall be put off or go off some time this year, and that I shall be paid for the losses I have sustained through the Indians acting as they have done.

I have, &c.,
(Signed)   A. DODS.

The Provincial Secretary to the Superintendent of Indian Affairs.

Provincial Secretary's Office,
21st July, 1874.

SIR,—In reply to your letter of the 16th instant, I have now the honour to forward for your information, copy of an Order in Council on the subject of the Indian Reserves.

I have, &c.,
(Signed)   JOHN ASH.

ENCLOSURE.

Copy of a Report of a Committee of the Honorable the Executive Council, approved by His Excellency the Lieutenant-Governor, on the 15th June, 1874.

On a Memorandum of the 13th day of June, 1874, from the Honorable Attorney-General, reporting that application has been made by the Indian Department to vary an Order in Council, dated the 25th July, 1873, which allots twenty acres of land to each head of an Indian family of five persons, by striking out the two last words, viz.: "five persons," so that the allotment shall read "twenty acres of land to each head of an Indian family," the Committee advise that the recommendation be approved.

Certified,
(Signed)   W. J. ARMSTRONG,
Clerk Executive Council.

The Superintendent of Indian Affairs to the Chief Commissioner of Lands and Works.

Indian Office,
Monday.

MY DEAR SIR,—Would you be good enough to give me any information at your disposal respecting a piece of the Cowichan Reserve, leased as a Mill-site—part of Section 17, Range VIII; also of the land taken up or sold to Pat. Brennan.

I have, &c.,
(Signed)   I. W. POWELL.

The Chief Commissioner of Lands and Works to the Superintendent of Indian Affairs.

Lands and Works Department,
Victoria, July 29th, 1874.

SIR,—In reply to your letter of Monday last, I have the honour to inform you that Patrick Brennan received a Crown grant for 20 acres of land in Cowichan District, being portions of Sections 15 and 16, Range III., (10 acres in each section) on June 21st, 1871. With regard to the "mill site" on Section 17, Range VIII, Quamichan District, Mr. W. F. Crate applied for a Crown grant of a portion of this section, amounting to 2¼ acres, on the 6th August, 1869.

Mr. Crate, in a letter from this department, dated August 17th, in the same year, was informed he could lease the said property for a term of 7 years, paying an annual rental of $15.

No lease was ever made out or rental paid.

Mr. W. F. Crate, I understand, died some time since.

I have, &c.,
(Signed)   ROBERT BEAVEN.

The Superintendent of Indian Affairs to the Chief Commissioner of Lands and Works.

Indian Office, Victoria,
July 31st, 1874.

SIR,—I have the honour to inform you that the survey of the Musqueam Indian Reserve, lately undertaken by my orders, is now finished, and that the quantity of land is insufficient to give each head of a family an allotment of 20 acres. The actual number of families in the tribe is 70, consequently 1,400 acres of land will be required to make up the full quantity. Of this the present reserve contains 314 acres, 114 of which is quite useless.

I now make application for 1,197 acres, and request that the surveyor may be allowed to choose the land in the immediate vicinity, or as near the present reserve as may be found practicable.

The Islands marked B B B in the enclosed diagram, with the Sections C C and F, on Sea Island, are particularly desired by the Indians for grazing lands.

I should be glad if your immediate consideration may be given to the above request, so that advantage may be taken of the presence of the surveyor in that locality.

I have, &c.,
(Signed)   I. W. POWELL.

The Chief Commissioner of Lands and Works to the Superintendent of Indian Affairs.

Lands and Works Department,
Victoria, 6th August, 1874.

SIR,—I have the honour to acknowledge the receipt of your letter, dated 31st ultimo, having reference to the survey of the Musqueam Indian Reserve.

And in reply would ask how you ascertain the actual number of families in each tribe, and also what is your definition of the head of an Indian family, and are you prepared to reduce the acreage of reservations, where the necessary number of Indians do not reside.

(Signed)   ROBERT BEAVEN.

The Superintendent of Indian Affairs to the Chief Commissioner of Lands and Works.

Indian Office, Victoria,
August 7th, 1874.

Sir,—I have the honour to acknowledge the receipt of your letter of the 6th inst., and in reply state: 1. That actual numbers of families are ascertained by counting individuals. 2. Every adult who has a wife or children is head of a family. 3. I understand in cases where reservation exceeds quantity of land allowed to a tribe (*i. e.* 20 acres to every head of a family) that due allowance is to be made for such excess, either by cutting down or otherwise, as may be mutually agreeable to Dominion and Local Governments.

As the survey party under Mr. Howse is now awaiting your reply to my letter of the 31st, and as any delay is attended with considerable expense, may I beg to be favoured with the same at the earliest possible moment.

I have, &c.,
(Signed) I. W. POWELL.

The Chief Commissioner of Lands and Works to the Superintendent of Indian Affairs.

Lands and Works Department,
Victoria, 10th August, 1874.

Sir,—I have the honour to acknowledge the receipt of your letter of 7th inst., giving me the information asked for in my letter of the 6th inst.

And beg to inform you that in the absence of necessary information, I much regret that I find it impossible to send an immediate definite reply.

As a matter of course, it is presumable that the number of families could only be ascertained by counting, but it is very important that the Provincial Government should know who supplied the information, whether it is taken under oath or how, and whether any penalty can be imposed for making a false return.

There are several other points in connection with the subject that require the fullest investigation before unsurveyed land in the vicinity of a reservation could be granted, and I would respectfully suggest that Mr. Howse's party be not detained there, after they have completed the surveys you have instructed them to make.

I am unable to advise the extension of present reservations, until positively informed that you are authorised to reduce as well as increase such reservations, and that you are prepared on behalf of the Dominion Government to guarantee that the Indians will agree quietly to reduction, if the Provincial Government agree to an increase.

I have, &c.,
(Signed) ROBERT BEAVEN.

The Superintendent of Indian Affairs to the Chief Commissioner of Lands and Works.

British Columbia,
July 31st, 1874.

Sir,—I have the honour to acquaint you that the area of the Tsowassen Reserve is inadequate to give allotments of 20 acres of cultivatable land to each family, a large portion being swampy and useless except for grazing purposes; the exact area required is 68 acres.

I have now the honour to apply that a further quantity of 100 acres (to the eastward and adjoining the present reserve) be laid aside for the use of the Indians of this place. There are 18 families, and the total quantity of land marked on the official plan of this reserve is 490 acres.

I have, &c.,
(Signed) I. W. POWELL.

The Chief Commissioner of Lands and Works to the Superintendent of Indian Affairs.

Lands and Works Department,
Victoria, 6th August, 1874.

SIR,—I have the honour to acknowledge the receipt of your letter, dated 31st ultimo, in reference to the Tsowassen Reserve ; but I am not aware that any land was returned to the Dominion Government, as an Indian Reserve, under that name or in that locality.

Would you, therefore, in order to clear up this point, kindly enclose your copy of reserves, which shall be immediately returned after being again compared with the copy in this Department.

I have, &c.,
(Signed) ROBERT BEAVEN.

The Superintendent of Indian Affairs to the Chief Commissioner of Lands and Works.

Indian Office, Victoria,
August 7th, 1874.

SIR,—I have the honour to acknowledge the receipt of your communication of the 6th inst., regarding the Tsowassen Indian Reserve. I now send you book of tracings as the only record of any land having been reserved for this band of Indians. I may add that I am informed there are several tribes of Indians for whom lands have been reserved by former Governments, but which were omitted in the schedule furnished the Dominion Government at the time of union.

The Tsowasson Reserve may have been one of these (I presume unintentional) omissions.

Future and perhaps grave mistakes would be avoided if all reserves of land intended for Indians were placed upon the Schedule. Great dissatisfaction prevails now among the Indians, especially those on the mainland, in regard to their lands and the non-recognition of their pre-existing rights, but it would, indeed, be attended with serious consequences were any piece of land (hitherto reserved for any tribe) used for any other purpose merely because the same had been left out of the schedule.

I have, &c.,
(Signed) I. W. POWELL.

The Superintendent of Indian Affairs to the Provincial Secretary.

Indian Office, Victoria,
August 5th, 1874.

SIR,—I have the honour to enclose for your consideration, copy of a Petition from the Indian Chiefs of the Fraser River and surrounding country, on matters relating to their land Reserves.

I have, &c.,
(Signed) I. W. POWELL.

ENCLOSURES.

Peter Ayessik to the Superintendent of Indian Affairs.

New Westminster, July 14th, 1874.

SIR,—Having been, along with some others, commissioned by the Chiefs to present our common petition to you, we have come down to New Westminster yesterday and, after consultation, we came to the conclusion to send the petition by mail.

You have told Alexis and myself not to go down till you send notice.

We expect to hear from you, through Rev. Father Durieu, at New Westminster.

I have, &c.,
(Signed) PETER AYESSIK,
Chief of Hope.

To the Indian Commissioner for the Province of British Columbia :—

The petition of the undersigned, Chiefs of Douglas Portage, of Lower Fraser, and of the other tribes on the seashore of the mainland to Bute Inlet, humbly sheweth :—

1. That your petitioners view, with a great anxiety, the standing question of the quantity of land to be reserved for the use of each Indian family.

2. That we are fully aware that the Government of Canada has always taken good care of the Indians, and treated them liberally, allowing more than one hundred acres per family ; and we have been at a loss to understand the views of the Local Government of British Columbia, in curtailing our land so much as to leave, in many instances, but few acres of land per family.

3. Our hearts have been wounded by the arbitrary way the Local Government of British Columbia have dealt with us in locating and dividing our Reserves. Chamiel, ten miles below Hope, is allowed 488 acres of good land for the use of twenty families: at the rate of 24 acres per family ; Popkum, eighteen miles below Hope, is allowed 369 acres of good land for the use of four families : at the rate of 90 acres per family ; Cheam, twenty miles below Hope, is allowed 375 acres of bad, dry, and mountainous land for the use of twenty-seven families: at the rate of 13 acres per family; Yuk-Yuk-y-yoose, on Chilliwhack River, with a population of seven families, is allowed 42 acres: 5 acres per family; Sumass, at the junction of Sumass River and Fraser, with a population of seventeen families, is allowed 43 acres of meadow for their hay, and 32 acres of dry land; Keatsy, numbering more than one hundred inhabitants, is allowed 108 acres of land. Langley and Hope have not yet got land secured to them, and white men are encroaching on them on all sides.

4. For many years we have been complaining of the land left us being too small. We have laid our complaints before Government officials nearest to us ; they sent us to some others; so we had no redress up to the present ; and we have felt like men trampled on, and are commencing to believe that the aim of the white men is to exterminate us as soon as they can, although we have always been quiet, obedient, kind, and friendly to the whites.

5 Discouragement and depression have come upon our people. Many of them have given up the cultivation of land, because our gardens have not been protected against the encroachments of the whites. Some of our best men have been deprived of the land they had broken and cultivated with long and hard labour, a white man enclosing it in his claim, and no compensation given. Some of our most enterprising men have lost part of their cattle, because white men had taken the place where those cattle were grazing, and no other place left but the thickly timbered land, where they die fast. Some of our people now are obliged to cut rushes along the bank of the river with their knives during the winter to feed their cattle.

6. We are now obliged to clear heavy timbered land, all prairies having been taken from us by white men. We see our white neighbours cultivate wheat, peas, &c., and raise large stocks of cattle on our pasture lands, and we are giving them our money to buy the flour manufactured from the wheat they have grown on the same prairies.

7. We are not lazy and roaming-about people, as we used to be. We have worked hard and a long time to spare money to buy agricultural implements, cattle, horses, etc., as nobody has given us assistance. We could point out many of our people who have, those past years, bought, with their own money, ploughs, harrows, yokes of oxen, and horses ; and now, with your kind assistance, we have a bright hope to enter into the path of civilization.

8. We consider that 80 acres per family is absolutely necessary for our support, and for the future welfare of our children. We declare that 20 or 30 acres of land per family will not give satisfaction, but will create ill feelings, irritation amongst our people, and we cannot say what will be the consequence.

9. That, in case you cannot obtain from the Local Government the object of our petition, we humbly pray that this our petition be forwarded to the Secretary of State for the Provinces, Ottawa.

Therefore your petitioners humbly pray that you may take this our petition into consideration and see that justice be done us, and allow each family the quantity of land we ask for.

And your petitioners, as in duty bound, will ever pray.

(Signed)   PETER AYESSIK, Chief of Hope,
And 109 others.

I hereby testify that the Chiefs above referred to met together in my presence, and the above petition is the true expression of their feeling and of their wishes.

(Signed)   PETER AYESSIK,
New Westminster, July 14, 1874.   Chief of Hope.

The Provincial Secretary to the Superintendent of Indian Affairs.

Provincial Secretary's Office,
11th August, 1874.

SIR,—I have the honour to acknowledge the receipt of your letter of 5th inst., forwarding for my consideration a copy of a petition from the Indian Chiefs of the Fraser, and in reply I would recommend you to carry out the prayer of the said petition by forwarding the same to the Secretary of State for Canada.

I have, &c.,
(Signed)   JOHN ASH.

The Chief Commissioner of Lands and Works to the Superintendent of Indian Affairs.

Lands and Works Department,
Victoria, 10th August, 1874.

SIR,—I have the honour to acknowledge the receipt of your communication of 7th inst., and its enclosures.

As evident discrepancies exist between the schedule of Indian Reserves furnished by Mr. Pearse (the late Surveyor-General) to the Dominion and Provincial Governments and the book of tracings enclosed by you, I beg to be permitted temporarily to retain the same for a thorough examination, this department never having had the opportunity, to my knowledge, of inspecting these tracings in the form you have had them prepared.

A piece of land opposite New Westminster is shown in one of the tracings, which is clearly not an Indian Reserve. It is possible, therefore, that the person who has made them for you is not aware which are Indian Reservations.

I have, &c.,
(Signed)   ROBERT BEAVEN.

The Chief Commissioner of Lands and Works to the Superintendent of Indian Affairs.

Lands and Works Department,
Victoria, 13th August, 1874.

SIR,—I have the honour to return your book of tracings called "Mainland Indian Reservations," and to thank you for allowing me to examine it.

The difference, however, between it and the schedule furnished to the Dominion Government by Mr. Pearse, late Surveyor-General, is so noticeable that I need not particularize.

I wish, however, to call your particular attention to the fact, that the Reservations, New Westminster, as shown in Sheet No. 7, and Similkameen (left bank), Sheet No. 7, are not Indian Reservations.

I might also mention that the land classed in your Schedule as Burrard Inlet, No. 2, Sheet No. 1, and False Creek, Sheet No. 1, are identical. There is no land answering the description of Bonaparte, No. 2, Sheet 10, existing in that section of the country. That the two pieces called Katsey, Sheets 2 and 3, are identical.

That Matsqui 1 and 2, Sheet 2, are the same land as Matsqui A and B, Sheet 3.

That Stryen is omitted in your Schedule.

That land on Yale-Lytton road between 9 and 10 mile posts, Sheet No. 8, is also scheduled as Spuzzum.

I wish also to call your attention again to the fact that land surveyed under your instructions, near English Bluff, south of the mouth of Fraser River, as the Tsowassen Reservation, is not mentioned in Mr. Pearse's schedule.

I have, &c.,
(Signed)   ROBERT BEAVEN.

The Superintendent of Indian Affairs to the Provincial Secretary.

Department of Indian Affairs,
Victoria, August 15th, 1874.

SIR,—Pursuant to the arrangement of granting 20 acres of land to every head of an Indian family in British Columbia, I had the honour of applying to the Honourable Chief Commissioner of Lands and Works for land to make up deficiency in the present reserves of Musqueam and Tsowassen. The Honourable Chief Commissioner informed me, in reply (10th August), that he is unable to advise the extention of *present* reservations until positively informed "that you are authorized "to reduce as well as increase such reservations, and that you are prepared, on be-"half of the Dominion Government, to guarantee that the Indians will agree quiet-"ly to reduction, if the Provincial Government agree to an increase."

As many of the present reserves do not contain *five* acres of land to each head of a family, the injustice with which Indians having such reserves would be treated in case they were not extended, and the serious complications which would at once be consequent upon such treatment are so great, that I sincerely trust the interpretation seemingly conveyed in the Honourable Chief Commissioner's letter, of confining the grant to new reserves, is not that intended by the Government in lieu of *all* reserves containing 20 acres to every head of a native family.

As to the reduction alluded to, according to the Order in Council I had the honour of transmitting on the 15th of May, and the reply of the Local Government, 15th of June, I imagined the Dominion Government could not claim more than the acreage agreed upon in any reserve, and therefore in cases where the quantity of land exceeded 20 acres to each Indian family, such excess would no longer be a part of any reserve, unless some special arrangement were made to the contrary.

Agreeably to such an understanding, and with a view of promoting peace among the Indians, I have been authorized, at considerable expense, to survey all reserves, with a view to allotment on the basis agreed upon ; and to promise them that this arrangement would be faithfully carried out.

Surveyors are now at work in Cowichan, and on Fraser River reserves, and were any delay to take place in granting me lands to make good deficient reserves, not only would valuable time and money be wasted, but great uneasiness among Indians would be at once engendered. I therefore trust that I may be authorized to obtain land in instances of deficiency as they arise, upon my furnishing the Government with a correct census of the number of heads of families, and the number of acres therefore required. On my part I will at once notify you of excess in any reserve which may be surveyed for allotment. This was the basis of my agreement with the Honourable the Attorney-General, and I beg to append a copy of his telegram sent in order to allow me *to promise the same to the Indians at any official visitation.*

It would be too great an undertaking on my part to guarantee quietude on the part of the Indians generally, because throughout the interior, from whence I have just returned, where Indians possess many horses and cattle, *and have no grazing lands*, they consider 20 acres to each head altogether insufficient.

I have, &c.,
(Signed) I. W. POWELL.

TELEGRAM.
Victoria, 12th June, 1874.

To Dr. Powell, Lytton.

Twenty acres to each head of Indian family granted on condition agreed; could not send sooner. Forty rejected.

(Signed) GEO. A. WALKEM.

The Provincial Secretary to the Superintendent of Indian Affairs.

Provincial Secretary's Office,
27th August, 1874.

SIR,—In reply to your letter of the 15th instant, on the subject of extending certain present Indian Reserves, I have the honour to acquaint you that the decision of the Government shall be conveyed to you at as early a date as practicable after the return of His Excellency the Lieutenant-Governor.

I have, &c.,
(Signed) JOHN ASH.

The Provincial Secretary to the Superintendent of Indian Affairs.

Provincial Secretary's Office,
2nd September, 1874.

SIR,—With reference to your letter of the 15th ultimo, on the subject of extending present Indian Reserves, in which you mention that, pursuant to the arrangement for granting 20 acres of land to every head of an Indian family in British Columbia, you had applied to the Chief Commissioner of Lands and Works for land to make up deficiencies in the present Reserves of Musqueam and Tsowassen, and that that officer had acquainted you in reply that he was unable to advise the extension of present Reservations; I have the honour to refer you to my letter of the 28th July, 1873, in which you are notified that all future Reserves for Indians will be adjusted on the basis of 20 acres of land for each head of a family of five persons, and from which you will perceive that the Chief Commissioner in reply, was only carrying out the Order in Council on which my letter was based. The question of the extension of present Reserves was not touched upon in the above Order in Council, but on the return of the Lieutenant-Governor the subject will be fully considered and the views of the Government thereon definitely conveyed to you.

With reference to your offer to furnish correct census of the number of heads of families, I have to remark that before proceeding to make any survey of Indian Reserves it would appear most desirable that you should furnish the Chief Commissioner with a correct census of the native population of the Province, or at least of the district proposed to be surveyed, the Province having been previously arranged by you into convenient districts for this purpose. Such census should convey the number of men, women, and children, and the number of heads of families should be exactly ascertained.

With regard to Reserves not yet made, it would be very desirable that before they are located you should point out if they are in a block (the requisite number of acres being therein contained), or whether it is proposed to reserve small tracts here and there in different directions. With reference to your remarks as to the quietude of the Indians, I desire to point out to you that it is incumbent on the Government of the Province to preserve peace and order equally among the natives as among the white population.

I have, &c.,

(Signed) JOHN ASH.

The Superintendent of Indian Affairs to the Provincial Secretary.

Indian Office, Victoria,
September 2nd, 1874.

SIR,—I have the honour to acknowledge the receipt of your letter of this date, in answer to mine of the 15th ult., and in reply to state that, in view of the trouble which would at once be created among the Indians should it be fully decided by the Provincial Government that the proposed quantity of twenty acres to each family is not to apply to those having claim to present Reserves, I shall anxiously await the receipt of the communication you propose to furnish me on the return of His Honour the Lieutenant-Governor.

I have, &c.,

(Signed) I. W. POWELL.

The Deputy Superintendent of Indian Affairs to the Provincial Secretary.

Indian Office, Victoria,
September 3rd, 1874.

SIR,—Mr. Mohun, surveyor to the Indian Department, has just returned from Chemainus (for orders). He informs me that several plots of land which had been surveyed and laid off as Indian Reserves, and on which the Indians have lived for a number of years and partially cultivated, are not laid down in the official maps, copies of which were lately made at the Lands and Works Office, and forwarded to him.

Would you be good enough to inform me, at your earliest convenience, if the Provincial Government ignores the various reserves, which are omitted in the schedule prepared by the Lands and Works Department (presumed to contain all existing Indian Reserves), viz., Tsowassen, Chemainus, Range VIII, part of Sections 8 and 9, and a section at Cowichan adjoining Harris' landing, with others not now named.

I enclose a letter on the foregoing subject from Mr. Mohun, to which I beg to call the attention of the Provincial Government.

(Signed) H. MOFFATT.

ENCLOSURE.

Mr. Mohun to the Superintendent of Indian Affairs.

Chemainus, 1st September, 1874.

SIR,—I have the honour to inform you that after making various surveys in Chemainus, I received from you a tracing from the official map of that District, which I find omits, doubtless through inadvertence, a reserve occupied by the Chemainus Indians, containing about eighteen or twenty acres, being part of R. VIII, S. 8 and 9, and the only one belonging to this tribe in the settlement.

I may mention for your information that this reserve was laid out by Mr. Pearse, whom I then accompanied, in 1863 : that it is well known and recognized, both by whites and Indians, and that one of the old posts marked "Indian Reserve" is still in existence.

I trust you will instruct me at your earliest convenience, as to the course to be pursued in defining—

1st. Reserves in surveyed Districts which may not be shown on the maps forwarded me from time to time, and

2nd. Those in unsurveyed Districts which are, and have been for years past, in the undisputed possession of the Indians.

I would, however, most respectfully, but earnestly, urge upon your consideration the fact that to pass without surveying these, after the promises that have been made to the Indians, will lead to most serious complications, and imperil life and property throughout the settlements.

If I have exceeded my province in making these remarks, I have done so only from a deep sense of the deplorable results likely to ensue even from a temporary postponement of the work.

          (Signed)   EDWARD MOHUN, C.E.

The Superintendent of Indian Affairs to the Provincial Secretary.

Indian Office, Victoria,
21st September, 1874.

DEAR SIR,—Referring to your letter (official) of the 27th ultimo, I should be glad to have your further reply if now convenient.

Could you, at the same time, give me an answer to Mr. Moffatt's letter (enclosing Mr. Mohun's) of Sept. 3rd.

Two parties of surveyors are now out, and as their future continuance in their present service greatly depends upon the nature of your letter, you will pardon my wish to obtain it as soon as possible.

          (Signed)   I. W. POWELL.

The Provincial Secretary to the Superintendent of Indian Affairs.

Provincial Secretary's Office,
September 21st, 1874.

SIR,—With reference to the application from your Department on the subject of the extension of certain existing Indian Reservations, I have the honour to acquaint you that the information respecting Indian affairs, for which you have been asked by the Honourable Chief Commissioner of Lands and Works must be given before an answer can be returned by the Government.

I have, &c.,

          (Signed)   JOHN ASH.

The Superintendent of Indian Affairs to the Provincial Secretary.

Indian Office, Victoria,
September 28th, 1874.

SIR,—Referring to your letters of the 2nd and 21st September, I have the honour to state for the information of the Government, that I have called in the two survey parties who have been engaged in surveying Reserves here and on the mainland. I also regret to state that I have not a doubt of the dissatisfaction of the Indians which will follow delay in adjusting all Reserves upon the basis (I thought previous to your letter of the 2nd inst.) mutually understood and agreed upon; to avoid which, and to put an end to all disputes between Indians and white settlers, these surveys, for the purpose of allotting to each Indian twenty acres of land, have been undertaken by the Dominion Government.

In respect to your letter of the 21st inst., I should be glad to furnish any information in my power to the Chief Commissioner of Lands and Works, in addition to that fully conveyed in my letter to him on the 7th ultimo, although I am at a loss to understand any connection "information" therein alluded to may have with the enquiries contained in my letter of the 15th ult., and the enclosure of Mr. Moffatt to yourself of the 3rd instant.

I regarded the manner of taking the census, etc., as a mere question of detail ; and as I informed the Chief Commissioner, in my personal conference with him, I should be glad to have it subscribed to as correct, under oath, or taken in any way satisfactory to the Government : my great desire being to settle these land questions for the Indians with the least possible delay, and put an end to anxiety which I know exists among white settlers of the interior, on account of anticipated troubles with Indians who are dissatisfied with their present Reserves.

I have, etc.,
(Signed) I. W. POWELL.

The Provincial Secretary to the Superintendent of Indian Affairs.
Provincial Secretary's Office,
28th September, 1874.

SIR,—In reply to your letter of the 15th ultimo, on the subject of the interpretation to be given to the Order in Council regulating the extent of the Reservations to be made wherever necessary throughout the Province for Indian purposes, I have now the honour to state that the said order was not intended to affect or unsettle Reservations already established, but that its operation is altogether confined to the cases in which, at the time of Confederation, aboriginal tribes or communities were not provided with lands set apart for their separate and exclusive use.

I am, however, authorized to state that the Government will consider any special claim made by you on behalf of an Indian community, where it can be shown to the satisfaction of the Chief Commissioner of Lands and Works that the circumstances warrant a departure from the general principle laid down in the said Order in Council. I have, &c.,

(Signed) JOHN ASH.

P. S.—I take this opportunity of calling your attention to the fact that the acknowledgment made by you in previous correspondence, that existing Indian Reserves do not in some cases allow of 20 acres of land being allotted to each head of a family, is a proof that the Provincial Government in agreeing to furnish 20 acres in future, has been more liberal than it was called upon to be by the Terms of Union, which stipulate that tracts of land of such extent as it has hitherto been the practice of the British Columbia Government to appropriate for that purpose, shall from time to time be conveyed by the Local Government to the Dominion Government in trust, for the use and benefit of the Indians, on application of the Dominion Government. (Initialed) J. A.

The Superintendent of Indian Affairs to the Provincial Secretary.
Indian Office, Victoria,
September 28th, 1874.

SIR,—I have the honour to enclose an application from David Salacalton (a christianized Indian of Chilliwhack), to be allowed to pre-empt land. Also a paper signed by a number of well-known settlers endorsing the said application. I beg to add, that this Indian has been employed by me as a servant, and I have pleasure in commending his petition to the favourable consideration of His Honour the Lieut.-Governor in Council.

(Signed) I. W. POWELL.

The Provincial Secretary to the Superintendent of Indian Affairs.

Provincial Secretary's Office,
8th October, 1874.

SIR,—In reply to your letter of the 7th instant, I have the honour to acquaint you that agreeably to your suggestion the Governor-General's proclamation exempting the Indians of British Columbia from the operation of the 8th Section of Cap. 21, 1874, will be published in the next issue of the Government *Gazette*.

I have, &c.,
(Signed) JOHN ASH.

Mr. Lenihan to the Provincial Secretary.

Victoria, British Columbia,
October 8th, 1874.

SIR,—I have the honour to enclose herewith, for the consideration of His Honour the Lieutenant-Governor in Council, the copy of a letter of the Reverend Father Grandidier, of Okanagan Mission in this Province, on the subject of Indian affairs, and addressed to the Editor of the *Victoria Standard*, also the copy of a letter of the Right Rev. Bishop D. Herbonez of British Columbia, to myself, referring to the same.

I consider the subject of these documents one of such vital importance as to call for immediate and careful consideration from the Provincial Government, emanating as they do from two gentlemen of such eminence, whose positions afford them the greatest possible facilities for acquiring the most thorough and correct knowledge of the subject upon which they write. The information possessed by those gentlemen is derived from a long and close intercourse with the Indians of this Province, which entitles them to speak in their behalf, and I feel assured their views will receive at the hands of the Government that careful attention which the importance of the subject demands.

I believe the Government will agree with me in the opinion that the cause of the Indians is very fully, justly, and ably stated by the Rev. Father Grandidier. The arguments adduced by the Rev. gentleman appear to me so convincing, that I cannot conceive how the Government can hesitate for a moment in conceding to the Indians demands so just and reasonable.

It is needless for me to inform the Government of British Columbia of the deep and earnest solicitude with which the Dominion Government regard all that concerns the well-being and happiness of our Indian fellow-subjects. I may, however, be permitted to state for the information of the Provincial Government, that the Dominion Government stands ready to render every assistance in its power to improve the material and social condition of the Indians of this Province, relying with the fullest confidence upon receiving the cordial and hearty assistance and co-operation of the Government of British Columbia in the furtherance of these very important interests.

No doubt the Government is aware that liberal grants were voted at the last session of the Dominion Parliament, to assist and encourage the Indians of this Province to engage in agricultural pursuits, as also for the promotion of the education of Indian children. I have reason to know that these grants will be still further augmented in future, as the requirements of the Indians may demand.

It is a source of just pride and congratulation to every true and loyal subject of our beloved Sovereign Queen Victoria to be able to point to the success which has crowned Her wise and benignant rule of Her Indian subjects.

As the humble servant, and in the name, of the Dominion of Canada, I appeal with confidence to the wisdom, the liberality, and patriotism of the Government of British Columbia to deal with this grave question in such a manner as will hereafter redound to its honour and shed fresh glory and lustre on the British Crown.

His Honour the Lieutenant-Governor is aware of the authority under which I write. I trust it may be sufficient to entitle me to the privilege of addressing the Government of British Columbia.

I have, &c.,
(Signed) JAMES LENIHAN.

ENCLOSURE No. 1.

St. MARY'S, September 24th, 1874.

To Mr. James Lenihan. Indian Commissioner, Victoria, B. C.

DEAR SIR,—I send to the editor of the *Standard* a letter from the Rev. Father Grandidier, wherein you can see that dissatisfaction amongst the Indians of the Upper Country about their land is far from abating. Bad feelings amongst them are increasing so much that I really fear we may have soon serious troubles. They do not speak to their missionaries about their warlike intention, because they know very well that we are against war, yet their frequent meetings, councils of chiefs, and messengers, induce many of our missionaries to believe that there may be some plotting going on. For myself, I am inclined to believe that it is time to take some steps in order to satisfy the Indians, as more delay would very probably expose the Province to a disastrous war. I find myself in duty bound to write these few lines to you.

I have, &c.,
(Signed) † LOUIS O. M. J.,
Bishop of Miletopolis, N. A. of British Columbia.

ENCLOSURE No. 2.

Okanagan Mission,
August 28th, 1874.

To the Editor of the Victoria Standard:—

SIR,—In your issue of the 12th instant you have an article entitled "An Indian War," which has called my especial attention. In it you attribute with correctness the never ceasing strife between the white and the Indian on the American side to the iniquitous treatment inflicted upon the latter. Your reflections have forciby drawn mine to our native tribes, and to their present dissatisfaction about their lands, which dissatisfaction has not abated, for the visit of Colonel Powell, Indian Commissioner, has not had all the results which were anticipated from it.

At Kamloops the Shuswap Indians gathered to welcome him, expecting that their grievance would be redressed. They exposed to him their needs, their earnest and unanimous wish to have more land. By the improvements which they had already accomplished on their reservations, without help from anybody, by their sole efforts, and by the census of their cattle, they showed him that theirs was no idle wish.

The Commissioner was pleased with them and gave substantial proofs of his interest, for which they feel very grateful; but for the land question it was out of his power to settle it according to their wish.

When the Dominion Government took charge of the Indian tribes of British Columbia it was proposed to adopt the same policy towards them as towards their brothers of the other Provinces, and grant each family a large quantity of land. To this proposition the Local Government objected, and would not grant more than twenty (20) acres. Is it just and expedient for the Government to grant the natives as small a portion of land as possible? None will think so.

Before the settlement of this Province the natives were in possession of it. There was no one to restrain them in that possession. Their horses had wide pasture lands to feed upon. The whites came, took land, fenced it, and little by little hemmed the Indians in their small reservations. They leased the land that they did not buy and drove the cattle of the Indians from their own pasture land. Many of these reservations have been surveyed without their consent, and sometimes without having received notice of it, so that they could not expose their needs and their wishes. Their reservations have been repeatedly cut off smaller for the benefit of the whites, and the best and most useful part of them taken away till some tribes are corralled on a small piece of land, as at Canoe Creek or elsewhere, or even have not an inch of ground, as at

10

Williams Lake. The natives have protested against those spoliations, from the beginning. They have complained bitterly of that treatment, but they have not obtained any redress.

Is that treatment according to the dictates of Justice? Who will wonder at the dissatisfaction that has been growing amongst the Indians? The land was theirs and their forefathers before the whites came; that land has been wrenched from them in virtue of might, not right; not a cent has been given them to extinguish their title to the land. They have been left to struggle on the parcel of land allotted them without any encouragement, any help, any agricultural implements from any quarter, and, because they are forbearing and peacefully disposed, they are to be granted the minimum possible of land.

I appeal to every impartial mind, is that treatment according to Justice? And are not the natives justified in now claiming their rights? Reverse the case, and place the whites in the place of the Indians, which white settler would bear with it? And it is not correct to say that no injustice has been done to the Indians in taking away their land because they did not cultivate it. For they were the owners of the land, and the title to a property is not rendered valueless because the property is left to decay. Our American neighbours have recognized that title, since they have passed a treaty with all the tribes whose land they come to occupy. Whether they fulfilled that treaty or not is not the question; but they recognize the Indian title to the land, although those lands were in the same condition then as it was here when the whites came. Besides their lands were valuable to the Indians for hunting, and now the game is receding far away before the whites. It was valuable to them for their horses, and now their horses and cattle have no ground to feed upon, and would starve in some places were it not for the forbearance of some white settlers.

In former times the Indians did not cultivate land; now, taught by the example of the whites, they see its value. They are not unwilling to let the whites have the greater and the best portion of it, but not the whole or nearly so. Children and owners of the soil, they want a sufficient share of it to get a living from it. They do not think that when a white man can pre-empt 320 acres and buy as much more, besides the facility of leasing more, that they are unreasonable in asking 80 acres of their own land per family; and in that they are supported by the example of the Dominion Government's conduct towards the other Indians, if they claim that it is to use it. And already on their reservations, or most of them, they carry on farming as far as their limited means and knowledge permit it. Both will improve in time, as the already effected improvement is a convincing proof. They must not be judged according to what they have been in past times, but according to what they are, and promise to be, useful and industrious men. It is better for every settler to have the Indians fixed contentedly on farms than wandering discontentedly, and looking with anxious eyes on the fat of the land which they are not allowed to share.

Then it is but just to deal fairly by them, and lay for their use reservations amply sufficient for their future wants. For the reservations which are to be laid over are to be permanent for many generations.

But will not twenty acres be sufficient for each family? What is the purpose of the Government? To civilize and make useful men of them. The first step to do it is to reclaim them from their wandering life and attach them by bonds of interest to the soil.

But if the Indian leaves off his ordinary pursuits of life he expects to find a better compensation in the new means adopted by him to earn the livelihood of his family and his own. Will he find it in a tract of twenty acres? Will those twenty acres be all good cultivated land easy of irrigation? Probably not. Supposing them however to be so, how can he get from them a comfortable living for his family?

Actually the Indian cannot live as he used to formerly; his contact with the whites has created for him new and imperious needs which must be satisfied, in the way of clothing and food. Besides his family he will have to find enough of food on his twenty acres to keep his horses and cattle. Having no natural meadows whereon to cut hay, he will have to sow grass on a large piece of his twenty acres, for already the Indian begins to raise cattle, and the census taken last Spring shows 436 heads of horned cattle and about 1,300 horses between seven tribes, and they are only beginning. What will it amount to in ten or twenty years if they have land enough to feed them? Having set aside the part for hay they will cultivate the cultivable balance of their twenty acres; after a few years that land being light soil will require manure, but where will the Indian find it? Where are they to keep their horses and cattle to save manure? How many heads can they keep on twenty acres summer and winter, after the needs of their families have been attended to? Then what can they do with their exhausted land, without means of fertilizing it, and without any more of it to sow, while the old piece is left to rest? If a white man can scarcely eke out a living with his 320 acres how can an Indian do it with 20? They will have twenty (20) acres while the present head of the family lives, but at his death, his sons dividing his inheritance, will have ten or even five acres for their lot. Are such prospects attractive enough to lead the Indians to leave off their wanderings and turn all their energies to cultivate the soil?

Is it possible to beleive that the Indians can, any more than anybody else, live with their families out of the produce of 20 acres, keep horses and cattle there and meet all expenses? Besides, a good part of the reservation, with a few exceptions, is either overflooded in summer, or parched for want of water which cannot be brought there, covered with timber, or strewn with rocks, as any visitor may convince himself.

Out of 320 acres a man may pick out the best spot to cultivate and make a living; out of twenty acres it is impossible; which white family would like to try it? And still they have more means and knowledge at their command than the Indians.

If the Government be sincere in its intention of civilizing the Indians, let sufficient land be alloted to them; as it is at present it is either too much or far too little; too much if the Government does not want them to cultivate their farms and live from the produce, too little by far if it does.

The question is too important for the welfare of the country to stop at half measures. But those who want to cultivate on a large scale can pre-empt land as any other man, after they have obtained a special authorization from the Governor. That permission may be refused, and would be if many applications were sent, for that special permission is required against Indian pre-emption, and it is not the Government policy to let Indians pre-empt. Besides, suppose the permission granted, how can an Indian who has nothing, no provisions, no money, no implements of agriculture, remain for ten months on his claim with his family? When he leaves he cannot engage a white man, another Indian cannot take his place, so that in his absence to procure food for his family his land may be jumped.

Pre-emption is but a nominal right to the Indian for whom it was not intended, and whose condition does not allow him to fulfil the provisions of the law.

The natives are now quite awake to the necessity of following the example of the whites. They look into the future with fear for themselves and their children if they do not do so; they want reasonable means for doing it, and consequently demand 80 acres of a farm for each head of a family, and extensive mountain pasture for their cattle, so as to allow them to increase their number every year and improve their own condition. This they have asked from the Indian Commissioner; they are anxious to obtain no money, nor any other compensation will they accept in its stead.

The Indians of this country, as a people, are honest, peaceful, law-abiding, and well disposed towards the whites; none can complain that they have done him any harm. On the contrary, they are industrious and of great service to the whites. Let not their good qualities be turned against their interests, but be one reason the more to secure to them the means of becoming useful members of society. If they obtain the right which they claim, the good feeling that reigns between them and the whites shall be strengthened for ever. The settlers need not entertain any fear of them; we shall never see in our midst the heart-rending scenes which desolate so many homes amongst our neighbours; and the comparison which you draw to the advantage of our Government and of its just treatment of the natives will remain an undisputed truth.

But if the Indians are persistently refused their demands, if they are deprived of their fathers' land without any hope of redress from the proper authorities, their dissatisfactions will increase, meetings shall be held again, as it has been about their grievances, until they come to an understanding, the end of which I am afraid to foresee. We may have very serious disturbances, which it might be impossible to suppress except at the cost of human life and large expenditure of money, as our past experience has taught us with the Chilcotin Indians; and those were only a handful of men, whilst the present dissatisfaction pervades all the tribes living amongst the whites.

I beg to apologize for the length of this communication, but the matter is too important for me to keep silent. If it is my duty to teach the Indian to keep the commandments of God, and obey the just laws of man, it is no less my obligation to spare no effort in order that justice be done to them, and that peace and security be preserved in my adopted country.

Believe me to remain, etc.,
(Signed)   C. J. GRANDIDIER.

The Provincial-Secretary to Mr. Lenihan.
Provincial Secretary's Office,
12th October, 1874.

SIR,—I have the honour to acknowledge the receipt of your communication of the 8th instant, covering copies of a letter from the Rev. Father Grandidier to the Editor of the *Standard*, and of a letter from the Right Rev. Bishop D. Herbonez to yourself, on the subject of Indian Affairs in the Province of British Columbia, and with reference thereto to acquaint you that the same will be brought under the consideration of the Lieutenant-Governor in Council at the earliest opportunity.

In the meantime I desire to call your attention to the fact that all that it is "reasonable and just" to demand of the Provincial Government is that the 13th Section of the Terms of Union should be faithfully observed. Should the Dominion Government be of opinion that concessions beyond those provided for in the said section are necessary, it becomes the duty of that Government to make provisions accordingly.

I have, &c.,
(Signed)   JOHN ASH.

Mr. Lenihan to the Provincial Secretary.
Victoria, B. C.,
October 15th, 1874.

SIR,—I have the honour to acknowledge the receipt of your communication of the 12th inst., acknowledging mine of the 8th inst., and saying "the same will be brought under the consideration of the Lieutenant-Governor in Council at the earliest opportunity."

You are also pleased to say, "In the meantime I desire to call your attention " to the fact that all that is 'reasonable and just' to demand from the Provincial " Government is, that the 13th Section of the Terms of Union Act should be faithfully observed."

The Section referred to sets forth—" That the charge of the Indians, and the " Trusteeship and management of the lands reserved for their use and benefit, shall " be assumed by the Dominion Government, and a policy as liberal as that hitherto " pursued by the British Columbia Government shall be continued by the Dominion " Government after the Union.

" To carry out such policy, tracts of land of such extent as it has hitherto been " the practice of the British Columbia Government to appropriate for that purpose, " shall, from time to time, be conveyed by the Local Government to the Dominion " Government, in trust, for the use and benefit of the Indians on application of the " Dominion Government, and in case of disagreement between the two Governments respecting the quantity of such tracts of lands to be so granted, the matter " shall be referred for the decision of the Secretary of State for the Colonies."

A careful reading of this section, taken and considered in connection with all the other sections of the Terms of Union Act, and taking into account the very liberal provisions and stipulations of the same in favour of British Columbia, leads me to the conviction that the most liberal and enlightened interpretation should be given to the spirit and meaning of this particular section.

Permit me to ask, has this been done by the Government of British Columbia? and to what extent has it been "faithfully observed?"

It may also be well to enquire as to the "policy and practice" which has hitherto been observed by the Provincial Government on the question of Indian Reserves. Has it been well defined, regular, and uniform? By reference to the Report of the Superintendent of Indian Affairs for British Columbia for 1872 and 1873, page 20, and from which I extract three consecutive items, contained in the schedule of Indian Reserves by way of example. I find that the "Popcum" tribe, on the Fraser River, has a reservation of 369 acres, and I am credibly informed that there are only four (4) families upon this reserve, which gives an average of ninety-two acres to each family of good land.

Then there is the Chamiel tribe, in the same vicinity, having 448 acres, and my informant gives the number of families upon the reserve as twenty (20), which gives an average of twenty-four acres to each family. Again, there is the Cheam tribe, less fortunate than the other two named, having 375 acres for twenty-seven families, or an average of fourteen acres for each family.

Thus it is quite evident the "policy and practice which has hitherto been observed" has been neither well defined, uniform, or regular. The first named tribe having a maximum quantity of ninety-two acres of good land to each family, and the last mentioned tribe with a minimum of fourteen acres of poor land for each family; but putting the three tribes above mentioned together we find they have an average of twenty-four acres to each family, all situated upon the banks of the Fraser River, and where few or no cattle are kept, while the Government adhere strictly to a uniform "policy" of allowing only twenty acres to each head of an Indian family, and this too, in many cases, of the very worst quality, and for the Indians of the Mainland, many of whom have a large number of horses and cattle.

Therefore, in view of these facts, I most respectfully submit that a more liberal, well defined, and uniform "policy" should be adopted by the Government of British Columbia on the question of Indian Reserves, and more especially towards those Indians of the interior of the Mainland having a large number of horses and cattle, and with whom it appears no treaty has yet been made to extinguish the titles to their lands, which justice and equity should secure to them as the original owners and occupants of the soil.

In making this request I do not ask the maximum quantity and quality of land as given to the Popcum tribe (ninety-two acres to each family), but only that the Government may be pleased to grant, reserve, and set aside a sufficient quantity of the public lands of the Province, of good average quality, free from rocks and swamps, to secure to each head of an Indian family at least eighty acres of good average quality, together with continuing to him the right of pre-emption as under the existing laws and regulations; and that such reservations may be made, as far as possible, adjacent to and in connection with the present village sites, reservations, and favourite haunts of the Indians.

That, in addition to the limit of eighty (80) acres to each family, those having large herds of cattle and horses should receive sufficient land, over and above such limit, to answer their requirements, in consequence of being the owners of such horses and cattle.

While discussing this subject it may not be altogether out of place to remind the Government of British Columbia of the great advantage accruing to the Province by virtue of her Indian population, which will appear more clearly upon reference to Sections 2 and 3 of the Terms of Union Act, whereby she receives a handsome annuity from the Dominion Government anent her Indian population, which, in addition to the great advantages of the Indians as producers and consumers, and the assistance which they render in the development of the resources of the Province—if no higher view is to be taken of the question—claims for the Indians at the hands of the Government of British Columbia very great consideration.

Again, there is the large sum which the Dominion pays to the Province annually, over and above any revenue which she receives therefrom, should entitle her to ask that the Government of British Columbia should put the largest possible construction upon the spirit and meaning of the section of the Terms of Union Act to which you have done me the honour to call my attention.

In conclusion I would again most respectfully urge upon the Government of British Columbia, and on behalf of the Dominion Government, the wisdom and justice of at once laying aside for the use and benefit of the Indians of the Province, a sufficient quantity of the public lands as aforesaid, to convince them that their interests shall be scrupulously guarded, and thereby secure their loyalty and good will, and avert any danger to the peace of the Province or the lives and property of our white fellow citizens.

I have, &c.,
(Signed)) JAMES LENIHAN.

The Chief Commissioner of Lands and Works to the Superintendent of Indian Affairs.

Lands and Works Department,
Victoria, November 12th, 1874.

SIR,—I have the honour to enclose for your information, a copy of a letter received by this department from Mr. A. Dods, of Cowichan District, V. I., with reference to certain existing difficulties between that gentleman and the Indians in his immediate vicinity.

I have, &c.,
(Signed ROBERT BEAVEN.

ENCLOSURE.

Mr. Dods to the Chief Commissioner of Lands and Works.

Cowichan, Nov. 5th, 1874.

SIR,—You are aware that I have had considerable trouble with the Indians about my land. Yesterday was appointed for the trial of one for trespass; he disregarded the summons and a warrant was issued for his arrest. The constable, however, could not take him. The Indian defied him with a bayonet on a pole, surrounded by a lot of his friends. A number of men from the road party were called, and also neighbours, but they could not arrest him.

I would not now, by any means, write about it as I consider it is out of my hands, but that the Indian sent to me to say that if I would pay him he would go off. I told him that he must talk to Mr. Morley, but that I would send a paper to see what you would do.

The difficulty on the Indians' part could now, I feel assured, be settled by a sum of 100 or 150 dollars, and being reduced to a matter of dollars, is comparatively easily settled.

Dr. Powell expressed a willingness, when up here, to either pay the old man who has made all the bother or to pension him off on some small sum.

Will you please let me know what you can do, that I may stay proceedings if possible, as it would, of course, be to my own interest, as well as that of the Government, to settle with the Indians amicably.

I am, &c.,
(Signed) ARCH.'D DODS.

The Under Secretary of State to the Lieutenant-Governor.

Ottawa, 14th November, 1874.

SIR,—I have the honour to transmit to you an Order of His Excellency the Governor-General in Council, and of the Memorandum of the Honourable the Minister of the Interior therein referred to, on the subject of the Land question in British Columbia.

I am directed to request that you will have the goodness to bring the important subject to which these documents relate under the early consideration of your Government.

I have, etc.,
(Signed)   E. J. LANGEVIN.

ENCLOSURE No. 1.

Copy of a Report of a Committee of the Honourable the Privy Council, approved by His Excellency the Governor-General, on the 4th November, 1874.

The Committee of the Privy Council have given their attentive consideration to the Memorandum of the Honourable the Minister of the Interior, in reference to the unsatisfactory state of the Indian Land question in the Province of British Columbia, and they respectfully report their entire concurrence in the views and recommendations submitted therein, and advise that a copy of this Minute, when approved by Your Excellency, and of the annexed Memorandum, be transmitted to the Lieutenant-Governor of British Columbia, in the hope that the views entertained by the Dominion Government on this important question, as embodied in the said Memorial, may meet with an early and favourable consideration at the hands of the Government of British Columbia.

They further advise, that a copy of this Minute and annexed Memorandum be transmitted by Your Excellency to the Right Honourable Her Majesty's Secretary of State for the Colonies, accompanied by copies of such of the other documents submitted as the Honourable the Minister of the Interior may think necessary, to enable Lord Carnarvon to understand, in all its bearings, the great national question now seeking solution at the hands of the Dominion and British Columbia Governments.   (Certified)   W. A. HIMSWORTH,

Clerk Privy Council.

ENCLOSURE No. 2.

DEPARTMENT OF THE INTERIOR, OTTAWA,
November 2nd, 1874.

MEMO.

The undersigned is desirous of bringing under the consideration of the Governor-General in Council, the present unsatisfactory state of the Indian Land question in the Province of British Columbia.

In connection with this subject, he has had before him various reports and official documents, among others, a voluminous correspondence of Mr. Indian Commissioner Powell with the Local Government of British Columbia, in reference to the Order in Council of the 24th April last, respecting the Indian Reserves; also, the same Commissioner's report of a visit made by him to the Indian tribes in the interior of British Columbia during the past Summer; and lastly, an able and interesting communication from the Rev. C. J. Grandidier (a Roman Catholic missionary, residing among the Indians in the Interior) published in the *Standard* newspaper, Victoria, with letters from both the Indian Commissioners and from the Roman Catholic Bishop of British Columbia, commenting on Father Grandidier's communication; all of which reports and letters are herewith submitted.

A cursory glance at these documents, is enough to show that the present state of the Indian Land question in our Territory West of the Rocky Mountains, is most unsatisfactory, and that it is the occasion, not only of great discontent among the aboriginal tribes but also of serious alarm to the white settlers.

To the Indian, the land question far transcends in importance all others, and its satisfactory adjustment in British Columbia will be the first step towards allaying the wide-spread and growing discontent now existing among the native tribes of that Province.

The adjustment of this important matter is not a little complicated, from the fact that its solution requires the joint action of the Dominion Government and the Government of British Columbia, and involves a possible reference to the Secretary of State for the Colonies.

The policy heretofore pursued by the Local Government of British Columbia toward the red men in that Province, and the recently expressed views of that Government in the correspondence herewith submitted, fall far short of the estimate entertained by the Dominion Government of the reasonable claims of the Indians.

In the very last official communication, under date of the 12th ultimo, received through Mr. Commissioner Lenihan, the Provincial Secretary of British Columbia writes as follows:—

"In the meantime I desire to call your attention to the fact that all that is *reasonable* "and *just* to demand of the Provincial Government is that the 13th Section of the Terms "of Union should be faithfully observed. Should the Dominion Government be of opinion "that concessions beyond those provided for in the said Section are necessary, it becomes "the duty of that Government to make provision accordingly."

To explain the relative position of the Dominion and Local Governments in relation to this question, it is necessary to remember:—

That, under the operation of the 109th and 146th Sections of the "British North America Act of 1867," all the public lands of the Province of British Columbia are placed under the control of the Local Government;

That, by the 13th Article of the Terms of admission of British Columbia into Confederation, it is provided,—

"That the charge of the Indians, and the trusteeship and management of the lands "reserved for their use and benefit, should be assumed by the *Dominion Government*, and "a policy *as liberal as that hitherto pursued* by the British Columbia Government, should "be continued by the Dominion Government after the Union."

And it is further provided,—

"To carry out such policy, tracts of land of such extent as it has hitherto been the "practice of the British Columbia Government to appropriate for that purpose, shall from "time to time be conveyed from the Local to the Dominion Government, in trust for the "use and benefit of the Indians, on application of the Dominion Government; and in case "of disagreement between the two Governments, respecting the quantity of such tracts "of land to be granted, the matter shall be referred for the decision of the Secretary of "State for the Colonies."

When the framers of the Terms of admission of British Columbia into the Union inserted this provision, requiring the Dominion Government to pursue a policy *as liberal* towards the Indians as that hitherto pursued by the British Columbia Government, they could hardly have been aware of the marked contrast between the Indian policies which had, up to that time, prevailed in Canada and British Columbia respectively.

Whereas in British Columbia, ten acres of land was the maximum allowance for a family of five persons, in old Canada the minimum allowance for such a family was eighty acres: and a similar contrast obtained in regard to grants for education and all other matters connected with Indians under the respective Governments. Read by this light, the insertion of a clause guaranteeing the aborigines of British Columbia the continuance by the Dominion Government of the liberal policy heretofore pursued by the Local Government, seems little short of a mockery of their claims.

The first step taken by the Government of the Dominion in dealing with this subject, was the passing of an Order in Council, of the 21st March, 1873, recommending that eighty acres of land should be assigned by the Local Government of British Columbia to every Indian family of five persons.

To this recommendation (made in accordance with the general policy heretofore pursued in Old Canada in such matters, but without taking into consideration the bearing of the 13th Clause already referred to, securing a liberal policy for the Indians of British Columbia) the Government of that Province peremptorily declined to accede, alleging that the quantity of land which the Order in Council proposed to assign to the Indians was greatly in excess of what was found to be sufficient by previous local Governments, and the Indian Commissioner was notified that the Government of British Columbia had decided that the land reserved for the Indians should not exceed twenty acres for each head of a family of five persons.

Even this allowance of twenty acres for each head of a family, inadequate as it would have been considered by the Indians, has, by the interpretation lately put by the local authorities on their Order in Council granting it, been very materially reduced. They now hold that that Order in Council was intended to apply to new reserves only and not to the old reserves existing at the time of Union. Such, with the exception of the latter interpretation, was the position of the Indian land question in British Columbia when the duty of administering Indian affairs devolved upon the undersigned in his capacity of Minister of the Interior.

His first step in connection with the subject was to submit a memorandum to Council setting forth the facts of the case and recommending, as under the circumstances was inevitable, that the Order in Council of the 21st March, 1873, assigning eighty acres to each Indian family be rescinded, and that only twenty acres be allowed to each family, but also recommending, *inter alia*, that the Local Government should be invited to reconsider their Indian land policy with a view to co-operate in every way with the Government of the Dominion in satisfying the reasonable demands of the native tribes West of the Rocky Mountains.

This memorandum was approved by the Governor-General in Council on 24th April last.

Mr. Indian Commissioner Powell duly submitted this Order in Council to the British Columbia Government, accompanied by such arguments as he could use in favour of the adoption by that Government of a more liberal land policy toward the Indians.

The British Columbia Government, however, appear to be resolved to adhere to their determination not to go beyond the grant of twenty acres to each Indian family, and even that allowance, as already observed, is authoritively declared to be intended not "to affect or unsettle reservations before established, but is confined to the cases in which, "at the time of Confederation, the original tribes were not provided with land set apart "for their exclusive use."

The Indian Commissioner on being officially notified of the views of the Local Government, felt reluctantly obliged to arrest the surveys of the Indian Reserves in the Province—surveys which had been authorized by him, and which were then being proceeded with, on the understanding (sanctioned, as he believed, by the Local Government) that 20 acres of land were to be allowed to each Indian family, whether on the old reserves or otherwise.

This suspension of the surveys, though under other circumstances a necessary step, is calculated to aggravate the discontent and alarm of the Indians in reference to their treatment by the Government, and will, in a great measure, help to keep open the long pending dispute between the white settlers and the Indians in reference to their respective land claims; disputes which, in the summer of 1873, nearly led to an outbreak of the Indian population of the Province, and to the recurrence of which it was hoped these surveys would put an end.

How universal, deep-seated, and intense, the feeling of discontent among the Indians of British Columbia was, previous even to the last decision of the Local Government limiting the 20 acre grant, is unmistakably apparent in Mr. Commissioner Powell's Report of his visit to the native tribes last summer, and in the letters of the Roman Catholic Bishop of the Province, and Father Grandidier.

In this connection Mr. Commissioner Powell does not hesitate to write that—

"If there has not been an Indian War, it is not because there has been no injustice "to the Indians, but because the Indians have not been sufficiently united."

These gloomy anticipations are shared, not only by both the Indian Commissioners, but also by the white settlers generally in the Province, and are expressed still more strongly, if possible, in the communication already alluded to, of Father Grandidier and the Roman Catholic Bishop of the Province.

All concur in the opinion that, until the land grievances of which the Indians complain are satisfactorily redressed, no treatment, however liberal or humane in the way of money grants or presents, will avail to secure peace or contentment among them. As an evidence of the strength of this feeling of dissatisfaction, Commissioner Powell states that the Indian bands at Nicola and Okanagan Lakes wholly declined to accept any presents from him last summer, lest, by so doing, they should be thought to waive their claim for compensation for the injustice done them in relation to the Land Grants.

The views of the Roman Catholic Bishop and of Father Grandidier entirely accord, as we have said, with those of the Commissioners; and the opinions of those Reverend gentlemen are, it is thought, worthy of special consideration, from the fact that they speak with a thorough knowledge of the subject, acquired by a long residence among the Indians, and close and habitual intercourse with them.

The other principal land grievances of which the Indians complain, besides that of the insufficient quantity allowed them, as already referred to, may be briefly stated under two heads:—

1st. They complain that, in many instances, the lands which they had settled upon and cultivated have been taken from them without compensation, and *pre-empted* by the white settlers, and that in some cases their burial grounds have been thus pre-empted.

2nd. They complain that in consequence of the present state of the law in reference to pastoral land, their cattle and horses are systematically driven away from the open country by the white settlers who have taken leases of pastoral land in the neighbourhood.

All these several grievances have been, for many years past, the subjects of complaint among the Indians. But during the last two or three years they have assumed a more serious aspect than heretofore; partly from the fact that the Indians are now, for the first time, feeling practically the inconvenience of being hemmed in by the white settlers, and prevented from using the land for pastoral purposes; partly because the Indians are only now beginning to understand the value of agriculture and to desire the possession of land for cultivation; and partly, it may be, because they have been recently made aware of the liberal land policy extended to the Indians of North-West in recent Treaties, and naturally contrast this treatment with the policy meted out to themselves.

The Indians of British Columbia, especially those in the Interior of the Province, are intelligent and industrious, and likely to turn to good account any farming lands which may be assigned to them. Moreover they already own large herds of horses and cattle, and a liberal allowance of pastoral land is to them a matter of absolute necessity, to enable them to support their stock.

The undersigned feels that the Government of the Dominion cannot be charged with want of liberality in its dealing with the Indians of British Columbia since the admission of that Province into the Union. During the last two years the sum of $54,000 has been voted by Parliament for their benefit: and before the expiration of the current financial year, the whole of that large sum will probably have been expended, either in supporting Indian Schools, making surveys, distributing agricultural implements and seed, or for other objects calculated to promote their material and moral well-being.

When it is stated that prior to the admission of British Columbia into the Union, the entire annual expenditure of the Local Government on the Indians, did not exceed, at most a few hundred dollars; that as Mr. Commissioner Powell states:—

"Money payments by the Government, on account of the Native Race, have been "restricted to expenditure incurred by Indian outrages; and no efforts have been put "forth with a view to civilize them; it having been considered that the best mode of "treating them was to let them alone."

It cannot be alleged that, in this respect, the Government of the Dominion has failed on its part, to continue towards the Indians of that Province a policy as liberal as that previously pursued by the British Columbia Government.

In laying the foundation of an Indian policy in that Province, on the same permanent and satisfactory basis as in the other portions of the Dominion, the Government of the Dominion feel they would not be justified in limiting their efforts to what, under the strict letter of the Terms of Union, they were called upon to do. They feel that a great national question like this, a question involving possibly in the near future an Indian War with all its horrors, should be approached in a very different spirit, and dealt with upon other and higher grounds. Actuated by these feelings, the Government of the Dominion in its dealings with the Indians of British Columbia, has acted, as has been shewn, in a spirit of liberality far beyond what the strict terms of the agreement required at its hands; and they confidently trust that on a calm review of the whole subject in all its important bearings, the Government of that Province will be prepared to meet them in a spirit of equal liberality.

The policy foreshadowed in the provisions of the 13th Clause of the British Columbia Terms of Union is plainly altogether inadequate to satisfy the fair and reasonable demands of the Indians.

To satisfy these demands, and to secure the good-will of the natives, the Dominion and Local Governments must look beyond the terms of that agreement, and be governed in their conduct towards the aborigines by the justice of their claims, and by the necessities of the case.

The undersigned would, therefore, respectfully recommend, that the Government of the Dominion should make an earnest appeal to the Government of British Columbia, if they value the peace and prosperity of their Province,—if they desire that Canada as a whole should retain the high character she has earned for herself by her just and honourable treatment of the red men of the forest, to reconsider in a spirit of wisdom and patriotism the land grievances of which the Indians of that Province complain, apparently with good reason, and take such measures as may be necessary promptly and effectually to redress them.

In conclusion, the undersigned would recommend that, should the views submitted in this Memorandum be approved by the Governor-General in Council, a copy of the Order in Council passed in the case, with a copy of this Memorandum, be transmitted to His Honour the Lieutenant-Governor of British Columbia, with a request that he would take an early opportunity of submitting them to his Executive Government, and express the hope that the views of the Dominion Government therein embodied may obtain an early and favourable consideration.

He would further recommend, that copies of the Order in Council and the Memorandum, should also be transmitted by the Governor-General to the Secretary of State for the Colonies, accompanied by copies of such of the other documents herewith submitted as may be thought necessary to enable the Colonial Secretary to understand in all its bearings the great national question now seeking solution at the hands of the Dominion Government and the Government of British Columbia.

(Signed) DAVID LAIRD,
Minister of Interior.

The Superintendent of Indian Affairs to the Chief Commissioner of Lands and Works.

Indian Office, Victoria,
December 4th 1874.

SIR,—I have the honour to enclose a copy of the sworn statement of Mr. Mainguy relative to the boundary line of one of the Indian Reserves, Section 6, Range 8, at Chemainus. As Mr. Mainguy's evidence makes Section 6, Range 9, the boundary on the east side instead of the slough, as shown on the official map, would you be good enough to define the boundary line in order that I may be enabled to settle a dispute between the Indians and a Mr. McEwan, who states that he has been referred to me by yourself on the matter.

I have, &c.,
(Signed) I. W. POWELL.

ENCLOSURE.

I, the undersigned, Daniel Wishart Maniguy, of Chemainus, in the Province of British Columbia, Farmer, make oath and say :—That the piece or plot of land owned or pre-empted by me in the year 1863, being the eastern portion of Section 6, Range 8, Chemainus District, and bounded as follows, viz:—on the North by Section 7, Range 8; on the East by Section 6, Range 9; on the South by Section 5, Range 8; and on the West by the creek known as Butcher's Slough, was taken by the Government from me for an Indian Reserve, and that the boundaries above mentioned were in my presence pointed out to the Indians by the then Surveyor-General, the Hon. B. W. Pearse.

(Signed) D. W. MAINGUY.

Sworn before me at Chemainus, B. C.,
this second day of December, 1874.
(Signed)   HENRY FRY, J. P.

The Chief Commissioner of Lands and Works to the Superintendent of Indian Affairs.

Lands and Works Department,
Victoria, 7th December, 1874.

SIR,—I have the honour to acknowledge the receipt of your letter of the 4th inst., in reference to the boundaries of the Indian Reserve on Section (6), Range (8), Chemainus, and in reply, would beg to inform you that the official map of Chemainus shows that the Penalakhut Indian Reserve is bounded on the East by a straight line, commencing at the South-west corner of Section (6), Range (9) ; thence true North to Somenos Creek ; thence following the West bank of said creek to the range line between Ranges (8) and (9) ; thence true North along said line to the North-west corner of Section (6), Range (9) ; and does not include any portion of Section (6), Range (9), Chemainus District.

(Signed) ROBERT BEAVEN.
per STANHOPE FARWELL.

The Provincial Secretary to the Superintendent of Indian Affairs.

Provincial Secretary's Office,
8th December, 1874.

SIR,—I have the honour to acquaint you that a complaint has been brought before the Government by Mr. Calver, residing at Jervis Inlet, that he had been threatened and warned off his pre-emption at Seychelt by the Indians of that Inlet, and it is asserted that the Indians have taken this action in consequence of your not having visited them and distributed presents, as among other tribes.

I have &c.,
(Signed) JOHN ASH.

The Superintendent of Indian Affairs to the Provincial Secretary.

Department of Indian Affairs,
December 9th, 1874.

SIR,—I have the honour to acknowledge the receipt of your letter of the 8th instant, acquainting me that a Mr. Calver, residing at Jervis Inlet, had been threatened and warned off his pre-emption at Seychelt, by the Indians of that Inlet, and further, it is asserted that the "Indians have taken this action in consequence of " your not having visited them and distributed presents, as among other tribes."

In reply, I have the honour to state that I had previously been informed the Indians residing at Jervis Inlet claim the lands upon which Mr. Calver is located, and that they have warned Mr. Calver to leave because they have not been settled with in respect to these lands.

I would, with much deference, suggest that the pre-emption of lands in unsettled parts of the Province, before satisfactory arrangements have been made with the aborigines with regard to such settlement, is certain to lead to complaints and even more serious consequences than those conveyed in your letter. I may remind you that several tribes of Indians whom I have visited have refused the acceptance of presents while their claims to land are unrecognized; and, pending the definite and final agreement between the Provincial and Dominion Governments respecting the quantity of lands to be allowed all Indians of the Province, I am of opinion that any future visitation on the part of a Commissioner is not only unadvisable, but would be quite unproductive of the permanent benefit which such an interview, under other circumstances, ought always to secure.

I will, however, transmit a copy of your letter to the Honourable the Minister of the Interior, for his consideration and direction in the matter alluded to, and shall be glad to acquaint you with the nature of his reply as soon as received.

I have &c.,
(Signed) I. W. POWELL.

The Chief Commissioner of Lands and Works to the Superintendent of Indian Affairs.

Lands and Works Department,
Victoria, 2nd February, 1875.

SIR,—I have the honour to inform you that I am instructed by His Excellency the Lieutenant-Governor in Council, to inform you in reference to the application of David Polatchen, an Indian at Chilliwhack, to pre-empt land, that his request cannot be granted, in consequence of there being large tracts of unimproved land held by Indians in that vicinity, and that he had better cultivate some portion thereof.

I have, &c.,
(Signed) ROBERT BEAVEN.

The Superintendent of Indian Affairs to the Provincial Secretary

Indian Office,
Victoria, 27th February, 1875.

SIR,—I have the honour to request that you will kindly acquaint me with the manner in which Fines received under the Indian Liquor Act have been disposed of.

In view of the many inquiries made of myself, and the importance of having some proper mode of expending money which may be coming to any Indian Tribes in respect to the said law, I should be glad to receive the desired information as soon as convenience will permit.

I have, &c.,
(Signed) I. W. POWELL.

The Superintendent of Indian Affairs to the Attorney-General.

Indian Office, Victoria,
Victoria, 5th March, 1875.

SIR,—I have the honour to request that you may be good enough to inform me, 1ST.—As to the manner in which reserve lands were transferred to Indians; whether by Order in Council or other formal instrument: 2nd.—In setting apart Indian Reserves, has the Government ever retained any rights whatever to the same in respect to minerals, &c.?

I have, &c.,
(Signed) I. W. POWELL.

The Attorney-General to the Superintendent of Indian Affairs.

Attorney General's Office,
5th March, 1875.

SIR,—I have the honour to acknowledge the receipt of your letter of the 5th instant, and also of the 27th February, addressed to the Hon. Provincial Secretary, which has been referred to me.

I beg to inform you that when the pressure of business consequent upon the opening of the Session is removed, the matters referred to will receive attention.

I have, &c.,
(Signed) GEO. A. WALKEM.

The Superintendent of Indian Affairs to the Chief Commissioner of Lands and Works.

Indian Office,
Victoria, April 7th, 1875.

SIR,—I have the honour to request that you will be good enough to allow me to inspect the treaties made between the Hudson's Bay Company and the Indians of the Songish and Nanaimo Tribes, as contained in the record book at present in your Office.

Should you think it necessary that the book remain in your care, I shall be glad to return it safely.

I have, &c.,
(Signed)   I. W. POWELL.

The Chief Commissioner of Lands and Works to the Superintendent of Indian Affairs.

Lands and Works Department,
Victoria, April 7th, 1875.

SIR,—I beg to acknowledge the receipt of your communication of even date, requesting that you be permitted to inspect the record book containing the original treaties made between the Hudson's Bay Company and certain tribes of Indians on Vancouver Island. In reply I have the honour to forward, herewith, the record book referred to for your inspection.

I have, &c.,
(Signed)   STANHOPE FARWELL,
For the Chief Commissioner of Lands and Works.

The Superintendent of Indian Affairs to the Chief Commissioner of Lands and Works.

Indian Office,
Victoria, 10th April, 1875.

SIR,—I have the honour to return the book containing record of treaties between the Hudson Bay Company and certain Indian Tribes of Vancouver Island, and my thanks for your courtesy in allowing me to inspect the same. Would you be good enough, in accordance with your suggestion, to favour me with a copy of all matters contained in the book at your earliest convenience.

As the record relates purely and sorely to Indian Affairs, I should be glad if, through yourself, His Excellency the Lieutenant-Governor in Council would subsequently consider the propriety of placing this and any other documents referring to the same in my possession.

I have, &c.,
(Signed)   I. W. POWELL.

The Chief Commissioner of Lands and Works to the Superintendent of Indian Affairs.

Lands and Works Department,
Victoria, 12th April, 1875.

SIR,—I am instructed by the Hon. Chief Commissioner of Lands and Works to acknowledge the receipt of your letter of the 10th instant, returning the book containing records of treaties between the Hudson Bay Company and certain Indian Tribes of Vancouver Island, and requesting a copy of the same, and to inform you he will be most happy to permit any one of your staff making a copy of said records in this office.

I have, &c.,
(Signed)   J. GORDON VINTER.

The Superintendent of Indian Affairs to the Chief Commissioner of Lands and Works.

Indian Office,
May 12th, 1875.

SIR,—I have the honour to enclose a note from Mr. Morley, J. P., relative to a complaint of the bearer against a white man who has taken possession of the Indian's house and land at Plumper Pass. I should be glad to know if any pre-emption has been made at the place referred to, and if so, by whom?

Pending some definite settlement of the Indian Reserve question, I am of opinion that present difficulties will be multiplied if whites are allowed to pre-empt lands already occupied by Indians, though not contained in the Schedule of Reserves.

The land above referred to has been used as a fishing station.

I have, &c.,
(Signed)   I. W. POWELL.

ENCLOSURE.

Mr. Morley to the Superintendent of Indian Affairs.

Maple Bay, May 1st, 1875.

MY DEAR SIR,—The bearer hereof, an Indian named Charley from Plumper Pass, has been to complain that during his absence from his land near Plumper Pass, some white man had taken possession of his land, and wants to drive him on to some rocks. I cannot exactly tell the white man's name, but several settlers have gone to those Islands lately. The Indian has drawn a sketch map to show where his land is situated. I believe by applying at the Land Office you might find what person it is. If white settlers are allowed to take Indians' land and houses from them, it will be impossible to keep them quiet. I have told the Indians that you will see that justice is done to them. Two of the chiefs, Lowa and Cape-el, came with the Indian to complain. They have had a large potlash at Quamichan this week, but have been very orderly and quiet.

I forward the sketch map; the Indian made it in my presence. I do not know whether you understand it. Any instructions I will see carried out.

I have, &c.,
(Signed)   JNO. MORLEY.

The Chief Commissioner of Lands and Works to the Superintendent of Indian Affairs.

Lands and Works Department,
Victoria, May 12th, 1875.

SIR,—I have the honour to acknowledge the receipt of your letter of this date, in reference to an alleged complaint made to you by an Indian against a white man, who you state has taken possession of the Indian's land at Plumper Pass.

I have made enquiries from the Indian whom you sent to this office, and find that his name is "Charley," and that he belongs to a ranch situate opposite Clallam Bay, Washington Territory, and that they occupy land in the neighbourhood of Jordan River, on the South-west Coast of Vancouver Island.

I find also that this land that the Indian states is taken possession of by a white man, is situate on *Mayne Island*, and is known as Helen Point in Section 18 of that Island. This land has not been pre-empted recently, and I have not been able to find any Pre-emption Record of it in this Department.

I have assured the Indians that their just rights would always be respected by the authorities of this Province.

In reference to the latter clause of your letter, I can only remark that you assuredly must be aware that the pre-emption of an Indian Settlement is prohibited by Statute, and has been for years past; and to prove to you that such is the case,

I take the liberty of enclosing to you a copy of the "Land Act, 1875," *now in force*, and to call your attention to clauses 3 and 12, to the declaration forms 2 and 5, and to Clause 34 in reference to declarations.

I regret exceedingly that the Dominion Government have not long since thought proper to take the preliminary steps necessary to the settlement of the boundaries of Indian Reservations unadjusted prior to Confederation, and as embodied in the 13th Clause of the Terms of Union between Canada and British Columbia.

I have, &c.,
(Signed)   ROBERT BEAVEN.

The Lieutenant-Governor to the Secretary of State for Canada.

No. 49.

Government House,
Victoria, 18th August, 1875.

SIR,—With reference to your despatch of the 12th June last, I have the honour to enclose herewith, a Minute of my Executive Council, setting forth the views of my Government upon the subject of the "Indian Land Question" in this Province, which I beg you to have the goodness to submit for the consideration of His Excellency the Administrator of the Government. I also, at the instance of my Ministry, forward a duplicate copy of the said Minute, with the request that you will move His Excellency to transmit the same to Her Majesty's Principal Secretary of State for the Colonies.

I have, &c.,
(Signed)   JOSEPH W. TRUTCH.

The Under Secretary of State to the Lieutenant-Governor.

Ottawa, 15th November, 1875.

Sir,—Adverting to your despatch No. 49, of the 18th August last, and its accompanying Minute of your Executive Council, and also to previous correspondence on the subject, I am directed to transmit to you, for the consideration of your Government, a copy of an Order of His Excellency the Governor-General in Council, and of the Memorandum of the Acting Minister of the Interior therein referred to, on the subject of the Indian Land question in British Columbia.

I have, &c.,
(Signed)   EDOUARD J. LANGEVIN.

ENCLOSURE.

Copy of a Report of a Committee of the Honourable the Privy Council, approved by His Excellency the Governor-General in Council, on the 10th November, 1875.

The Committee of Council have had under consideration the Minute in Council of the Government of British Columbia of the 18th August last, adopting the recommendations contained in a Memorandum of the local Attorney-General, as the expression of the views of that Government as to the best method of bringing about a settlement of the Indian Land question, and submitting those recommendations for the consideration and assent of the Government of the Dominion.

They have also had before them the Memornadum herewith annexed, from the Honourable Mr. Scott, acting in the absence of the Honourable the Minister of the Interior, to whom the above-mentioned documents were referred, and they respectfully report their concurrence in the recommendations therein submitted, and advise that a copy thereof and of this Minute be transmitted for the consideration of the Government of British Columbia.

Certified,

(Signed) W. A. HIMSWORTH,
Clerk, Privy Council, Canada.

Department of the Interior,
Ottawa, 5th November, 1875.

MEMORANDUM:

The undersigned has had under consideration the Report of the Executive Council of the 18th of August last, adopting the recommendations contained in Memorandum of the local Attorney-General, the Honourable George A. Walkem, as the expression of the views of that Government as to the best method of bringing about a settlement of the Indian Land question, and submitting those recommendations for the consideration and assent of the Government of the Dominion.

The action of the British Columbia Government in this matter was no doubt brought about by the Order of Your Excellency in Counnil of the 4th November, 1874, on the subject of the Indian Reserves of British Columbia, which was communicated officially to the British Columbia Government by the Secretary of State.

The suggestions contained in Mr. Walkem's Memorandum, and adopted by the Order in Council of the British Columbia Government, are as follows:—

1. That no basis of acreage for Indian Reserves be fixed for the Province as a whole, but that each nation (and not tribe) of Indians of the same language be dealt with separately.

2. That for the proper adjustment of Indian claims the Dominion Government do appoint an agent to reside with each nation.

3. That Reserves of land be set aside for each nationality of Indians; such Reserve to contain, in addition to agricultural land, a large proportion of wild and forest land. Every application for a Reserve shall be accompanied by a Report from the agent having charge of the nation for whom the Reserve is intended; and such Report shall contain a census and give a description of the habits and pursuits of each nation and also of the nature and quantity of the land required for the use of such nation.

4. That each Reserve shall be held in trust for the use and benefit of the nation of Indians to which it has been allotted, and, in the event of any material increase or decrease hereafter of the members of a nation occupying a Reserve, such Reserve shall be enlarged or diminished as the case may be, so that it shall bear a fair proportion to the numbers of the nation occupying it. The extra land required for any Reserve shall be allotted from vacant Crown Lands, and any land taken off a Reserve shall revert to the Province.

5. That the present local Reserves be surrendered by the Dominion to the Province as soon as may be convenient, the Province agreeing to give fair compensation for any improvements or clearings made upon any Reserve which may be surrendered by the Dominion and accepted by the Province.

The suggestions in question are stated by Mr. Walkem as having been made by Mr. Duncan, in a letter which is appended to the Order in Council.

The undersigned would remark that the suggestions, as given by Mr. Duncan in the letter in question, do not correspond precisely with the propositions formulated by Mr. Walkem.

Mr. Duncan's suggestions are as follows:—

1. That no basis of acreage for Reserves be fixed for the Province as a whole, but rather that each nation of Indians be dealt with separately on their respective claims.

2. That for the proper adjustment of such claims let the Dominion and the Provincial Governments each provide an agent to visit the Indians and report fully as to the number and pursuits of each nation and the kind of country they severally occupy.

3. That the Provincial Government deal as liberally with the Indians as other Provincial Governments in the Dominion.

My opinion is that a liberal policy will prove the cheapest in the end, but I hold it will not be necessary in the interests of the Indians to grant them only cultivable lands ; rather I would recommend that a large portion of their Reserves should be wild and forest lands, and hence may be very extensive without impoverishing the Province, and at the same time so satisfactory to the Indians as to allay all irritation and jealousy towards the whites.

4. I think the Provincial Government might reasonably insist upon this with the Dominion Government: That no Indian shall be allowed to alienate any part of a Reserve, and in case of any Reserve being abandoned, or the Indians on it decreasing, so that its extent is disproportioned to the number of occupants, that such Reserve or part of a Reserve might revert to the Provincial Government.

Mr. Duncan adds:—"The existing Reserves are shown to be, by the corres-
"pondence, both irregular in quantity and misplaced as to the locality, by follow-
"ing tribal divisions, which is no doubt a mistake and fraught with bad conse-
"quences."

"My advice would be, in the meantime, simply to ignore them, as it certainly
"would not be wise to regard them as a precedent, and it would be impolitic to
"have two systems of Reserves in the Province, one tribal and the other national."

It will be observed that Mr. Walkem speaks of the appointment of an agent by the Dominion Government, whereas Mr. Duncan proposes that the Dominion and Provincial Governments shall each provide an agent to visit the Indians and report upon the question of Reserves.

While the undersigned is of opinion that in view of the very large experience Mr. Duncan has had amongst the Indians of British Columbia, and the marvellous success which has attended his labours amongst them, that gentleman's suggestions on matters of Indian policy are entitled to the greatest weight, and, while he concurs entirely in the general principles enunciated by Mr. Duncan, yet he thinks that both the suggestions of Mr. Duncan and the propositions of Mr. Walkem, adopted by the Government of British Columbia in their Minute of 8th August last, fail to provide a prompt and final settlement of this long-pending controversy.

Mr. Walkem provides merely that the agent shall make an *application* for a Reserve and *report* upon the subject, and Mr. Duncan recommends that the Dominion and Provincial agents shall *report* merely as to the number and pursuits of the Indians. Looking to Mr. Walkem's admission "that the Indians have undoubtedly
"become discontented, and that they are restless and uneasy as to their future,"
and to his further statement "that the Local Government have been keenly alive
"not only to the advantage but to the absolute necessity and *urgent importance* of
"a *speedy settlement* of all the questions connected with their Reserves," and again to Mr. Duncan's expression of opinion as to "the urgency and importance of the
"land question and its vital bearing on the peace and prosperity of the Province," the undersigned submits that no scheme for the settlement of this question can be held to be satisfactory which does not provide for its *prompt* and *final adjustment*.

In lieu, therefore, of the propositions submitted by Mr. Walkem and sanctioned by the Order in Council of the British Columbia Government, the undersigned would respectfully propose the following:—

1. That with the view to the speedy and final adjustment of the Indian Reserve question in British Columbia on a satisfactory basis, the whole matter be referred to three Commissioners, one to be appointed by the Government of the Dominion, one by the Government of British Columbia, and the third to be named by the Dominion and the Local Governments jointly.

2. That the said Commissioners shall, as soon as practicable after their appointment, meet at Victoria, and make arrangements to visit, with all convenient speed, in such order as may be found desirable, each Indian nation (meaning by nation all Indian tribes speaking the same language) in British Columbia, and, after full enquiry on the spot into all matters affecting the question, to fix and determine for each nation, separately, the number, extent, and locality of the Reserve or Reserves to be allowed to it.

3. That in determining the extent of the Reserves to be granted to the Indians of British Columbia, no basis of acreage be fixed for the Indians of that Province as a whole, but that each nation of Indians of the same language be dealt with separately.

4. That the Commissioners shall be guided generally by the spirit of the Terms of Union between the Dominion and the Local Governments, which contemplates a "liberal policy" being pursued towards the Indians, and, in the case of each particular nation, regard shall be had to the habits, wants and pursuits of such nation, to the amount of territory available in the region occupied by them, and to the claims of the white settlers.

5. That each Reserve shall be held in trust for the use and benefit of the nation of Indians to which it has been allotted, and, in the event of any material increase or decrease hereafter of the numbers of a nation occupying a Reserve, such Reserve shall be enlarged or diminished, as the case may be, so that it shall bear a fair proportion to the members of the nation occupying it. The extra land required for any Reserve shall be allotted from Crown Lands, and any land taken off a Reserve shall revert to the Province.

6. That so soon as the Reserve or Reserves for any Indian nation shall have been fixed and determined by the Commissioners as aforesaid, the existing Reserves belonging to such nation, so far as they are not in whole or in part included in such new Reserve or Reserves so determined by the Commissioners, shall be surrendered by the Dominion to the Local Government so soon as may be convenient, on the latter paying to the former, for the benefit of the Indians, such compensation for any clearings or improvements made on any Reserve so surrendered by the Dominion and accepted by the Province, as may be thought reasonable by the Commissioners aforesaid.

It will be observed that the preceding paragraphs, Nos. 3, 4, 5 and 6, are substantially the same as those submitted in the Memorandum of Mr. Walkem, approved by the Order in Council of the British Columbia Government.

The undersigned would further recommend that each Commissioner be paid by the Government appointing him, and that the third Commissioner be allowed ten dollars per day while acting, and that his pay and other expenses be borne equally by the Dominion and the Local Governments; and the undersigned would further recommend that if this Memorandum be approved by Your Excellency, a copy thereof and of the Minute of Council passed thereon be communicated to His Honour the Lieutenant-Governor of British Columbia for the consideration of His Government, and that another copy be placed in Your Excellency's hands for transmission to the Right Honourable the Secretary of State for the Colonies.

The whole respectfully submitted.

(Signed) R. W. SCOTT,
Acting Minister of the Interior.

APPPENDIX.

GAZETTE NOTICES OF INDIAN RESERVES.

PUBLIC NOTICE.

Kamloops and Shuswap Indian Reserves.

The Officer Administering the Government desires it to be notified that the claims of the Kamloops and Shuswap Indian Tribes to the tract of land extending for over forty miles along the right bank of the South Branch of Thompson River, from Kamloops to the Great Shuswap Lake, have been adjusted, and three portions thereof appropriated as reserves for the use of these tribes, viz:—

For the Kamloops Tribe—A tract of land, three miles square, at the junction of the North and South Branches of Thompson River, extending three miles up each branch from the point of their intersection.

For the Shuswap Tribe—Two tracts of land.

The first tract reserved is situated at the locality known as the Two-Creeks, about twenty-nine miles from Kamloops up the South Branch of Thompson River, extending two miles along the right bank of said river from the upper of the Two-Creeks, and about two miles back from the bank of the river to the shore of a large lake.

The second reserve is situated at the upper end of the Little Shuswap Lake on its north shore, and extends about two miles eastward from a small creek running into the lake half a mile west of the Indian Village, and about one mile back from the shore, including the Village Chapel and graveyard.

The Indian Reserves above described will be exactly surveyed and staked off immediately, and the remainder of the land hitherto claimed by the Indians along the north bank of the South Branch of Thompson River will be open to pre-emption from the 1st of January, 1867, before which date however no pre-emption records thereon will be received.

JOSEPH W. TRUTCH,
Chief Commissioner of Lands and Works
and Surveyor General.

Lands and Works Office,
New Westminster, October 5th, 1866.

Indian Reserve at Cowichan.

Lands and Works Office, Victoria, B. C.,
4th July, 1867.

The Governor desires it to be notified for the information of the public, that the following Sections of land only are reserved for the use of the Indians:—

COWICHAN DISTRICT.

Range I.,	Sections	11,	12,	13,	14,	15,	16,	17.
,, II.,	,,		12,	13,	14,	15,	16.
,, III.,	,,			14,	15,	16,

QUAMICHAN DISTRICT.

Range V., Sections 15, 16.
„ VI., „ 15, 16.
„ VII., „ 10 N. E. corner, 15 acres.
„ VII., „ 11 E. part, 30 acres.
„ VII., „ 10 N. half, 11, 13, 14, 15, 16, 17.

The mode of dealing with the remaining portions of the original Reserve will be publicly notified hereafter.

The Clem-clem-alats and Somenos District Reserves, other than those included in the above Schedule, remain as heretofore.

By Command,

B. W. PEARSE.

Indian Reserve at Chemainus.

His Excellency the Governor desires it to be notified that the following Reserves have been made in the Chemainus District, in Vancouver Island, for the use of the Indians, to wit :—

AL-HALT INDIAN RESERVE.—All that piece of land known as Section 5, Range VII., as shown on the Official Map of the Chemainus District, and containing 100 acres or thereabouts.

Also all that piece of land West of the Main Chemainus River, being part of Sections 8 and 9, Range VII. and VIII., as laid down by posts, but not yet surveyed.

PENAL-A-KHUT INDIAN RESERVE.—All that piece of land, being the Eastern portion of Section 6, Range VIII., extending Westwards as far as the creek commonly known as "Butcher's Creek," and otherwise bounded as shown on the Official Map of the said District.

The Islands at the mouth of the said Chemainus River are no longer reserved for the use of the Indians.

By Command,

B. W. PEARSE,
Assistant Surveyor-General.

Lands and Works Department,
July 3rd, 1867

Indian Reserves in Lytton and New Westminster Districts.

The Governor desires it to be notified that Reserves for the use of the Indians respectively residing thereon, have been defined and staked out at the undermentioned places, viz :—

IN LYTTON DISTRICT.

1. 47½ acres on Bonaparte River, near Cache Creek.
2. 575 acres on Deadman's Creek, near Savona's.
3. 918 acres on Nicola River, 9 miles below Nicola Lake.
4. 670 acres on the south-east shore of Nicola Lake, 4 miles from the head of the Lake.
5. 60 acres on the same shore of said Lake, about 2½ miles west of No. 4 Reserve.

IN NEW WESTMINSTER DISTRICT.

1. 390 acres. ⎫
2. 300 acres. ⎬ Squay-ya Reserves, on the Squay-ya Slough and Fraser River, at the mouth of Squay-ya Slough.
3. 80 acres. ⎭
4. Schu-ye Reserve, 490 acres, an Island in Fraser River, between the mouths of the Chilliwhack River and Ko-qua-pilt Slough.
5. Ko-qua-pilt Reserve, 175 acres, between the Ko-qua-pilt Slough and the Telegraph Road.
6. Is-qua-ahla Reserve, 160 acres, on the right bank of Chilliwhack River, adjoining and to the south of the Ko-qua-pilt Reserve.
7. Assy-litch Reserve, 45 acres, on the left bank of Chilliwhack River, opposite the Is-qua-ahla Reserve.
8. 128 acres, ⎫ Scokale Reserves, on both sides of Chilliwhack River, about
9. 30 acres, ⎭ 9 miles from its junction with Fraser River.
10. Yuk-yuk-y-yoose Reserve, 42 acres, on right bank of Chilliwhack River, south of and near to the Scokale River.
11. So-why-lee Reserve, 690 acres, on left bank of Chilliwhack River, above Cultus Creek, which bounds it on the west.
12. Scowlitz Reserve, 330 acres, on the left bank of Harrison River, at its junction with Fraser River.
13. Nicomin Reserve, 109 acres, on the right bank of the Nicomin or Harris' Slough, about 7 miles from its junction with Fraser River.
14. S'que-aam Reserve, 73 acres, on the left bank of Nicomin Slough, nearly opposite the Nicomin Reserve.
15. Klat-waas Reserve, 86 acres, on right bank of Nicomin Slough, about $1\frac{1}{2}$ miles from its junction with Fraser River.
16. Sumass Reserve, No. 1, 32 acres, on right bank of Fraser River, just above the mouth of Nicomin Slough.
17. Sumass Reserve, No. 2, 43 acres, on right bank of Sumass River, just above the mouth of Chadsey's Slough.
18. Upper Sumass Reserve, 440 acres, on left bank of Sumass River, about 2 miles above Sumass Lake.
19. Matsqui Reserve, No. 1, 96 acres, on left bank of Fraser River, about 2 miles below St. Mary's Mission.
20. Matsqui Reserve, No. 2, 52 acres, on Matsqui Prairie, near the Telegraph Station, about one mile south of the left bank of Fraser River.
21. Wha-nock Reserve, 92 acres, on right bank of Fraser River, about four miles above Fort Langley.
22. Katzie Reserve, 58 acres, on left bank of Fraser River, opposite Katzie village.

Plans of the above Reserves may be seen at the Lands and Works Office, Victoria, and at the Office of the Assistant Commissioner of Lands and Works of the District in which the Reserves are respectively situated.

The land hitherto supposed to be included in these Reserves will be open for pre-emption on and after the 1st March, next ensuing.

By Command,

JOSEPH W. TRUTCH.

Lands and Works Office, Victoria,
   18th December, 1868.

Indian Reserves for New Westminster District.

Notice is hereby given that Reserves for the use of the Indians respectively residing thereon, have been defined and staked out at the undermentioned places, viz :—

IN NEW WESTMINSTER DISTRICT.

No. 1. Thirty-five (35) acres on the North Shore of Burrard Inlet, immediately opposite the Vancouver Island and British Columbia Spar, Lumber and Saw-mill Company's Mill.

No. 2. Thirty-seven (37) acres on the South shore of False Creek, about half a mile from English Bay.

No. 3. One hundred and eleven (111) acres on the North shore of Burrard Inlet, about one mile West of the North Arm.

Plans of the above Reserves may be seen at the Lands and Works Office, Victoria, and at the Office of the Assistant Commissioner of Lands and Works, at New Westminster.

By Command,

JOSEPH W. TRUTCH.

Lands and Works Office, Victoria,
November 25th, 1869.

REPORT

OF THE

GOVERNMENT OF BRITISH COLUMBIA

ON THE SUBJECT OF

INDIAN RESERVES.

Copy of a Report of a Committee of the Honorable the Executive Council, approved by His Honour the Lieutenant-Governor on the 18th day of August, 1875.

The Committee of Council concur with the statements and recommendations contained in the Memorandum of the Honorable the Attorney-General, on the subject of Indian Affairs, dated 17th August, 1875, and advise that it be adopted as the expression of the views of this Government as to the best method of bringing about a settlement of the Indian Land Question.

Certified,
(Signed)   W. J. ARMSTRONG,
Clerk of the Executive Council.

The undersigned begs leave to submit, for the consideration of His Honour the Lieutenant-Governor in Council, the following Memorandum on Indian Affairs:—

For some time past the Government of the Province have endeavoured, but without success, to arrive at some practical solution of what is termed the Indian Land question. The negotiations with the Dominion on the subject have been based on the 13th Article of our Terms of Union agreed to in 1871, which reads as follows:—

"The charge of the Indians, and the trusteeship and management of the lands "reserved for their use and benefit, shall be assumed by the Dominion Government, and "a policy as liberal as that hitherto pursued by the British Columbia Government shall "be continued by the Dominion Government after the Union.

"To carry out such policy, tracts of land of such extent as it has hitherto been the "practice of the British Columbia Government to appropriate for that purpose, shall "from time to time be conveyed by the local Government to the Dominion Government "in trust for the use and benefit of the Indians on application of the Dominion Govern-"ment; and in case of disagreement between the two Governments respecting the "quantity of such tracts of land to be so granted, the matter shall be referred for the "decision of the Secretary of State for the Colonies."

It will thus appear—

1st.—That Canada assumed the charge of the Indians and the trusteeship and management of their lands;

2nd.—That a policy towards our Natives as liberal as that of the Colonial Government of British Columbia (prior to Confederation) should be continued by the Dominion Government.

3rd.—That this Province should, after Confederation, convey to the Dominion, in trust for the use of the Indians, tracts of land similar in extent to those which had been set apart for their use by British Columbia when governed directly by the Imperial Authorities.

4th.—That any disagreement with respect to the extent of such lands should be referred to the Secretary of State for the Colonies for his decision.

Upon these four distinct terms the 13th Article is based. It need scarcely be stated that there is a marked difference between a stipulation to establish a general policy and an agreement to supply certain detailed assistance " to carry out such policy." Referring to the Report of the Hon. the Minister of the Interior, adopted by Minute of the Privy Council of the 4th of November, 1874, it will be observed that the Minister fails to draw such a distinction, and harshly condemns the Indian *policy* of the Crown Colony "as little short of a mockery of the claims" of the Indians, because the *aid* given to it in the shape of land and for education fell short of that given in old Canada.

The value of the above distinction will presently appear in discussing the several points in the order laid down. Although the question of *What assistance in land shall British Columbia now give to enable the Dominion to carry out her Indian policy?* is the real issue between the two Governments, it appears to be absolutely necessary to give a short sketch of the Indian policy of the Crown Colony, with a view of removing the very unjust impressions respecting it which have been created in the public mind by the publication of the Report of the Minister of the Interior. Superior to this reason is the undoubted right of the Imperial Government (to whom the Indian correspondence has been referred) to a full explanation respecting the charges preferred in the Report, of mal-administration of a policy established under their directing influence. In justice also to the past and present Governments of British Columbia, as well as to its people at large, a thorough consideration of the Minister's Report is demanded. With these remarks the undersigned now proposes to deal with the three last propositions above set forth, as the first condition may be considered as disposed of.

With respect to the second proposition, that the Indian policy of Canada shall not be less liberal than that of the Crown Colony of British Columbia it is not intended to give more than a brief statement of the Colonial Policy as it was pursued prior to 1871 ; nor would such a statement have been necessary had the Colonial Indian System been better understood by the Dominion Government.

The policy of the Dominion aims at a *concentration of the Indians upon Reserves*, while that of the Crown Colony, besides granting Reserves in cases where the Indians preferred them, courted rather an opposite result. The Colonial Policy was first inaugurated under the auspices of the Imperial Government in 1858, the date of the foundation of the Crown Colony. Under this policy the Natives were invited and encouraged to mingle with and live amongst the white population with a view of weaning them by degrees from savage life, and of gradually leading them by example and precept to adopt habits of peace, honesty, and industry. It is true that this step was not unattended with some of the well-known evils which are unfortunately inseparable from the attempted fusion of savage and civilized races, but these defects it was believed would in time have been largely removed by the application of proper remedies.

The Dominion Commissioner for Indian Affairs, resident here, has asserted (*vide* Report) that—

"Money payments by the Government, on account of the native race, have been "restricted to expenditure incurred by Indian outrages, and no efforts have "been put forth with a view to civilize them, it having been considered that "the best mode of treating them was to let them alone."

This is certainly a very strong and positive statement, and one which undoubtedly leads the reader to infer that the Crown Colony (which is meant by the word "Government") had cruelly neglected the Indians and left or "let them alone" in their savage condition, to struggle for life against the inroads of aggressive white settlers, who, as the complaint in the report states, "*in many instances* took from them the lands "which they had settled upon and cultivated, and in some cases, their burial grounds." (*vide* Report.)

Upon referring to the books and vouchers of the Treasury Department, it appears that between 1858 and 1871, money payments by the Colonial Governments on account of the Native race were, apart from expenditure caused by "Indian outrages," extensively made for various purposes. Considerable sums were, from time to time, paid for laying off and Surveying Reserves in the lower country and in the interior; for settling boundary and other disputes, whether amongst themselves or with white settlers ; and for specific expenses incurred in protecting and upholding their civil rights of property in our Courts of Law. Under a local Ordinance very large amounts were, from the earliest days, spent solely in the interest of the Indians, in the effort to suppress the "liquor traffic" amongst them. The expenditure on this account is composed of payments for the fuel consumed by Ships of War, for Steamers, for the salaries, travelling expenses, and allowances of Magistrates, Pilots, Police, and Witnesses engaged in this service. By instructions from the Government, the Natives were exempted from paying tolls and direct taxes levied on the community at large for the construction of public highways and bridges; nor were Customs Duties exacted upon the animals and merchandize—sometimes of no inconsiderable value—which the members of a tribe from time to time imported across the boundary line from American soil. These abatements—large in the aggregate—are virtually "money payments" on Indian account. Pecuniary aid was given to the sick and destitute, and to a large extent in cases of epidemics such as small pox. Treating the life of the Indian with as much respect and consideration as that of his civilized neighbour, Inquests were held, when necessary, in cases of untimely death. These proceedings were often, and almost always in the interior, attended with considerable outlay. In the administration of justice gratuities were sometimes given at the instance of a Judge on circuit, or of a District Magistrate, to deserving Indians. With a view of encouraging their feelings of loyalty and strengthening their fidelity and attachment to the Crown, a general invitation was annually extended to the various tribes within reach to meet at some central point in the lower country for the purpose of celebrating the birthday of Her Majesty. Nearly 4,000 Indians responded to the call in 1865, and large numbers attended at each subsequent meeting. On such occasions the Governor met them in person, and distributed the liberal money and other prizes amongst the successful competitors in games and in water sports. Presents of food and clothing to the Indians assembled were added; and the opportunity thus afforded was improved by giving them good counsel and advice for their future well-being. On other occasions, badges of value were given to meritorious chiefs, who with their followers received blankets, food, and articles of dress.

The system of "gifts" to the Native tribes was not, however, a prominent feature in the Colonial Policy. It was followed more in obedience to Indian tradition than from convictions of ultimate good. The practice was therefore countenanced rather than encouraged, as it was opposed to the main principles of assimilation in the higher degree of the native and civilized races and of the consequent treatment of the Indian as a fellow subject. Instead of this mode of assisting them, habits of self reliance were inculcated, and the advantages of well directed labour were impressed upon them. The time too was opportune for putting these lessons into practice, as labour was scarce and in great demand. Every Indian therefore who could and would work—and they were numerous—was employed in almost every branch of industrial and of domestic life, at wages which would appear excessively high in England or in Canada. From becoming labourers, some of the Natives after a time, stimulated by example and by profit, engaged on their own account in stock-breeding, in river boating, and in "packing," as it is termed, as carriers of merchandize by land and by water; while others followed fishing and hunting with more vigour than formerly to supply the wants of an incoming population. The Government frequently employed those living in the interior as police, labourers, servants, and as messengers entrusted with errands of importance. It may here be mentioned that in the payment or distribution of public rewards (however large) for the apprehension of criminals, the claims of the Indian and of the white man were treated alike. It is not of course suggested that any payments for services rendered are payments "on account of the Indians." The facts are merely stated to illustrate some of the features of the general policy pursued towards them. They were taught by association with the civilized races and by the course pursued in our Courts, where justice was meted out with even hand to all classes and races, to appreciate and respect the laws of the country. A special enactment provided that when "any Aboriginal Native" was "destitute of the knowledge of God," or was an unbeliever "in religion or in a future state of rewards and punishments," the evidence of such Native might be received in any civil or criminal cause upon his making a "solemn affirmation," or a simple "declaration to tell the truth" [Revised Statutes, No. 74]. Their lives and their property were jealously guarded. From humane motives, two penal statutes with stringent provisions were in early days passed—one, to prevent the spoliation of their graves and burial grounds—the other, as its caption reads, "To prohibit the sale or gift of intoxicating liquors to Indians." [Revised Statutes, Nos. 69 and 85].

Thus far it will be seen that no discriminating lines were drawn between the Natives and other races, save in the interest of the former. In disposing however of the Crown Lands, the Colony, for obvious reasons, made a distinction between the Indians and other resident British subjects. This may best be shown by quoting Section 3 of the "Land Ordinance, 1870."—

Sec. 3. "Any male * * * British subject of the age of 18 years or over, "may acquire the right to pre-empt any tract of unoccupied, unsurveyed, and unreserved "Crown Lands (not being an Indian Settlement) not exceeding 320 acres * * East "of the * * Cascade Mountains, and 160 acres * * in the rest of the Colony. "Provided that such right * * shall not * * extend to any of the Aborigines "of this Continent, except to such as shall have obtained the Governor's special per- "mission in writing to that effect."

This Section needs little comment. It is a transcript of the law of 1860 [Proclamation No. 17] as afterwards amended. The Indians, although denied the right of pre-emption which the Act gave to other British subjects, were permitted to pre-empt Crown Lands provided the Governor was satisfied that they could fulfil the usual conditions upon which the land was sold. As late as 1872, a Fort Langley Indian received permission to pre-empt 100 acres of land upon his practically proving that he could intelligently cultivate it. [Appendix A.] The above Section is now in force, but the practice of giving these permissions has been discontinued, lest it should interfere with the Dominion policy of concentrating the Indians upon Reserves.

Tracts of land or Reserves were also set apart by the Crown for the use of some of the tribes. As an invariable rule they embraced the village sites, settlements, and cultivated lands of the Indians. Several of the Reserves though rich in soil and situated in the centre of white settlements, are, however, unfortunately unproductive to the country, owing partly to Indian indolence and partly to the attractions of good wages offered by the white population.

To secure the Indians in peaceable possession of their property generally, the Colonial Legislature conferred upon the District Magistrates extensive powers (not even possessed by the Supreme Court) to remove and punish by fine, imprisonment, or heavy damages and costs any person unlawfully "entering or occupying" their Reserves or Settlements, or damaging their "improvements, crops, or cattle." [Revised Statutes, No. 125.]

To effectually carry out their general Indian Policy, the Colonial Government appointed the Magistrates resident in the several Districts to act as Indian Agents. As such their manifold duties may be summed up in the statement that they advised and protected the Indians in all matters relating to their welfare.

It has been said that no system of Education, in its restricted sense, was established on behalf of the Indians. While this is admitted, it may also be stated that the Government merely deferred the subject, believing that it was far more important in the interests of the community at large to first reclaim the Natives from their savage state and teach them the practical and rudimentary lessons of civilized life. How this was done has been already explained.

Since writing the above, the undersigned has fortunately obtained a copy of a despatch, addressed in 1870, by the Governor of British Columbia to the Secretary of State for the Colonies, respecting the Colonial Indian Policy. [Appendix B.] This document strongly and ably bears out many of the views and opinions above expressed.

Such is but an imperfect sketch of the Colonial Indian Policy which was founded in 1858 and determined in 1871. It was based on the broad and experimental principle of treating the Indian as a fellow subject. The principle was, at least, a lofty one, and worthy of an enlightened humanity. Like others of its kind, it had its trials; but it also had its rewards, for, through its influence, the Colony was enabled on the day of Confederation to hand over to the trusteeship of the Dominion, a community of 40,000 Indians—loyal, peaceable, contented, and in many cases honest and industrious. This fact is in itself the best commentary that can be offered upon the policy pursued towards the Indians during the 13 years preceding Confederation.

All policies or systems are open to more or less abuse; and the Colonial Indian Policy laid no claim to exclusive immunity in this respect. It has been shown that laws, unquestionably wise and humane, were enacted in the interest of the Indians. If, "in many instances," their cultivated patches or, "in some cases," their "burial grounds" have, as they complain, been unjustly taken from them, the law provided a sure and speedy remedy. The undersigned, however, takes the liberty of thinking that their statements in this respect are exaggerated. If such instances do exist they are exceedingly few in number—three or four at most—and are probably capable of satisfactory explanation. The Indians of this country number about 40,000, and are settled over an area of 220,000 square miles. It is doubtful whether any parallel exists of so large a number of savage tribes, a vast majority of whom never saw a white face until 1858, being successfully controlled and governed by, comparatively speaking, a mere handful of people of a European race. The country has been singularly free from the graver classes of crime among the Natives. Excepting an outbreak of a serious character in 1864 and a few acts of violence committed by Indian marauders on the North-West Coast, breaches of the law have generally been confined to cases of theft, to common and aggravated assaults, and to inter-tribal feuds. In nearly every instance the origin of Indian crime may be traced to the evasion of the Indian liquor laws.

Since Confederation the Indians have undoubtedly become discontented. Hopes of visionary wealth, to be acquired without labour, have been excited in the minds of some of the tribes; for it is a notorious fact that 80 acres of land were promised, of course without authority, to each head of an Indian family before the question of Reserves was even laid before the Provincial Government. When the policy of the Dominion supplanted that of the Colony, the several Indian Agencies established by the latter lapsed, and have not been replaced. It is not suprising therefore that the Indians, left as they have been for the last four years without that counsel and advice which they formerly received from those in authority, should have become uneasy and restless as to their future.

Before passing to the 3rd and 4th propositions it seems necessary to first call attention to that portion of the Report of the Minister of the Interior which inferentially charges the Local Government with a want of proper regard for the rights of the Indians, and with the grave responsibility of unnecessarily impeding a settlement of the question of Reserves or, as it is called in the correspondence, the Indian Land Question. It is to be regretted that this charge should have been made, as it cannot with justice be sustained. In this matter the Minister has probably acted upon insufficient information, both as to the general views of the Provincial Government upon the subject of Reserves, and as to the special reasons which dictated the course they have hitherto pursued.

It is almost needless to state that the Local Government have been keenly alive, not only to the advantages, but to the absolute necessity and urgent importance of a speedy settlement of all questions connected with the Reserves. The favorable influence which it would exert in the future cannot be overrated. Peace would be ensured, and prosperity would not fail to follow the improved condition and social elevation of the Indian. The fruits of his labour might at first fall short of expectation; but in time their value would be gradually increased by well directed training. The importance of the tribes, as large consumers and as labourers, is fully understood and appreciated. The Provincial Government feel that these facts in themselves entitle the Indians to a kind and liberal treatment. Their claims to consideration rest moreover on much higher grounds. The common dictates of humanity, apart from the moral lessons of education, silently but eloquently appeal to our better nature to shun oppression, and to protect and assist the ignorant and helpless. Such principles of action are not new. They have been happily engrafted upon our Constitution which, in the case of the Indian, views a disregard of his rights as oppression, and that oppression as a synonym for slavery.

Strongly holding the above views and convictions, the Provincial Government have, with great reluctance, felt compelled to differ in opinion from the Dominion Government on the subject of Reserves. A request by the Dominion for any reasonable and discriminating acreage of cultivable land for the use of the Indians is one which, on grounds above stated, could not but recommend itself to the favourable consideration of the Government of the Province. But in considering the demands already made, the Local Government felt constrained to keep in view not only the present condition and probable future of the Province, but the habits and pursuits of our Indians. That negotiations on the subject have hitherto failed is a matter of extreme regret; but is also a misfortune for which the Government here cannot justly be held responsible. The real causes of this failure are attributable to the want of proper information on the part of the Dominion Government of the physical structure of this country and of the habits of the Indians. At least such is the opinion plainly indicated in the annexed portion of a letter lately addressed to the Minister of the Interior by Mr. Duncan, an Indian Missionary remarkable not less for his unselfish devotion to the cause of the Indians than for his marvellous success amongst the tribes of the North-West Coast. [Appendix C.]

It will be observed that he has advised the Indian Department to defer the question of Reserves, and to appoint a Resident Indian Agent in each district. This Agent, he suggests, would, from his local knowledge, give trustworthy advice to the Government respecting "the number, wants, and pursuits of the Indians under his charge, the nature "of their country * * * and the most suitable locality and quantity of land required." "Without such advice," Mr. Duncan adds, "I cannot see how the Government can be "expected to act fairly or wisely in dealing with the subject." Though this language is addressed to the Dominion Government, it applies with equal, and indeed with greater, force to the Government of the Province, as they are responsible for the manner in which they dispose of the public lands, from which the Reserves will, of course, be taken.

The undersigned has also received a letter [Appendix D] from Mr. Duncan on the same subject of Reserves, in which he says,—"I am persuaded that the whole difference" between the two Governments on the land question, "springs from the fact that no "definite information is before the Provincial Government" on the subject. Reading both communications it will be found that he condemns the old, or Colonial, Reserves as being misplaced and too limited in area, and suggests that they therefore be abandoned for more eligible lands. He also disapproves of the Dominion land scheme as submitted for adoption by the Province.

The gravity of the interests directly involved in the applications of the Dominion for Provincial lands for the Indians, will best be understood by reference to the following figures, and by contrasting them with the extent of land prescribed by the Terms of Union, as they are interpreted:—

For present purposes the Indian population may be assumed to be 40,000.

 1st.—Terms of Union.—10 acres to each Indian family ....   80,000 acres;

 2nd.—21st March, 1873.—Request by Dominion for 80 acres of average quality for each family of five persons, and old Reserves to be regulated accordingly, equal to.................   640,000 acres;

 3rd.—In reply the Province offered 20 acres to each head of a family of five persons, which the Indian Department was authorized by the Dominion Authorities to accept, equal to   160,000 acres;

 4th.—15th May, 1874.—In lieu of the above, a further request was made for 20 acres to each head of a family or, as understood, for each Indian adult (the adults being about three-tenths of the Indian population), equal to........................   240,000 acres;

 This was assented to in the case of future Reserves; but the Provincial Government declined to include past Reserves in this agreement. They, however, offered to consider any special claim which might arise in respect of the latter.

 [NOTE.—From each of the above quantities, the acreage of the old Reserves must, of course, be deducted. The amount cannot be stated with accuracy in the absence of complete surveys. It, however, represents but a very small fraction of the quantities stated.]

This statement at once shows the very grave nature of the responsibility which rested upon the Provincial Government in dealing with such large tracts of agricultural land. Without definite information they felt it impossible to come to any intelligent conclusion upon the subject. Under all the circumstances, and bearing in mind what Mr. Duncan has stated, it would appear that they were fully justified in hesitating to accede to propositions which might not only retard the future settlement of the Province but prove to be, both illjudged, and illtimed in the interests of the present settlers and of the Indians themselves.

The enlargement of past Reserves is in many instances practically impossible, as they are surrounded by white settlements. The proposal to implement any deficiency of their acreage from lands more or less distant from them is open to grave objections. Every individual of a tribe which is provided with a reservation, regards the land as his home, and as the common property of the community to which he belongs. This being the case, the Indian Department would have to decide the difficult question of selecting the individual who should, in their opinion, be compelled to part from his tribe, his friends, and the home to which he had long been attached by the strongest natural ties, to settle on land selected for him perhaps at a distance from his reserve. The division of the old Reserves into 20-acre allotments, as contemplated, would also be attended with great difficulty, except some scale of compensation were settled upon, as any one such allotment might include all the cultivated land of the tribe. The settlement of such cases as the above may be said to properly rest with the Indian Department; but it is equally clear, that the Province would be responsible for enforcing this settlement, and suppressing any disturbances which might be caused by attempts to force unwilling Indians to accept what they might consider unjust.

Passing now to the third and fourth propositions, which may be dealt with together, it remains for the Provincial Government to consider what assistance in the shape of land they will give to the Dominion Government to carry out their Indian policy. The 13th Article binds the Province to give the same quantity of land as in practice the Crown Colony gave. This quantity seems to have been settled at ten acres to each Indian family, as appears by the following extract from the Speech of Governor Douglas to the Legislative Council in 1864. [British Columbia Sessional Papers, 1864.]:—

"The Native Tribes are quiet and well-disposed. The plan of forming Reserves "of land embracing the village sites, cultivated fields, and favourite places of resort of "the several tribes, and thus securing them against the encroachment of the settlers, "and forever removing the fertile cause of agrarian disturbance, has been productive of "the happiest effects on the minds of the Natives.

"The areas thus partially defined and set apart in no case exceed the proportion of "ten acres for each family concerned, and are to be held as the joint and common pro- "perty of the several tribes, being intended for their exclusive use and benefit, and "especially as a provision for the aged, the helpless, and the infirm."

It may be broadly stated that uniformity of acreage in the Reserves is practically impossible in this country. A uniform acreage that might appear desirable and just in Ontario, where there is abundance of good agricultural land, would, if adopted here, be fraught with mischief to the Province at large. The physical features of British Columbia are not only varied in themselves in the most positive manner, but they widely differ from those of all other sections of the Dominion. The natural laws of accommodation have produced equally marked distinctions between the several tribes of the Province; nor is there much more analogy between these tribes as a body and the tribes that inhabit the Plains and the Eastern Provinces.

In order to deal intelligently with the subject of Reserves it appears desirable that the habits and pursuits of our Natives should be duly considered, with a view of determining some general principles upon which in future a fair distribution of our public lands may be based. The physical structure of each locality should also be borne in mind. In the absence of that full and definite information, which Mr. Duncan considers indispensable, the following general remarks may be offered, especially as they are not likely to conflict with the Indian policy suggested by that gentleman.

Apart from tribal divisions and differences of dialect, the Indians may be divided into three classes :—
1. Fishermen and hunters;
2. Stock-breeders, and farmers on a small scale;
3. Labourers.

The first class naturally constitutes a very large proportion of the Indian population. It includes about 30,000 "Coast Indians," who live on the seaboard, besides two or three thousand Indians who live in the Interior and in the Southern parts of the Province. The request of the Dominion for a uniform acreage of land for all the tribes, necessarily implies that each male adult of this and of all other classes is to be withdrawn from his present occupation, and taught to cultivate the land allotted to him. If this course be carried out, a serious injury will be inflicted upon the Indians and the Province. Our numerous bays, inlets, and rivers contain inexhaustible supplies of the finest fish. Otter, seal, and other useful products are also easily obtained. The long experience and acquired skill of both fishermen and hunters might, instead of being diverted to other purposes, be turned to excellent account by qualified Indian Agents resident amongst them. No good reason exists why "Fisheries," such as those established by our merchants on Fraser River for curing and exporting salmon, and other merchantable fish, should not be erected in suitable places for the benefit of the Indians, and be in time profitably controlled and conducted by themselves. Many of the Indians are now employed in this industry as fishermen, at one dollar, or four shillings sterling, a day. The business requires but little mechanical skill, and that they already possess. Their beautiful canoes and well executed carvings in ivory, stone, and wood are good proofs of this. The experiment might be made at a very small outlay, especially as all the necessary appliances—a few tools and some tinware excepted—are almost within their reach. In the comparative cost of labour they would possess an enormous advantage as long as wages remain at their present high figures. The Merchant, instead of embarking in such ventures himself, would doubtless find it more profitable to purchase his supplies from the Indian "Fisheries," which would thus at the outset be relieved of the responsibility of finding a foreign market for their goods. The establishment of lumber mills and other industries would unquestionably follow success in this direction.

The hunter's skill might likewise be turned to good use. It is a notorious fact that valuable fur-bearing animals—large and small—are wastefully and even wantonly destroyed at unseasonable periods of the year. The mountain ranges which supply this class of animals are, generally speaking, wholly unfit for agricultural purposes. The experience and superior intelligence of the Indian Agent would again be usefully called into play. The hunter would be taught to regard these localities as fur-preserves, to avoid indiscriminate slaughter, to kill only at proper seasons of the year, and to carefully protect a source of wealth which he is now gradually but too surely destroying. The fur trade of the Province, with all its present disadvantages, is one of considerable importance, and might be greatly increased. Under these circumstances, any care taken to preserve and foster it would be well bestowed. The Indians upon whom this trade almost wholly depends, would largely reap the benefits of its good management. These views upon this branch of the subject have been communicated by Mr. J. W. McKay, a gentleman who has had thirty years experience amongst the Indians of the Province.

Reserves.

From the above general remarks it is reasonable to suppose that large tracts of agricultural lands will not be required for the class of Indians referred to. Those who cannot be employed usefully, in the manner indicated, in fishing or hunting, might require and fairly expect farming lands. The other portion of the community would be provided for in other ways, by reserving their fishing stations, fur-trading posts and settlements, and by laying off a liberal quantity of land for a future town-site. In the mountain ranges, the most eligible localities for the hunter's purpose might be selected and reserved as fur-bearing preserves.

Stock-breeders and Farmers.

With respect to this class of Indians who are a useful portion of the community, it must be conceded that their herds of horses and cattle require as much pastoral land for their support as equal numbers of stock owned by the white settlers. The pastoral leases complained of in the Minister's report will, however, soon be determined and a fruitful source of irritation will thus be removed. As suggested by Mr. Duncan, a liberal allowance of farming lands should be made, provided that the general outlines of the Indian Policy which he recommends for adoption in the Province be followed.

Labourers.

In the present infancy of British Columbia, the Indians of this class have proved invaluable in the settled portions of the Province. Little can be added to what has already been said with respect to their employment and kind treatment by the white population. It may be mentioned, however, that our lumber mills alone pay about 130 Indian employés over $40,000 annually. Each individual receives from $20 to $30 per month and board. An average of $25 gives the total of $40,000 as a clear annual profit made by 130 natives. This information has been obtained from one of the principal mill-owners. Such is one of the results of the Colonial policy. It is needless to say that it would require an enormous amount of farming produce to yield the same, or even one-half of this annual profit, to a similar number of Indians. Reserves of agricultural land for such labourers would be worse than useless, for if they got them they would be bound to occupy and cultivate them, and this they could not do without loss to themselves and loss of valuable and trained labour to the Province. Discarding, however, from consideration, the mere matter of pecuniary loss or gain, it clearly appears that the employment of the Indians at such centres of labour, possesses other and higher advantages than those described, as it tends to centralize the Natives and their families in places easy of access to the Missionary and to the School-teacher.

This Memorandum has reached a greater length than was anticipated by the undersigned; but he has felt that the importance of the subject required such information as the Provincial Government could give respecting their past and present views upon the Indian land question, in order that erroneous impressions may be removed, unnecessary complications be avoided, a practical land scheme be devised, and the Indian question finally settled to the mutual satisfaction of both Governments.

The following suggestions for the settlement of the subject have been made by Mr. Duncan. [Appendix D.]

1st. That no basis of acreage for Indian Reserves be fixed for the Province as a whole; but that each Nation (and not tribe) of Indians of the same language be dealt with separately:

2nd. That for the proper adjustment of Indian claims the Dominion Government do appoint an Agent to reside with each Nation:

3rd. That Reserves of land be set aside for each Nationality of Indians. Such Reserves to contain, in addition to agricultural land, a large proportion of wild and of forest land. Every application for a Reserve shall be accompanied by a Report from the Agent having charge of the Nation for whom the Reserve is intended; and such Report shall contain a census and give a description of the habits and pursuits, and of the nature and quantity of land required for the use of such Nation:

4th. That each Reserve shall be held in trust for the use and benefit of the Nation of Indians to which it has been allotted; and in the event of any material increase or decrease hereafter of the members of a Nation occupying a Reserve, such Reserve shall be enlarged or diminished as the case may be, so that it shall bear a fair proportion to the members of the Nation occupying it. The extra land required for any Reserves shall be allotted from vacant Crown lands, and any land taken off a Reserve shall revert to the Province:

5th. That the present local Reserves be surrendered by the Dominion to the Province as soon as may be convenient; the Province agreeing to give fair compensation for any improvements or clearings made upon any Reserve which may be surrendered by the Dominion and accepted by the Province:

The undersigned has the honor to recommend that the above suggestions be adopted, and that, if this Memorandum be approved, His Honor the Lieutenant-Governor be respectfully requested to forward a copy thereof, and of the Minute of Council referring thereto, to the Dominion Government, for their consideration and assent; and he further recommends that another copy be sent to the Dominion Government, for transmission to the Right Honorable the Secretary of State for the Colonies.

(Signed) GEO. A. WALKEM,
Attorney-General.

Victoria, 17th August, 1875.

APPENDIX A.

Copy of a Report of a Committee of the Honorable the Executive Council, approved by His Honour the Lieutenant-Governor on the 3rd day of December, 1872.

On a Memorandum dated 2nd December, from the Honorable the Chief Commissioner of Lands and Works, reporting that an Indian named Charlie has been living on an Island opposite Langley for some time, under an assurance from the late Mr. Brew that his possession of the land would be secured to him. The Indian has erected a house and has cleared some of the land. He also has cattle and poultry. The Island is overflowed every year at high water. The Indian raises wheat, turnips, potatoes, Indian corn and onions. He has planted apple trees also. The Island contains about 100 acres, and the Chief Commissioner of Lands and Works recommends that His Excellency the Lieutenant-Governor be respectfully requested to give Charlie permission to pre-empt, under the provisions of the "Land Ordinance, 1870."

The Committee advise that the recommendation be approved.

(Certified) JAMES JUDSON YOUNG.
Clerk Executive Council.

APPENDIX B.
Governor Musgrave to Earl Granville.

(Copy.) GOVERNMENT HOUSE, BRITISH COLUMBIA,
29th January, 1870.

MY LORD,—I have had the honour to receive your lordship's despatch, No. 104, of the 15th November, 1869, transmitting copy of a letter from the Secretary of the Aborigines' Protection Society, relative to the condition of the Indians in Vancouver Island.

2. If the statements made in Mr. Sebright Green's letter, forwarded to your lordship by the Society, were statements of facts, they would be a matter of great reproach to the Colonial Government; but I have satisfied myself that his representations are in some cases quite incorrect, and in others greatly exaggerated. As the circumstances alleged and referred to by Mr. Green were antecedent to my acquaintance with the Colony, I referred his letter to Mr. Trutch, the Commissioner of Lands and Works and Surveyor-General, for a report; and I now enclose a memorandum from that officer upon the subject. From other sources of information I have every reason to believe Mr. Trutch's statements to be correct.

3. It is very difficult, if not impossible, to place Indian tribes exactly in the same position as more civilized races, but they do, substantially, enjoy equal protection from the Government; and I believe that those of them who are most in contact with the white population quite understand that this is the case. Complaints are frequently brought by the Indians in the neighbourhood of Victoria before the Police Magistrate, against each other. And since my arrival here, Indians have been the principal witnesses in trials for murder.

I have, &c.,
(Signed) A. MUSGRAVE.

Memorandum on a letter treating of condition of the Indians in Vancouver Island, addressed to the Secretary of the Aborigines' Protection Society, by Mr. William Sebright Green.

Mr. Green's letter contains a series of allegations against the Government, most of which are so entirely inconsistent with facts, and in the remainder the truth is so strangely distorted, that his statements in this matter, and the deductions drawn by him therefrom, urgently require to be met with most distinct and positive refutation.

It is not true, as he avers, that in this Colony we have "no Indian Policy whatever;" that "there are no Indian Agents;" and that "the only friends the Indians have in the Colony are the Missionaries." On the contrary, for the past ten years at least, during which I have resided in this Colony, the Government appears to me to have striven to the extent of its power to protect and befriend the Native race, and its declared policy has been that the Aborigines should, in all material respects, be on the same footing in the eye of the law as people of European descent, and that they should be encouraged to live amongst the white settlers in the country, and so, by their example, be induced to adopt habits of civilization. In the more settled districts the Indians now reside mostly in the settlements, working for the white settlers, eating similar food, and wearing similar clothing, and having, to a great extent, relinquished their former wild, primitive mode of life. In these respects the native race has undoubtedly derived very material benefit from their contact with white people, whilst it is undoubtedly equally certain that it has thence contracted a large share of the vices, and attendant disease which have ever been inevitably entailed by European races, on the Indians of this continent amongst whom they have settled.

This policy towards the Indians has been consistently carried out, so far as I am aware, by successive Governors, and under it the Indians have assuredly, as Mr. Green states, "been made amenable to English laws;" but it is somewhat more than exaggerated to write, as he has done, that the Indians have been "suffered to shoot and kill one another within rifle-shot of the city, without interference." It may be, and I believe is, a fact, that during the past ten years there have been instances of Indians having shot and killed one another in the outskirts of Victoria without having been apprehended; but they certainly have not been suffered to do so. On the contrary, had they been detected in the commission of such crimes, they would most assuredly have been tried and punished according to English law. In fact, Indians have been tried for this very crime in Victoria and hanged. At the trial of all such offenders counsel have been assigned by the judge for their defence, unless specially provided by themselves or their friends, precisely as though they had been white men. For it must be pointed out that Mr. Green is again positively incorrect in stating, as he has done, that the defence of Indians is a "mere matter of chance." There is no more of the element of chance in this respect, as regards an Indian on his trial, than would affect a white man similarly circumstanced. Money must, of course, always have its effect in securing the services of able counsel and in other ways, when a man is under trial for any offence against the law; but in this respect a poor Indian is no worse off than a poor white man, indeed, he is probably not so friendless, as the judges in this colony have always made it their special care that Indians on trial should be at least at no disadvantage on account of their being Indians.

The Magistrates, too, throughout the Colony, are the especially constituted protectors of the Indians against injustice. They are, in fact, "Indian Agents" in all but the name, and I am confident that they have so performed this well-understood branch of their duty, that as full a measure of protection and general advantage has been bestowed on the Indians through their agency by Government, out of the pecuniary means at its disposal for this purpose, as could have been afforded to them through the medium of a special Indian Department.

The Indians have, in fact, been held to be the special wards of the Crown, and in the exercise of this guardianship Government has, in all cases where it has been desirable for the interests of the Indians, set apart such portions of the Crown lands as were deemed proportionate to, and amply sufficient for, the requirements of each tribe; and these Indian Reserves are held by Government, in trust, for the exclusive use and benefit of the Indians resident thereon.

But the title of the Indians in the fee of the public lands, or of any portion thereof, has never been acknowledged by Government, but, on the contrary, is distinctly denied. In no case has any special agreement been made with any of the tribes of the Mainland for the extinction of their claims of possession; but these claims have been held to have been fully satisfied by securing to each tribe, as the progress of the settlement of the country seemed to require, the use of sufficient tracts of land for their wants for agricultural and pastoral purposes.

In 1850 and 1851, shortly after the first settlement at Victoria by the Hudson Bay Company—at that time grantees from the Crown of the whole of Vancouver Island, with full executive powers of Government—their agent, Governor Douglas, made agreements with the various families of Indians then occupying the south-eastern portion of the Island, for the relinquishment of their possessory claims in the district of country around Fort Victoria, in consideration of certain blankets and other goods presented to them. But these presents were, as I understand, made for the purpose of securing friendly relations between those Indians and the settlement of Victoria, then in its infancy, and certainly not in acknowledgment of any general title of the Indians to the lands they occupy.

In reference to the Cowichan settlement, it appears from the records—for I cannot speak of this matter from personal knowledge, as I had no official connection with Vancouver Island until the year before last—that portions of the Cowichan Valley were surveyed by Government and sold in 1859. The settlement dates, therefore, from that year, although the unoccupied lands in this district were not thrown open for preemption until 1862. When these lands were surveyed, certain sections, containing in all 4635 acres, were set apart as reserves for the use of the Cowichan Indians, and are now held in trust by Government for that purpose, with the exception of about 500 acres which have been since withdrawn from this reservation, with the consent, as appears from the recorded correspondence in this office, of the Indians interested therein.

I can find no record of any promise having been made to these Indians that they should be paid for the lands in the Cowichan Valley which they may have laid claim to, nor can I learn that any such promise has ever been made. But it is probable that the Cowichans, when the white people began to settle among them, may have expected and considered themselves entitled to receive for the lands, which they held to be theirs, similar donations to those which had been presented to their neighbors, the Saanich Indians, years previously, as before mentioned, on their relinquishing their claims on the lands around their villages. It is further very likely that it was Governor Douglas' intention that such gratuities should be bestowed on this tribe, although no direct promise to that effect had been made; and, in fact, presents of agricultural implements and tools were authorised to be made to them through this department last year, although no demands for payment for their lands had, to my knowledge, been made by these Indians of Government.

It is unfortunately only too true that the law forbidding the sale of liquor to the Indians, although efficacious in the country districts, especially on the mainland, is virtually inoperative in Victoria and its neighbourhood, as its provisions, strict as they are, are evaded by an organized system between white men who make the vile liquor for this trade, and the Indian traders who purchase it in quantities, to be retailed to their Indian customers on the reserve. Government has endeavored to suppress this most baneful traffic, but the profits are so considerable that those engaged in it in a wholesale way cannot be tempted to become informers; and it is only occasionally that even the minor agents are apprehended and punished, whilst the principal offenders, some of whom it is hinted are most respectable persons, cannot be traced. It is easy for Mr. Green to say, "he could point out at least a dozen men known to be engaged in this nefarious traffic;" but it would no doubt have been difficult for him to have proved this, which he asserts as a known fact, otherwise he would surely have evidenced his earnestness in the cause of those on whose behalf he writes, by giving such information to the police as might have led to the punishment of these offenders.

Prostitution is another acknowledged evil prevailing to an almost unlimited extent among the Indian women in the neighborhood of Victoria; but the prevention of this vice is at least as difficult to effect here as in more civilized communities, and the only direct step towards this result that appears open for Government to take would be to remove the entire Indian population to a distance of some miles from Victoria; a course against which the Indians themselves, and the majority of the white inhabitants, would strenuously protest, for a variety of reasons; but this course must certainly be adopted before any measures for the improvement in this respect of the moral and social condition of the Indian population can be carried into effect with any hope of success.

In direct refutation of the charges of utter neglect and inhuman treatment of the Indians at Victoria during the prevalence of small-pox in 1868, which Mr. Green makes against Government, it will be sufficient for me to recount what came under my own observation in reference to this subject.

Some time during the autumn of that year, whilst this disease was at its height, Mr. Young, at that time acting Colonial Secretary, called my attention to a leading article in that morning's *British Colonist*, of which Mr. Green was then editor, which contained most exaggerated representations of the horrible condition of the Indians on the reserve at Victoria under this visitation, and charges against Government of having utterly failed to take any steps to prevent the spread of the fell contagion, or to alleviate the sufferings of those attacked by it, or even provide for the burial of its victims; statements, in fact of a character and tenor identical with the charges which are so broadly made in the letter now under reference. Mr. Young informed me, that although he knew these statements had no foundation in fact, he was then going to investigate the matter thoroughly, and would be glad if I would accompany him. Accordingly, Mr. Young, Mr. Pemberton, Police Magistrate of Victoria, and myself, went at once to the Indian reserve, and spent some hours in inspecting the Indian houses, hospital, graveyard, &c., and in inquiring into the arrangements that had been made by the Police Magistrate, with the assistance of the Rev. Mr. Owens, at that time resident on the reserve in charge of the Church of England Indian Mission thereon, and who also joined us in our inspection.

We found but few—only three—cases of small-pox then existing on the reserve, and these cases were in care of an attendant, paid by Government, in a building erected by Government specially as an Indian Small-pox Hospital, and under medical treatment also provided by Government. Those who had died on the reserve and in the town of Victoria had been decently buried, to the number of about fifty, that being the number of newly-made graves. We could not verify whether these represented all the deaths up to that time from small-pox among the Indians; but we certainly saw no dead bodies of Indians left unburied on the reserve, or elsewhere in the neighborhood of the town; nor did we learn that even one such dead body had been found "on the rocks outside the harbor," where Mr. Green says "hundreds of bodies were left unburied." The shanties which had been occupied by the small-pox patients, together with their clothes and bedding, had been carefully burnt; and from all that we saw on the reserve, and from the information furnished to us by the Rev. Mr. Owens, Mr. Pemberton, and others, we were satisfied that all practicable measures were being taken for the proper care of the Indian sufferers from small pox, and for the prevention of the spread of the disease.

I will only add, in confirmation of the correctness of the impressions we then formed to the above effect, that this subject was brought under discussion during the last Session of the Legislative Council by the late Dr. Davie, then Member for Victoria District, who, speaking of his own knowledge, as he had been unremitting in his professional services to Indians as well as to white persons afflicted with small-pox, and who, being one of the medical officers appointed by Government for this purpose, had frequently visited this reserve on such charitable errands, bore testimony to the zeal and unthinking disregard of the danger of contagion which had been exhibited by those to whom the duty of taking care of the Indians during the late visitation had been entrusted.

I have since ascertained that the deaths from small-pox among the Indians in 1868, amounted to eighty-eight, and that about two thousand dollars were expended by Government in the care of, and medical attendance on, these sufferers, and in the burial of the dead.

Most of the Indians from the outlying districts along the Coast fled from the City in their canoes, by the advice of the authorities, but under no compulsion, at the first outbreak of the contagion, but, unfortunately, not in time to escape its ravages; for they carried the infection with them, and those attacked by the dreaded disease on their way homeward were left by their friends on the shore to perish unattended.

Many Indians died in this way, in addition to those whose deaths were registered; but I am unable to perceive what measures it was in the power of Government to take, other than those which were adopted for the protection and succour of the white and Indian population alike.

I will only remark further, on the general subject of the condition of the Indians in the Colony, that it is unhesitatingly acknowledged to be the peculiar responsibility of Government to use every endeavour to promote the civilization, education, and ultimate christianization of the native races within our territory, and that any practical scheme for advancing this object which it would be within the scope of the pecuniary ability of the Colony to carry into effect would be adopted with alacrity.

At present this good work is almost exclusively in the hands of the Missionaries of various denominations, and much has been effected by their labours in those stations where the Indians under their teaching are not subject to those temptations which seem almost inevitably to overcome them when brought into close contact with the white population of the towns. But Government, although giving cordially to these missions every countenance and moral support in its power, has found it impracticable to grant them any pecuniary aid, from the consideration that, by so doing, it would be involved in the invidious position of appearing to give special state aid to particular religious bodies.

(Signed)   JOSEPH W. TRUTCH.

APPENDIX C.

Copy of part of a letter on Indian Affairs addressed to the Minister of the Interior, Ottawa, by Mr. Duncan, May, 1875.

Thus I have sketched the origin and growth of Metlakahtla, that from the facts and experience thereby shown, I may have good and safe grounds for recommending the following simple policy or principles of action to the Government in their future dealings with the Indians of British Columbia:—

A clear, practical, and satisfactory Indian Policy is now undoubtedly called for and is of vital importance to the prosperity of the Province. The problem of Indian affairs too, is confessedly difficult and solemn, hence I feel in duty bound to tender my humble aid to the Government toward its right solution.

Not having any personal or party ends to serve, but simply a desire to promote the spiritual and temporal interests of the Indians with whom my lot is cast, I will open my mind freely, and trust that what I have to say will be received by the Government in a like spirit of candour.

Let me then first assure the Government, that I believe the present organization of the Indian Department in British Columbia can never work successfully, and that however sincerely desirous those who now exercise the management of Indian affairs may be to do their duty, to my mind so palpably defective and misdirected are their labours, that I fear when the Government and the public come to look for results, they will be sorely disappointed.

The first anomaly that strikes one, is the isolated existence of the Department from the influence and control of the Lieutenant-Governor of the Province.

Such an arrangement, however easy it may work in Provinces nearer Canada, will prove, I am fully persuaded, both perplexing and injurious to the Indians of British Columbia. Its tendency will be to lower the Lieutenant-Governor in their estimation; retard their loyalty; and engender toward the white race antagonism of interests.

The Governor of the whites being no longer regarded as the guardian of their welfare, they will cease to respect him; while the Indian Commissioner, though he may succeed in enlisting their friendship, yet, from having no authority among or over the whites, will fail to inspire them with that salutary reverence so necessary to their good government.

It is to be hoped that this impolitic state of things may soon be remedied, and that, with an Indian Commissioner by his side, the Lieutenant-Governor, as the representative of the Queen, may continue to be looked up to by the Indians as the head of all authority and public interests in the Province; and that though they may feel themselves inferior to the whites in political and social standing, yet, that at least they have one and the same Governor, who will administer their affairs as impartially, and guard their interests as sacredly, as he does those of their otherwise more favored brethren.

I will now proceed with my suggestions for an Indian Policy which I propose to place under the heads of *Surveillance, Reserves,* and *Gifts.*

First, Surveillance.—This I conceive to be the proper starting point for commencing a right policy in Indian affairs; for without surveillance no satisfactory relationship can ever exist between the Government and the Indians.

But in looking at this subject I would ask the Government to lose sight of the tribal divisions of the Indians, which are so numerous and perplexing, and regard only the natural division of languages, of which I suppose there are some ten or twelve in the Province; each language being spoken, judging roughly, by about four to five thousand persons.

To each of these languages I would recommend the Government to appoint a Superintendent, or more properly speaking, a Sub-agent, who should also be a Justice of the Peace. This Sub-Agent should of course reside among his Indians and identify himself with their interests. He should be a married man of good character and a total abstainer from intoxicating drink. He must be a man of courage, patience, of orderly and industrious habits, and one who could command the respect of his people. He should possess some knowledge of medicine and of building, and be of a practical turn of mind. It should be his aim, as soon as possible, to learn the language of his Indians, and acquaint himself with their country, their pursuits, wants, and difficulties; all which he should duly record and report upon to the Chief Commissioner in the Province. His duties for the Indians would consist in preserving the peace in their midst, helping any in sickness or distress, teaching and aiding the community to open up the resources of their country and to build themselves good houses, and thus lead the way to their becoming an industrious and prosperous people.

I would recommend that at first the Sub-Agent take up his quarters *pro tem.* with the principal tribe in his district, but that as soon as he shall have become acquainted with the country he shall choose out a good central position for his station or head quarters, and erect his house on a site suitable for a future Native town. Before he moves he should make his plans fully known to his Indians and then encourage them to settle around him, without regard to tribal or sub-tribal distinctions.

As soon as possible after moving to the central station, I would recommend that he should choose out a Native constable or two, and gradually increase the staff until he has a corps sufficiently strong for all emergencies. Simultaneously I would recommend he should select a Native Council with whom he should deliberate upon all matters affecting the public weal within his district.

The expense of these two Native forces would be but trivial if the plan as at Metlakahtla be adopted. There the council have only a badge of office, which consists of a cape trimmed with scarlet, while the constables have each a simple uniform about every five years, and are remunerated for their services only when sent on special duty.

For the protection and encouragement of the Sub-Agent I would recommend that his station be visited once annually by the Governor or Chief Commissioner, and that his salary be not less than fifteen hundred dollars ($1500) a year, with allowances for medicine and canoe hire.

Next as to Reserves:—

Here again I would ask the Government to lose sight of scattered tribes, and rather be prepared when the time comes to grant a large district for the use and benefit of all the Indians of one language; that is, I would recommend one large Reserve for each tongue as the principle to be kept in view, and as opposed to having some ten or fifteen smaller reserves for each language if tribal divisions were followed.

But in practice this recommendation might require modifying in some cases, as where the Indians of the same tongue are very much scattered, or are divided by natural barriers which render their pursuits and means of living so dissimilar that their coming all on one reserve is impracticable. In such cases two, or at most three, reserves might be required.

In addition to the reserve for each tongue, I would earnestly beg the Government to hold in trust for the benefit of each tribe its respective fishing station, though it may not come on the reserve and be only occupied (of course) part of the year. To allow the whites to pre-empt or occupy *such clearings* would not only be a great injustice but would, I am sure, be a fruitful source of trouble to the Province.

As the question of Reserves is one of *vital importance* both to the Indians and the Government, and serious evils may result from precipitancy, I would propose that the subject wherever possible should lie over until the Government Agent before alluded to has taken up his position in each district; and after he has learnt the number, wants, and pursuits of the Indians under his charge, and the nature of their country, he should duly advise the Government accordingly, thus pointing out the most suitable locality and the quantity of land required by his particular Indians.

Without such advice I cannot see how the Government can be expected to act fairly or wisely in dealing with the subject.

Further, I would suggest as matter for caution that whatever system be adopted in granting reserves, that the Government will not sanction the establishing of an *Indian Settlement* on or near the *border* of a reserve where it might at once or at some future day be in proximity to a *White Settlement*, but rather order that all new and permanent Indian towns or villages shall be built as far from the settlement of the whites, or where such settlements are likely to arise, as the reserve in each case will allow.

Further, I look to the reserve question if rightly settled greatly to aid in remedying the present scattered condition of the Indians, and thus rendering them accessible to the Christian Missionary and Schoolmaster: for unless they become more collected it would seem impossible that education or civilization should ever reach them as a whole.

Next as to Gifts:—

In no matter affecting the Indians can the Government do more good or harm than in the matter of gifts.

Money may be spent to a large amount upon the Indians and yet tend only to alienate, dissatisfy, and impoverish them if wrongly applied; whereas a small sum rightly administered will yield much good both to the Indians and the country at large.

The policy of dealing out gifts to individual Indians I consider cannot be too strongly deprecated, as it is both degrading and demoralizing. To treat the Indians as paupers is to perpetuate their baby-hood and burdensomeness. To treat them as savages, whom we fear and who must be tamed and kept in good temper by presents, will perpetuate their barbarism and increase their insolence. I would therefore strongly urge the Government to set their faces against such a policy.

The Indians of British Columbia are by no means poor in the usual meaning of the word, i.e. they are not poor as to resources, but are ignorant, indolent, and improvident, and hence need a guiding and friendly hand before they can become a prosperous people. Thus may I recommend the Government in making pecuniary grants for Indian use to lose sight of individuals altogether, even chiefs not excepted, and rather spend the money on *Public Works* which shall benefit the community as a whole and be a palpable and *lasting* evidence of the interest the Government take in their welfare.

Of course such openings [for thus helping the whole community would be set before the Government, from time to time, by the Agent, with the consent and approbation of the Native Council, and each proposition or call for help would stand or fall on its own merits; but, speaking generally, pecuniary aid might be well applied in opening up roads, helping all who built at the Government Station to erect good houses, by providing, say, windows, nails, &c.; also assisting Indians in companies to open up any new industry: making this, however, a fundamental rule, only to assist those who are endeavouring to rise higher in social life and are law-abiding subjects of Her Majesty.

Thus I would have the Government to employ their money grants, and the Agent his energies principally to build up a good and substantial *Native town* for *each language*, and as central as possible for all the tribes of the same tongue.

These central Government Stations being started, a *Government School* might be established in each, and good openings would thus be made for Religious Societies to step in with their aid, and no doubt a Minister would soon be provided for each such station and thus for each tongue in the Province.

The three gentlemen—the Agent, the Minister, and the Schoolmaster—thus severally employed, and aiding and encouraging each other, might reasonably be expected to bring about such a state of things as would warrant the town at no very distant date being incorporated and have its own Native Magistrate, and thus cease to belong to the Indian Department or need an Indian policy.

(Signed)   WILLIAM DUNCAN.

APPENDIX D.

Mr. Duncan to the Hon. G. A. Walkem.

VICTORIA, 6th July, 1875.

SIR,—Having read over the correspondence between the Provincial Government and the Indian Department, in reference to the question of Land Reserves for the Indians, I have now the honor to submit to you, for the consideration of the Government, the following remarks which contain my views on the subject.

Of the urgency and importance of the Land question, and its vital bearing on the peace and prosperity of the Province there can be no doubt. The Provincial Government will, I feel sure, readily endorse all that appears in the correspondence on these points.

The questions to settle appear to be:—
1. *Who* among the Indians shall be entitled to land?
2. What *number of acres* shall be granted to each Indian so entitled?
3. What is to be done with *existing Reserves?*

Taking the first question:—

The mode approved by the Government appears to be, that *each family of five* is to receive certain lands, while some of their correspondents urge rather to regard *every male adult* as eligible. With the latter idea I fully concur, as it seems to me the only workable course to pursue.

I should pity the officer appointed to carry out the arrangement about families; nothing but complication and annoyance would ensue, and ultimately (in my opinion) the plan would be thrown aside as untenable.

As to the 2nd question.—The Dominion Government ask for eighty (80) acres for each family of five persons, while the Provincial Government offer only twenty (20) acres for such family.

I cannot believe the great difference between the demand in the one case, and the offer on the other, denotes the comparative respect for the Indians' welfare as held by the two Governments. No, I am persuaded that the whole difference springs from the fact that no definite information is before the Provincial Government as to the number and pursuits of the Indians in respective localities or the kind of land to be reserved for their use.

I can fully understand that the Provincial Government are reluctant to impede the progress of the Province by handing over to the Indians what might in some localities prove to be the whole of the cultivable lands, without their having much prospect or any guarantee that such lands will be utilized; hence I beg to make the following suggestions:—

1st. That no basis of acreage for Reserves be fixed for the Province as a whole, but rather that each nation of Indians be dealt with separately on their respective claims.

2nd. That for the proper adjustment of such claims let the Dominion and the Provincial Governments each provide an agent to visit the Indians and report fully as to the number and pursuits of each nation and the kind of country they severally occupy.

3rd. That the Provincial Government deal as liberally with the Indians as other Provincial Governments in the Dominion. My opinion is that a liberal policy will prove the cheapest in the end; but I hold it will not be necessary in the interests of the Indians to grant them only cultivable lands; rather I would recommend that a large proportion of their Reserves should be wild and forest lands, and hence may be very extensive without impoverishing the Province, and at the same time so satisfactory to the Indians as to allay all irritation and jealousy towards the whites.

4th. I think the Provincial Government might reasonably insist upon this with the Dominion Government,—that no Indian shall be allowed to alienate any part of a Reserve, and in case of a Reserve being abandoned, or the Indians on it decreasing, so that its extent is disproportioned to the number of occupants, that such Reserve or part of a Reserve might revert to the Provincial Government.

As to the 3rd question:—The existing Reserves are shown to be by the correspondence both irregular in quantity and misplaced as to locality by following tribal divisions, which is no doubt a mistake and fraught with bad consequences.

My advice would be in the meantime simply to ignore them, as it certainly would not be wise to regard them as a precedent, and it would be impolitic to have two systems of Reserves in the Province,—one tribal and the other national.

My opinion is that if the Dominion Government will establish sub-agents for each language or nation of Indians, and place and employ those agents as I have recommended, that the Indians will without any outside pressure be drawn and gradually gather round such agency and ultimately be willing to abandon the small and petty Reserves they now occupy, and especially so, if the Provincial Government offer to compensate them for the improvements or clearing of any lands they are willing to resign.

I enclose you a copy of part of a letter I have lately had the honor to present to the Indian Department, at Ottawa, on Indian affairs. I have, &c.,

(Signed) WILLIAM DUNCAN.

www.ingramcontent.com/pod-product-compliance
Lightning Source LLC
Chambersburg PA
CBHW020246170426
43202CB00008B/249